P9-DFZ-970

Judy Glattstein

MADE
FOR THE
SHADE

Color photographs by Judy Glattstein

*Illustrations by Dave Grindek,
Erin O'Toole, and Redenta Soprano*

CONTENTS

Virginia bluebells pair nicely with daffodils.

A mass planting of dogtooth violet, *Erythronium* 'Pagoda'.

Swamp habitat.

Illustrations
Erin O'Toole: Page 10; Redenta Soprano: Pages 42, 43;
Dave Grindek: Pages 60, 61.
USDA Plant Hardiness Zone Map reprinted courtesy Agricultural
Research Service, USDA.

Dedication
To my husband Paul Glattstein, whose acceptance of my horticultural
obsessions has been a foundation and support throughout the years.
Though he may claim to believe I make up all that Latin jargon, he
understands quite well *amor.*

Copyright ©1998 by Judy Glattstein

All rights reserved.
No part of this book may be reproduced in any form, by photostat,
microfilm, xerography, or any other means, or incorporated into any
information retrieval system, electronic or mechanical, without the written
permission of the copyright owner.

All inquiries should be addressed to:
Barron's Educational Series, Inc.
250 Wireless Boulevard
Hauppauge, New York 11788
http://www.barronseduc.com

International Standard Book No. 0-7641-0512-4

Library of Congress Catalog Card No. 98-20098

Library of Congress Cataloging-in-Publication Data
Glattstein, Judy. 1942-
    Made for the shade / Judy Glattstein.
        p. cm.
    Includes bibliographical references (p.   ) and index.
    1. Shade-tolerant plants. 2. Gardening in the shade. I. Title.
    SB434.7.G58   1998
    635.9'543—dc21   98-20098
                                                                      CIP

Printed in China
9 8 7 6 5 4

Combination of sedges, fern croizers, and skunk cabbage leaves.

A woodland pond in Japan makes a lovely mirror for azaleas in bloom.

Japanese primrose, seen here with skunk cabbage.

ACKNOWLEDGMENTS

Every gardener has someone special who helped nurture this passion for plants. I'm fortunate that there were/are several special someones. John Osborne, mentor, friend, and source of many plants made for the shade. He, alas, is gone but some special plants that started me off "into the woods," and many good memories, are still with me. H. Lincoln Foster and Timmy Foster, both influential in my development as a gardener, have also passed away. He would patiently answer my endless questions, and she impressed upon me the importance of tending what's been planted even after you move on to other plants. Helen Muller, dear friend, has taught me that, when one season is less than perfect, there's always next year. Sydney Eddison, whose fine garden expertise, witty conversation and merry laugh makes lengthy discussions seem all too short.

Authors, like gardeners, also never go it alone. To Guy DeSapio, my lawyer and agent, whose expertise and endless patience resulted in the contract for this book, grateful thanks. Lewis Tucci of Kew Professional Photo Labs made sure that the information in First Interlude was correct, and comprehensible. Their expert film processing means any less-than-ideal pictures are my doing, not shoddy processing (and there's always the circular file.) Mark Miele, my editor at Barron's Educational Series, Inc. believed in my vision for this book and helped "make it so." To John Reed and the staff at the New York Botanical Garden's LuEsther T. Mertz Library, my thanks: first for turning me loose in the stacks, and second for making sure I surfaced again. And to all the students in classes I've taught, thanks for making sure I keep in mind what you need to learn, so we'll all have fun and enjoy our travels down the garden path.

FOREWORD

Given the choice of a garden in full sun or one in shade, I would always opt for the shady one. Not that I don't like sun, but shade is so much more forgiving and the subtleties of changing light patterns on contrasting leaf shapes and textures, not to mention colors, never cease to intrigue me. There is a gentleness about shade that I find mysterious and beguiling; it reminds me of a cool, leafy glade in my grandmother's garden where as a child I would play hide-and-go-seek between spotted Japanese aucuba bushes underplanted with fragrant lily-of-the-valley.

At a time when gardening books are flooding the marketplace, relatively few seem to be written from practical experience. Fewer yet address plants that not only thrive in but often require shaded conditions. Judy Glattstein is a knowledgeable, dirt-under-the-fingernails sort of gardener, and she is intimately aware of the difference that light shade versus partial shade has on plant growth. Moreover, she talks in depth about how to measure the shade in your own garden. She gives us the benefit of her many years of gardening experience, not only with accurate descriptions of plants of all sorts—trees, shrubs, ground covers, perennials and the like—but by suggesting interesting and often unusual companions for them, and in different soil types. And she does not gloss over or shy away from the difficult aspects of gardening in shade—how to handle poor, dry soil conditions in spots under conifers, for example, and how *not* to provide an ongoing buffet bar for the deer. So this book serves not only as a reference work but also a design tool.

Although the most passionate gardeners have extensive collections of nursery catalogues, it is always useful to be alerted to new companies, especially those that specialize in a particular genus or group of plants. Judy casts her net far and wide, and her extensive appendix of nursery sources includes a wide range of mail-order businesses, each with a brief description of their stock. I have already made a list of those unfamiliar to me. How many times have I heard would-be gardeners wail "I can't grow anything—my garden is all shade." All they need is a really good book to help them on their way. *Made for the Shade* was written for them, and for the countless experienced gardeners and designers looking for sound reference information and to expand their plant palette.

Ruth Rogers Clausen

The Dynamics of a
SHADY GARDEN

A springtime community of shrubs, bulbs, perennials, and ground cover makes an inviting entry up the steps and into the garden.

The Dynamics of a
SHADY GARDEN

Delicate leaf texture and color make the red, cut-leaf Japanese maple a popular small tree for the shady garden.

Choices

Gardening is about choices: Which plants will be added and encouraged to grow; which will be weeded out. How they should be combined to create a beautiful landscape. Will this be a lot of work, not only in the beginning but also down the road? How to have a garden that is a pleasure, not a chore.

Every gardener wants a beautiful garden. Often, our expectations are raised by visions of paradise presented on television, in magazines, and books. But those extravagantly colorful herbaceous borders of England are set in sunlight on the lawn and it just doesn't work in a woodland. If you tried but failed to achieve that kind of dream landscape, you should not doubt your own capability as a gardener. With an understanding of what goes on in the shade, and an appropriate selection of plants, the shady garden can become a beautiful, magical place. Don't let disappointment reduce your dream garden from beautiful to simply anything that grows. That would be sad, for woodland gardens are special places. They can be formal, informal, or naturalistic, and serenely green or brightly colorful. Woodland gardens are not the same as sunny sites. You must select different plants, and use them in appropriate combinations. The dynamics of shade require a different approach to design and a different palette of

Pairing plants brings a cut-leaf Japanese maple, ajuga, and red begonias together for a superb result.

plants. If you understand your site, you'll know where to begin.

As a result of trees already on the site or deliberately introduced, gardens become shadier as they mature. Baffled by what is seen as limitations and restrictions of shade, most gardeners look for easy answers. They cover the ground where grass fails to grow with pachysandra, myrtle, or ivy and add some predictable perennials such as hosta and astilbe. They use impatiens for summer color. These obvious solutions utilizing a limited selection of plants are often a novice gardener's response to shade. Of course, it is possible to simply plug a few plants into the landscape and have them survive, but most often, the results will leave you dissatisfied. As a horticulturalist I focus on plants as the answer to solving landscape problems, and, over the years I've found more and more plants that are made for the shade, everything from trees and shrubs to vines and ground covers, perennials and annuals. With more plants to choose from, and a better understanding of how to create useful plant combinations, you can realize your dream and create an attractive garden in the shade. A diversity of perennials, useful annuals, and all sorts of trees and shrubs can enhance a

suburban woodland garden or shaded city terrace. Garden design—how you use what you choose—is extremely important.

It is the effective use of plants in combination that brings a garden into the "Wow!" class from the "That's nice" category; for example, red-leaved Japanese maple is a popular choice when you want a shade-tolerant small tree. It has dainty, attractive leaves with summer and fall interest, and a lovely overall vaselike shape. Regularly, I see a Japanese maple tree that has simply been plopped into a lawn where its thin, easily injured bark is at the mercy of lawn mowers or string trimmers. Moreover, grass does nothing to enhance the Japanese maple's appearance. As a designer, it is important for me to create a garden to my client's taste, rather than the one I'd make for myself on that site, and the nice thing is that there are always options. Now, instead of grass, picture a ground cover of burgundy-leaved ajugas, accented in the summer with a few plants of scarlet red fibrous-rooted begonias or impatiens. Not only have you simplified maintenance, you've created an attractive garden display.

Having selected plants, think about placement. Rather than a circular bed cut into the

A wonderful foliage effect is made with the pairing of *Hosta* 'Halcyon' and Japanese painted fern.

The Dynamics of a SHADY GARDEN

lawn with the tree in the center for a bull's-eye effect, consider shaping the bed into an ellipse, an egg shape, with the tree at the broader end. If you want something more subdued, less colorful than burgundy and red, instead of ajugas, consider hostas, perhaps the most ubiquitous of perennials ever hastily shoved into a shady corner. Don't grab the first one you trip over on a visit to a nursery or garden center. Choose one of the glaucous, blue-leaved cultivars such as 'Halcyon' or 'Blue Cadet'. Combine the hostas with the hoar-frosted lacy fronds of Japanese painted fern, add white-flowered impatiens, and you've created a pleasing, cool, summer-long display for the edge of a shady terrace. If the ajuga appeals to you but deer eat your hosta, choose what pleases *you*, and what works in your garden situation. Use burgundy-leaved ajuga with Japanese painted fern and still add summer color with impatiens, which could be scarlet red, pink, violet, or white. Good design is about aesthetically pleasing combinations of plants that grow well in a particular site.

Exciting gardens are the product of healthy, well-grown plants, combined with panache. Very often, just rearranging plants already growing in your garden can do the trick. You must learn to work with the seasonal dynamics of a shaded garden. Inappropriate plants struggling with unsuitable conditions will always look terrible, and plants chosen for rarity alone cannot guarantee success.

City Gardeners

City gardeners deal with a type of shade that is different from the type that exists in suburban or rural settings. Their gardens, surrounded by buildings, have more uniform shade and less of a seasonal shift. The situation is compounded by adjacent masonry buildings, concrete sidewalks, and asphalt paving that soak up summer heat during the day, then warm during what should be cooler nights. Adjacent buildings also create wind tunnels; pavement intercepts natural rainfall. From a gardener's perspective, however, the greatest influence on the quality of light reaching the ground is that provided by plants themselves.

Shade from Plants and Trees

Simply put, taller plants shade shorter ones. In a woodland, the layering is obvious. Tall canopy trees, smaller understory trees, shrubs, and herbaceous plants create distinct layers or zones. But not all forests are the same. Across the United States different woodland communities include the coniferous forests of the northern tier of states, mixed deciduous forests along the Atlantic coast, oak-hickory forests further inland, the distinctive mangrove swamps of subtropical Florida, evergreen and aspen forests of the Rocky Mountains lower slopes, and the Pacific Northwest old-growth forests.

A forest community. From left to right: a canopy tree, an understory tree, a shrub, and herbaceous plants.

Where competition is most severe, as in the constant, usually dry shade of conifers, undergrowth will be sparse. The shade under spruces is dense and heavy. Pines are somewhat better but still create an umbrella of bothersome dry, dark shade. Norway maples and beech spread just as dark a shadow, and their shallow roots also create a parching dryness; however, a few plants can survive even in the dark shade of greedy rooted maples. Dry shade is specifically addressed in the chapter that follows.

Oaks and tulip poplars are ideal deciduous trees. As well as dappling light from above, their branches are high enough off the ground to permit sunlight to slide in at the edge. Additionally, they are tap-rooted, reducing competition for moisture and nutrients. Some trees—birches and locusts—cast the most gossamer veils of shade. In the favorable conditions provided by deep-rooted trees and lighter shade, garden potential increases and understory growth is richer, more diverse.

Herbaceous Plants

Over time, the different layers of the forest have evolved a strategy favorable to all. At winter's end the sunlight reaches the woodland floor interrupted only by the bare branches overhead. When growth begins in the late winter or early spring, the herbaceous plants are the first to awaken. Their cycle of growth, flowering, and seed production are geared to the availability of sunlight, which provides the energy required for growth. Light that reaches the forest floor is reduced as woody plants leaf out. Some familiar spring-blooming geophytes (bulbous, cormous, or tuberous plants) such as snowdrops, daffodils, and winter aconites, are ephemeral: after flowering they promptly retire back underground and remain dormant through summer, fall, and winter. Native wildflowers such as Virginia bluebells, *Mertensia virginica*; and Dutchman's

In early spring a woodland path in my garden is lined with *Narcissus poeticus*, flowering in profusion before the trees awaken into growth.

breeches, *Dicentra cucullaria*; even a few perennials such as bleeding heart, *Dicentra spectabilis*; and the less-familiar yellow-flowered, buttercuplike *Adonis amurensis*, also follow this pattern. Their absence is only visual. Ephemeral plants need their garden space year-round. With careful selection, such deceptively bare places can be concealed by appropriate ground covers, summer annuals, or the burgeoning leafy growth of more conventional perennials growing adjacent to their sleeping neighbors.

Such familiar perennials as hosta and astilbe follow a more traditional pattern. They begin growing in mid- to late spring, go dormant in late summer or fall, and rest in the winter. Still others, such as Christmas rose, *Helleborus niger*; Nippon lily, *Rohdea japonica*; and Christmas fern, *Polystichum achrostichoides*, are evergreen. These perennials add invaluable foliage texture to the winter landscape. Immediately you can see various categories for herbaceous plant selection, based on flowers, foliage, and growth cycles.

Shrubs

Shrubs are the next group of plants to begin their cycle of growth. While most are chosen for their flowers, there are other characteristics

11

The Dynamics of a SHADY GARDEN

to look for. Shrubs with attractive berries or seed pods provide an ornamental display at a time when flowers are often scarce. Viburnums have clusters of blue-black fruits that often persist well through the fall, while hollies have fruits as red as sealing wax. The berries may also attract birds to the garden. Deciduous shrubs may have an interesting form in the winter, their bare branches perhaps displaying decorative bark colors and textures. Few coniferous shrubs are shade-tolerant. Broad-leaved, shade-loving evergreen shrubs such as mountain laurel, *Kalmia latifolia*; leucothoe, *Leucothoe catesbei*; and andromeda, *Pieris japonica*, are especially attractive in northeastern winter gardens. There are some appealing choices for southern and southeastern regions with milder winters, such as Burford holly, *Ilex cornuta* 'Burfordii', and Japanese fatsia, *Fatsia japonica*.

Understory Trees

Understory trees awaken after the shrubs have begun their growth. Perhaps most familiar is our native flowering dogwood, *Cornus florida*. This elegant little tree seems to have it all: beautiful white flowers in the spring, bright red berries attractive to birds, and a lovely form in the winter. Another fine example is the Japanese maple, *Acer palmatum*. Though the flowers are less interesting than those of flowering dogwood, spring leaf growth is fresh and delicate, fall color is superb, and the form of the bare tree in the winter is matchless.

Canopy Trees

Last of all, the canopy trees stretch, awaken, and send forth new leaves. Ideal for the shade gardener are deep-rooted, high-branched trees such as white oak, *Quercus alba*. Under their sheltering branches may be grown a wide range of smaller trees, shrubs, perennials, and bulbs. Not all trees are so garden-friendly. Consider Norway maple, *Acer platanoides*. Greedy roots close to the soil surface suck up moisture and nutrients, dense low branches cast heavy shade, and fallen leaves in the fall compact into a good imitation of roofing felt, making a dense, slimy blanket that is difficult for perennials and bulbs to penetrate. Still worse, Norway maple is a copious producer of tremendous numbers of fertile seed that develop into great numbers of rapidly growing young trees that crowd out native growth. Popular because it is quick growing and easily transplanted, Norway maple should be banned from further sale and use. Like loosestrife, *Lythrum salicaria*, in wetlands, this once-welcome exotic has become a noxious weed.

The Yearly Cycle

The yearly cycle of plant growth influences the characteristics of the woodland beyond the obvious pattern of waxing and waning shade. What goes on underfoot is also important. All plants, even evergreens, shed their leaves. Deciduous trees and shrubs are blatantly conspicuous about this. Now they have leaves; now they don't. (The trees on an acre of deciduous woodland drop a ton or more of leaves and twigs every year. As we'll see, this has important implications for garden maintenance, mulches, and organic matter in forest soils.) A fall walk through a pine forest quickly reveals that conifers also shed leaves. The fresh, fragrant carpet of bright golden tan needles is part of the pine tree's natural cycle. Broad-leaved evergreens such as the evergreen magnolias tend to drop their leaves in a more noticeable manner, simply because of the resulting clutter underfoot.

Not long to wait before these maple leaves let loose of the branch and drift to the ground, cycling nutrients between tree and earth.

When leaves are shed, they form a blanket on the earth, joining a continuous discard of twigs, small branches, and large branches. This layer is a natural mulch that decays to add organic matter to the soil. Take heed: Plants that are grown in shady gardens that evolved in woodlands expect a layer of mulch. It serves to reduce evaporation, moderates soil temperature, and provides suitable growing conditions. The amount of organic matter this litter returns to the soil, and how quickly, depends on what it is composed of and where (geographically) this is happening. In the tropics, decay occurs so rapidly that most of the biomass is tied up in living plants. In boreal forests, decay is slowed both by low temperatures and the rot-resistant nature of the conifers' resin-coated needles. Litter simply builds up in a relatively undecayed form,

the deep sterile duff in a pine forest. Deciduous leaves break down more quickly.

Decomposition and Replenishment

The microorganisms that promote decay begin their activity as the soil temperatures reach about 50° F. The softer the material, the more readily it breaks down—leaves faster than branches, deciduous leaves more quickly than evergreen foliage. Also, smaller pieces with a greater edge:area ratio are processed more efficiently by the microorganisms. If you run dry fall leaves through a shredder, or go over them with a lawn mower, they decay more quickly than if left whole. Organic matter is used up, cycled into plant growth, recycled into the soil, around and around; in gardens, it must be constantly replenished. In a naturalistic woodland, the process can follow the patterns of nature. In a more structured, organized, formal garden, leaf raking becomes a seasonal part of garden maintenance. The material that is removed must be replenished. Mulching with shredded leaves rather than pine bark chips readily renews the organic material and provides a use for leaves that might otherwise be raked away and discarded. This efficient use of fallen leaves has become especially important now that communities across the country no longer permit the disposal of yard waste at landfills. Alternatively, fallen leaves can be collected, composted, then dug into the soil in a partially decayed state.

It is necessary to understand the constraints and differing conditions of shade, not the absence of light but rather the changes in light's availability. This continuum of conditions—from light shade, dappled light, part shade or, heavy shade, to stygian gloom—controls which plants can grow. Yes, some situations are more limiting than others. Deep-rooted, high branched oaks permit a wider range of plants to grow beneath their friendly shade than do greedy, shallow-rooted beech trees. Dry shade forces the gardener to select

The Dynamics of a SHADY GARDEN

from a smaller list of plants than in more moderate situations. There are, however, plants for every situation. Use imaginative design to make creative use of familiar plants in interesting combinations. Understanding shade helps you to better grow the plants you already have, and evaluate new ones as they become available. Learn to assess your site.

Evaluating Light and Shade

The quality of light varies with the time of day. Morning and late afternoon light slants in at an angle. Filtered through more atmosphere, the light is less intense than it is at midday. Seasonal changes in the earth's orbit as the planet dances around the sun are pronounced. The soft highlights of early morning on spring's first flowers, or long slanted shadows of a golden afternoon in early fall, contrast with the short dark shadows of summer noon. *Analemma*, from the Latin word for sundial, is a graduated scale having the shape of a figure eight on its side, which shows the sun's declination and the equation of time for each day of the year. This declination, the angular distance north or south from the celestial equator, is measured along a great circle passing through the celestial poles. But this effect is known, even if nameless, to any gardener. Only at the equator are night and day fixed at 12 hours each; elsewhere the sun's rising and setting shifts along the horizon, and the hour of its appearance and descent varies.

A sunny garden is defined as one that receives a minimum of six hours of direct sunlight each day, and (though there are regional differences) wherever you live, day length is significantly extended beyond this during the growing season. The closer you approach the poles, the more pronounced the seasonal shift. In London, further north than New York City, the mid-May sun begins to rise at 4:00 A.M. and starts to set at 9:00 P.M.

Some Examples of Designs for Shady Gardens

Gardens are patterns imposed on the landscape. This arrangement can be formal or informal and is determined by the designer. Plants are chosen for the garden based on aesthetics and their suitability for local growing conditions. Native plants do not impose a naturalistic design upon the landscape, nor exotics a precise display. Foundation plantings, which include native American mountain laurel, are as commonplace as those with exotic Japanese pieris and rhododendrons.

Example 1
Darrell Morrison, a noted landscape architect specializing in such designs, chose to use only native plants at the Atlanta History Center. Red maple, *Acer rubrum*, and hop hornbeam, *Carpinus caroliniana*, are the dominant and understory trees planted in the lower, somewhat moist, partially shaded wooded area. The shrub layer is provided by a couple of deciduous rhododendrons: *Rhododendron canescens*, and the sweetly fragrant *R. viscosum*. For the ground plane Morrison selected a native geophyte, *Zephyranthes atamasco*, to arise amidst cardinal flower, *Lobelia cardinalis*, and great blue lobelia, *L. siphilitica*, all woven together with sensitive fern, *Onoclea sensibilis*.

Rather than select a limited palette of plants that thrive wherever planted, Morrison instead chose to exemplify natural conditions. Where the site grades into a swale, shifting light and moisture gradients define separate plant communities. He filled the hollow with drifts of northern sea oats, *Chasmantheum latifolium*. For semishaded areas a mix of bracken fern, *Pteridium aquilinium*; fire pink, *Silene virginica*; and blue star, *Amsonia tabernaemontania*, provide foliage and flowers to good effect. The woodland combination of hay-scented fern, *Dennstaedtia punctiloba*; white woods aster, *Aster divaricatus*; May apple, *Podophyllum peltatum*; and meadow rue, *Thalictrum dioicum*, is yet more shade-tolerant. What lovely diversity! Variations in shade and moisture sieve the plants, encouraging some here, others there. This close level of attention to detail reaps handsome rewards.

Example 2

A simple garden on Long Island uses a mix of local native plants and exotic species from abroad. Highbush blueberries, *Vaccinium corymbosum*, were transplanted from elsewhere on the property and replanted near the house in the dappled shade of oak trees. The tall, straggly character of the shrubs was accentuated by careful pruning to reveal their twisting form. A mix of Christmas fern, *Polystichum achrostichoides*; lungwort, *Pulmonaria saccharata*; and small spring-flowering geophytes created a simple ground plane planting. This is a handsome and interesting change from the usual foundation planting. Highbush blueberries have clusters of bell-like white flowers in the spring, berries that attract the birds that harvest before the homeowner, good red fall color if there is sufficient sunlight, and attractive red bark on the young twigs for winter interest.

Example 3

Highbush blueberry bushes were used to create a copse in a Connecticut garden. This was not the original intent, which was to raise blueberries for the table, but after several years the birds were better at harvesting than the owner, and she decided to use the shrubs an ornamentals. Pruned high, they became

An aficionado would find beauty in a collection of hosta at Cornell Plantation in Ithaca, New York, while others might find them perhaps a bit repetitious.

the canopy for a plethora of familiar and exotic perennials: forget-me-nots, primroses, lungworts, hellebores, rare arisaemas from Japan, and many different small bulbs, for the owner is a skillful plantswoman who delights in raising unusual plants from seed.

Example 4

On the west side of another Connecticut house, a small patio is shaded by the slope of the land and adjacent trees, and bordered with an informal hedge of white azaleas, *Rhododendron mucronatum* `Delaware Valley White'. The desired planting for summer interest was expected to be simple, to need limited maintenance, and to be attractive when the owners would sit outdoors in the evening. White shows best in low light, and foliage and flowers in this color were chosen. August lily, *Hosta plantaginea*, with its glossy, apple green leaves and deliciously fragrant white flowers, was the perennial element, with seasonal color provided by white impatiens, and *Caladium* `Candidum' (which has white leaves with green veins and margins). Although only three different kinds of plants were used for this tiny bed 5-feet long by 18-inches deep, it was attractive for four

The Dynamics of a SHADY GARDEN

months, from June until frost. In fact, the impatiens survived the first few light frosts, sheltered as they were by the site.

Example 5

A Georgia garden belonging to a hosta expert has, as might be expected, an incredible collection of hostas in all manner of shapes and sizes, from tiny, 3-inch-high *H. venusta* to 5-foot-wide clumps of `Blue Mammoth'. There were hostas with heavily veined, seersucker-like leaves, others with smooth, shiny leaves, and everything between. Green, gray, blue, yellow, variegated, I even saw a yellow-leafed hosta with a white edge. What relieved the potential monotony of the owner's preoccupation with a single genus was his inclusion of other woodland plants that enjoy similar growing conditions. Hellebores, especially *H. x orientalis*, liriopes, several ferns, Solomon's seals, ajugas, and others, were shoe-horned in among the dominant hostas.

Sometimes it is not even an entire garden that stays in my mind, just a vignette: chartreuse blades of Bowle's golden grass, *Milium effusum* `Aureum' coming through the spring purple leaves of *Viola labradorica*; the apple green flower clusters of bear's foot hellebore, *H. foetidus*, against the polished red bark of red-twig dogwood in a North Carolina garden one January, or a massive planting of Lenten rose, *Helleborus x orientalis*, flowering in abundance with blossoms of white, soft pink, rose, and plum, in the shade of tall tulip poplars.

Whether your plant selection is a simple combination of a few plants or a complex blend of many, exotics and/or natives, chosen for daytime viewing or at dusk, is a personal matter; attention to detail is something all gardeners should cultivate.

As you read on, you will come across mention of zones. Please refer to the map on page 17. The USDA Plant Hardiness Zone Map divides the country into 11 different major climatic zones. A zone is an area of the country that has roughly the same average minimum temperature.

Who could say leaves are uninteresting after looking at this pairing of Labrador violet and Bowles golden grass, *Milium effusum* 'Aureum'?

16

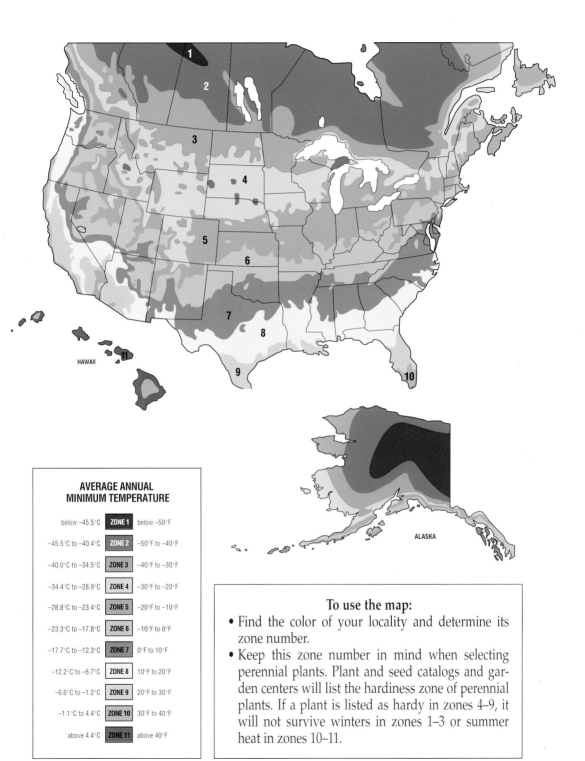

AVERAGE ANNUAL MINIMUM TEMPERATURE

below −45.5°C	ZONE 1	below −50°F
−45.5°C to −40.4°C	ZONE 2	−50°F to −40°F
−40.0°C to −34.5°C	ZONE 3	−40°F to −30°F
−34.4°C to −28.9°C	ZONE 4	−30°F to −20°F
−28.8°C to −23.4°C	ZONE 5	−20°F to −10°F
−23.3°C to −17.8°C	ZONE 6	−10°F to 0°F
−17.7°C to −12.3°C	ZONE 7	0°F to 10°F
−12.2°C to −6.7°C	ZONE 8	10°F to 20°F
−6.6°C to −1.2°C	ZONE 9	20°F to 30°F
−1.1°C to 4.4°C	ZONE 10	30°F to 40°F
above 4.4°C	ZONE 11	above 40°F

To use the map:
- Find the color of your locality and determine its zone number.
- Keep this zone number in mind when selecting perennial plants. Plant and seed catalogs and garden centers will list the hardiness zone of perennial plants. If a plant is listed as hardy in zones 4–9, it will not survive winters in zones 1–3 or summer heat in zones 10–11.

First Interlude:
MEASURING SHADE

Winter is bare, and trees are only an outline, a brief structural sketch.

Skip this if you are happy with an eyeball estimation of the quality of shade in your garden. However, if you are, like me, as insatiably curious as Kipling's Elephant Child, have a somewhat scientific bent, and own a 35mm camera, read on.

My dilemma: How can shade be measured by gardeners? Our eyes and minds are not calibrated; if your mood is sunny, the garden is apt to appear brighter too. Accurately remembering the quality of light in spring is difficult in winter's obscurity. The goal is to achieve some objective measurement of shade without an overwhelming array of scientific devices. After all, gardeners come from many backgrounds, not necessarily engineering or science. What measuring device are we likely to have in common? One gadget found in many households and used

to measure light is the meter built into 35mm single lens reflex cameras. And you can use this kind of 35mm camera to determine the shifting quality of light within the garden throughout the year. (Sorry, a point-and-shoot or disposable camera just won't do.)

A camera with a 50mm lens is most suitable. If you have a zoom lens, be sure it is set to 50mm. A wide-angle lens will gather too much light and deceptively suggest it is brighter than in fact it is. A close-focus lens, such as a macro lens, reduces the amount of light available to the meter.

There is a balance, a relationship, between the shutter speed and the lens opening. If the shutter speed is slow, the lens opening can be small and still allow in enough light to take a picture. Under the same light conditions, if the shutter speed is fast, the lens will need to open more to allow the same amount of light to enter. Film speed sets up one of the parameters for how much light is necessary at particular shutter speeds. Set the film speed on your camera to ASA 100. You don't need to actually have any film in the camera, because you aren't taking pictures, just using the meter and its readings. Set the shutter speed to 1/125th of a second. In full sunshine on a cloudless day, that film speed and shutter opening would designate an aperture, or lens opening, of f/16.

For most lenses, this is the smallest opening, and f/2.8 is the widest lens opening. But we are not going to take our measurement in full sun; we will be in shade. Your camera will indicate if conditions are too dark for 1/125th of a second at f/2.8, perhaps with a light that blinks or flashes or in some manner says, "Not enough light for a picture under these conditions." In a heavily shaded deciduous woodland in the summer, this will indeed be the case. For example, on a sunny, cloudless day in my Connecticut garden, I got a summer reading of f/2.8 at 1/30th of a second. The camera's meter reading was for a wide open lens and two shutter speed settings slower than 1/125th. Moments later, in the sunny portion of my garden, the reading was f/11 at 1/125th. I suspect the latter reading was influenced by the fact that the garden simply did not have any sufficiently large, open expanse, and I had the woods as a backdrop. Standing in the open and focusing into the woods affects the measurement of light taken by the light meter. I got a reading of f/16 at 1/125th in a nearby meadow.

The relationship of different readings is that, keeping shutter speed constant, one-half as much light is available at a reading of f/8, and one-quarter as much at f/4, as a reading of f/16. Kodak used to provide printed guidelines with each roll of film. These advised a setting of f/8 to f/5.6 for cloudy or open shade conditions. The reading I got, of f/2.8 at 1/30th of a second in my summer woodland garden, translates into a light level in the woods of approximately 3 or 4 percent of what it was in the open. How was I able to see anything under those conditions? The human eye is amazingly adaptable. The iris opens, just like a camera lens, and the rods and cones in the retina process the available light. Subjectively, conditions are shady but not gloomy. Objectively, the woods are lovely, lit by coindapple splashes of sunlight, not excessively dark. That is why a light meter is useful for objectively comparing differences.

The readings you take at various times of year and in separate places in the garden provide an impartial appraisal. In mid-October, a few months after my midsummer research, the woodland reading I got was f/4 at 1/125th of a second. Fall color was just about at peak, with flowering dogwood a deep plum purple. The oaks were also in leaf, with some still rather green, but the black birches, *Betula lenta*, were almost completely bare. Apparently it was the leaf drop on this species that resulted in such a significant difference. At the winter solstice, the reading I got was twice as bright—f/5.6 at 1/125th of a second. Though the day was brilliantly sunny with a clear blue sky, the numerous shadows of the tree trunks striping the ground were not as sharply hard-edged as summer shadows; the quality of the light is softer.

If these measurements intrigue you, you might want to compare morning, noon, and afternoon variations. For readings such as these, do not use clock times. Rather, a set period after sunrise and before sunset will more suitably span the seasons' differences. There is no list that correlates f stops and plants, but the relationships soon become clear.

Reduce the number of other possible variables, and choose conditions that are as consistent as possible. Since sunrise and sunset shift throughout the year, high noon on a sunny day is the time to take your readings. Stand in the shade under the trees or that of adjacent buildings, and focus at the

First Interlude: MEASURING SHADE

distance. If you stand in the open and focus into the woods the reading will be erroneous as ambient sunlight throws the meter off. The converse is also true: If you stand in shade and focus into the open, sunnier area, the meter will also give an inaccurate reading.

You should plan to take at least four readings, one in each season: midwinter when there should be the least shade in a deciduous woodland even if daylight is weaker; again in the spring and fall; and in midsummer, when shade will be heaviest. The longest day, arbitrarily marking summer's start, is the solstice around June 22nd. In Connecticut that day is 15 hours, 17 minutes

long. Usually deciduous trees are fairly well leafed out by then. Winter's solstice, the year's shortest day, falls on or about December 22nd. In Connecticut it is 9 hours, 5 minutes long, a significant 40 percent shorter. Commonly, deciduous trees and shrubs are then at their barest, having long since dropped their leaves. For spring and fall do not choose the equinox, when day and night are of equal length. These are fixed dates, around March 21st and September 23rd. And, as gardeners know, spring and fall begin on different dates as the season moves across the country. You will have to decide for yourself when local conditions are suitable for seasonal measurement.

Primula 'Moonlight' is just one perennial that is made for the shade.

Problem Shade/
PROBLEM
TREES

How shady is my garden?
Now you can figure that out

PROBLEM TREES

Attractive chartreuse flowers in early spring adorn spicebush, an excellent choice for moist, shady sites.

Shade is one parameter, one condition. Learning to understand shade is the first, and major, step. Especially where shade is moderate and site conditions favorable—good levels of organic matter and moisture in a soil that drains freely—you can grow a wide range of plants. As well as shade, gardeners need to consider water. When there are extremes of moisture, either dry or wet, plant options need to be refined yet again.

Dry Shade

Trees

Often the trees that create the shade add to the problem. Conifers—pines, spruces, firs, and hemlocks—cast deep, year-round shade. Their branches cover the ground like an open umbrella. Herbaceous plants are left thirsty and hungry, for the soil is not only dry, it is low in organic material and nutrients, and has an acid pH. Deciduous trees such as beeches and Norway maples are also difficult to work with, as they have greedy, spreading, shallow roots that grab available moisture and nutrients, again leaving little for herbaceous plants. In addition, Norway maples have large, very coarse leaves. After they drop in the fall, they mat down. By the spring, the result is a heavy, smothering, impenetrable layer, impossible for many perennials to penetrate. In such situations, you may be better off with attractive containers set on mulch.

Buildings and Walls

Trees are not the only culprit. Shade is also

cast by buildings and walls. Where there is a deep roof overhang, a rain shadow exists and the ground remains dry even when it rains. The building itself may prevent rain from reaching the ground next to its foundation on one side or another. Careful watering will correct this situation, but it is safest to use plants that accept dry conditions as well as shady situations.

Solutions

When shade is coupled with a lack of adequate water, the list of suitable plants shrinks dramatically. Few perennials accept the combination of shade and drought. Possibly the difficulty lies in the soil. A quick-draining, sandy soil holds little in the way of moisture or nutrients. If that is the case, you can improve conditions by amending the soil with moisture-retentive compost or leaf mold before you plant. It is better, and well worth the effort and expense, to prepare the site rather than individual planting holes. Remember also that organic matter gets used up and must be replenished on a regular, yearly basis. In addition, maintaining a constant, year-round mulch of shredded leaves or other organic material reduces evaporative loss of precious water, and, as it decays, adds organic matter to the soil.

Another solution is the creation of specialized planting beds raised above soil surface. Developed by John Neumer of the Delaware Chapter of the North American Rock Garden Society, and further refined by Jim McClements of Dover, Delaware, this is an easy, though lengthy process. It's best to begin in the fall since the project uses lots of leaves. Decide where you want the bed. Size is the next consideration, and that will be governed in large part by the materials you have available. In any case, the raised bed should not cover more than 25 percent of any tree's root area, the space determined by the outermost reach of its branches. Remove any desirable plants, and rake the ground clear of leaf litter,

mulch, and so on. It is suggested that you cover the soil with a layer of the water-permeable weed barrier landscape fabric. Do *not* substitute plastic mulch. Define the bed's perimeter with suitable material. In a formal garden you might choose cut stone for the edging, while mossy logs would be appropriate for a naturalistic setting.

In the fall, pile leaves 18 to 24 inches deep over the weed barrier. Don't skimp on the leaves, as they will shrink down considerably over time. Oak is best, but you can use other leaves except those of Norway maples, which mat like roofing felt. You can jump up and down on the heap every now and then, and children and dogs enjoy bouncing through the leaves too, but basically just forget about it and relax until the spring.

The mass of leaves, now shrunken and compressed by time, rain, and snow, should be covered with a 2-inch layer of coarse sand. Next, add a layer of composted cow manure. The dried bagged manure is fine. You need about 160 pounds for a 50-square-foot bed. Cover the sand and compost with a 4- to 6-inch thick layer of peat moss, about 16 cubic feet for a 50-square-foot bed. Make sure the peat moss is damp. If it is dry, leave a hose trickling into the bag for a couple of hours, then let it sit overnight before spreading it. Top the peat moss off with another inch of coarse sand, and disguise that with a cosmetic layer of shredded leaves to emulate the forest floor. Try to make this layered "lasagna" early enough in spring for seasonal rains to thoroughly soak the bed and further settle materials.

My version had a revision. One summer a windstorm ripped through the area, tearing limbs off trees and even uprooting them. When I passed a county work crew chipping everything up, it was more than I could resist. Offering a dumping site closer than the intended disposal site got me two huge truckloads of shredded material—for free. It was useless as mulch, for the combination of

Problem Shade/PROBLEM TREES

green leaves and chipped wood heats up very quickly and would harm plants. (See the information on composting in the Second Interlude, page 62.) By the next day the wooden handle of a grain scoop was warm to the touch just leaning against the pile for a few minutes. I would not substitute branches unless they were cut into very short pieces. The sand, composted manure, and peat moss will settle into the voids between the branches, resulting in uneven settling.

Much less laborious than double-digging, these raised beds provide maximum organic material and excellent drainage, making them the perfect home for all sorts of woodland plants from ferns to primroses, native trilliums to rare Japanese woodlanders. A yearly addition of shredded leaves, peat moss, and coarse sand should be applied late in the fall after the plants stop growing and go dormant. Plants will grow well for at least five years, longer if the initial leaf layer is generous and the annual top dressing is adequate.

Joann Knapp, a friend on Long Island, used water-holding polyacrylamide crystals to successfully grow primroses in her sandy soil. In the dry state, this answer provided by modern technology looks like coarse salt. Mixed into the soil, the crystals encapsulate the water, holding onto it until the water is utilized by the plants. One teaspoon of crystals absorbs a quart of water. Particles dehydrate, then rehydrate with the next available water. A few caveats:

• Never use the crystals in their dry state; always expand them with water first. (The first time she used the crystals, Joann mixed them in their dry state. The next morning she looked out on heaved primroses and expanded crystals bubbling out of the ground "like frog spawn.")

The flowers of *Trillium cuneatum* never open widely. No matter, their rich color and mottled leaves provide attraction enough.

• Secondly, dust the expanded material with dry soil. This separates them and make it easier to evenly mix the particles into the soil (like dusting blueberries with flour before mixing them with muffin batter.)

• Thirdly, use only 10 to 12 percent by volume of the expanded crystals. Too much results in soggy, sour soil that is just as bad for the plants as soil that is too dry. Some brand names are Terra-sorb©, Super-sorb©, and Hydro-gel©. Remember, these polyacrylamide crystals provide only water, not organic matter or nutrients that are necessary for plant growth.

It is necessary to set reasonable goals, even if it means revising your expectations. Dry shade is never going to provide a lush abundance. Nothing is more unappetizing than plants suffering a lingering death, neither actively growing nor decently dead. When you try new plants, remove them if they fail to thrive after a reasonable test period—perhaps they'll do better elsewhere in your garden. Do a site analysis: What type of tree provides the shade—conifer, broad-leafed evergreen, or deciduous? What is the soil type—clayey, loamy or sandy? Is moisture available only in the spring and the site dry at other times of year? An understanding of the year-round environmental conditions will help you choose appropriate plants. And there are appropriate, attractive plants for dry shade. A tidy ground cover, accented with a few perennials, can suitably "dress" the site.

Perennials for Dry Shade

Cast-Iron Plant, *Aspidistra elatior*
Thriving in the dimmest, darkest corners, cast-iron plant has a constitution that lives up to its common name. Numerous tough, shiny green leaves about 18 inches long by 4 to 5 inches wide, tapering to a point, arise from a creeping rhizome. Each individual leaf is on a separate stalk about 10 inches long. Cast-iron plant really prefers a moist but well-drained soil but is tolerant of heat and drought, and is hardy in zone 7 and south. Spring is a good time to divide your plants if they have gotten too large, or if you want more. As the rootstock is right at the surface of the soil, it is easy to figure out where to cut the plant apart. In zone 6 and cooler, treat your cast-iron plant as a container plant, taking it into the garden for a summer vacation, returning it indoors when the weather cools.

There is an elegant white-striped version, *A. elatior* `Variegata`, with attractive lengthwise white stripes on the leaves. Sometimes the variegated form reverts, and sends up an occasional plain green leaf that should be removed. Also be cautious about fertilizing, as too much nitrogen may cause plants to grow all green leaves. *A. minor* `Milky Way` is a delightful little charmer, with leaves only 6 to 10 inches long and 2 inches wide, also medium green but attractively spattered with small creamy, ivory-white spots.

White Wood Aster, *Aster divaricatus*
White wood aster, *Aster divaricatus*, is discussed in Perennials, beginning on page 125, in the section on perennials for fall interest.

Hay-scented Fern, *Dennstaedtia punctiloba*
It may seem strange to consider a fern as an option for dry shade since we think of them as plants for moist woodlands. The best fern for difficult dry sites is a fern that would not be tolerated in any less demanding situation. Hay-scented fern is an aggressive plant. Long, wiry, black rhizomes snake along or just below the soil surface, even wriggle their way between the stones of a wall. As long as there is some moisture available, new fronds will be produced throughout the growing season. An attractive yellowish green in color, the deciduous fronds are 15 to 30 inches long. I've seen these ferns grow in full sun in a parched site and I've also seen them as light airy ground covers in the dry sandy soil of an open woodland on Long Island. Hay-scented fern does need moisture while it is becoming established, but can then tolerate a surprisingly dry situation. Hardy from zone 3 to zone 8, this fern will take anything you throw at it. Be warned: This is not a plant for small, confined situations since hay-scented fern can get out of control if it gets into fertile, moist soil. Crushed or bruised fronds smell like new-mown hay.

Epimedium, *Epimedium* Species and Cultivars
Epimediums are well-known for their neat habits and undemanding requirements. Plant them, provide attention while they become established, go away for a decade or two, and the epimediums will still be growing where you left them. Related to the American vancouverias of the West Coast, epimediums come from the Mediterranean region into Asia. The Chinese and Japanese species require water in summer, but those from the Caucasus

and Mediterranean basin are drought-resistant plants that tolerate summer heat.

Epimedium perraldianum is from Algeria, and has glossy tough evergreen leaves. New leaves are bronze-copper in color when they first appear in the spring. The bright yellow flowers are quite attractive. This makes a showy, dense ground cover with good winter interest. Hardiness is somewhat debatable. The cultivar 'Fronleiten' is evergreen and hardy for me in USDA zone 6, a full zone hardier than the usually suggested USDA zone 7.

Native to Iran, *E. pinnatum* has tough, somewhat leathery, dark green leaves with spiny-toothed margins. The bright yellow flowers appear in the late spring in loose racemes of 12 to 30 flowers.

E. pinnatum ssp. *colchicum* from Transcaucasia and the Republic of Georgia, has larger, less prickly leaves, and bright yellow flowers. It has elegant foliage, damaged only at temperatures below 5°F.

From southern Europe, *Epimedium alpinum* is a good ground cover plant, with long rhizomes. Deciduous, the new leaves have a reddish flush when they appear in the spring, maturing to a bright fresh green. The flowers are very small, not particularly showy, with dark red sepals and yellow petals. There are several hybrid epimediums, of which the best for dry shade is *E. x warleyense* (*E. alpinum* x *E. pinnatum* ssp. *colchicum*), hardy to USDA zone 5. With long rhizomes, this makes a loose mat of leaves, light green with a reddish edge in the spring, and with attractive fall color. The coppery brownish flowers are produced in panicles of 10 to 30.

Euphorbia, *Euphorbia* Species and Cultivars

While the majority of euphorbias are sun

Unlike its sun-loving relatives, *Euphorbia amygdaloides robbiae* prefers shade, dry shade, where its evergreen foliage provides excellent year-round interest.

lovers, there are a couple that are fine plants for shade.

Wood Spurge, *Euphorbia amygdaloides*

This euphorbia has hard, almost woody stems 12 to 20 inches tall, creating a bushy effect. Evergreen leaves turn a rich, eye-catching reddish purple color in winter, and are dark olive green during the growing season. Unsuitable for heavy shade, use wood spurge in open woodland, forest clearings, perhaps facing down shrubs such as rhododendrons and mountain laurels. Good companion plants would be epimediums and bluebells, and either the purple or white form of annual honesty, *Lunnaria annua*, would create an attractive association. While the flowers on euphorbia aren't much, the bracts that surround them can be quite showy. In this instance they are a fresh chartreuse yellow, appearing in the late spring on the previous year's growth. There are several cultivars: 'Rubra' is more compact, with winter leaves and new growth in the spring flushed with purple-red; and 'Purpurea' with ruddy leaf color year-round and lime green flowers. *E. amygdaloides* var. *robbiae* has chartreuse flowers in the spring, handsome, broader, dark green rounded leaves in rosettes, a very robust growth habit, and it spreads widely by stolons. Cut the biennial flowering stems out after they bloom, right at ground level, as soon as they begin to look shabby. This encourages new growth, keeping the plants dense and thick and reducing potential competition from weeds. While plants in more open sites may suffer leaf damage in a cold winter, the more protected situation under a tree gives them the necessary shelter to carry them through unharmed. With caution, this can be grown in sheltered sites in zone 6, and is certainly a fine choice in zone 7.

Cypress Spurge, *Euphorbia cyparissias*
Cypress spurge has quite invasive spreading roots that quickly produce a solid mat of bright green shoots. In difficult dry sites this habit can be welcome, for cypress spurge will compete successfully with the worst tree roots, but only in light shade. Just remember: Cypress spurge needs room to run and will take space even if you don't provide it. Narrow, soft-needled, yellow-green leaves densely clothe 8- to 16-inch tall stems. The showy bracts are yellow when they first appear in April, turning reddish toward June.

Euphorbia polychroma (= E. epithymoides)
This is a clumping perennial to 2 feet tall, with robust stems forming rounded, almost spherical green domes. Most often grown in sunny sites, it is also suitable for lightly shaded areas at the edge of woodland. Bright yellow bracts appear in April and May. In particularly dry sites it may be only half as tall. Tough, showy, good in difficult places, this euphorbia may invade nearby areas by seed. There are a couple of selections occasionally available from specialist nurseries: `Emerald Jade` is smaller with attractive fall color;

`Sonnengold' is somewhat lower and more moundlike in form, and has particularly showy yellow bracts. Its chartreuse-yellow bracts would be elegant in combination with the blue flowers of forget-me-nots, *Myosotis sylvatica*, or Siberian bugloss, *Brunnera macrophylla*. For a crisp late spring display add the poet's daffodil, *Narcissus poeticus*, whose crystalline white petals surround a small orange cup rimmed with green.

Woodruff, *Galium odoratum*
Woodruff, *Galium odoratum* (= *Asperula odorata*) would be the perfect ground cover for dry shade except for the unfortunate fact that it is deciduous. Native to beech and mixed hardwood forests, the creeping roots spread widely, running right through any perennial in their path. Epimedium crowns are pierced, though larger cultivars seem undisturbed by this, and medium to large hostas are fine. Woodruff quickly develops into huge mats of soft green stems with whorls of leaves, in April or May tipped with delicate sprays of white flowers. With a scent like vanilla or fresh-mown hay that is most intense in dry stems, this herb is an important ingredient for Maibowle, that symbol of spring made from Rhine wine flavored with strawberries

Woodruff has a delicate appearance, which conceals a sturdy, spreading nature.

and a stem or two of woodruffs. Be careful when disposing of excess woodruffs; a patch I had dug, rolled up like a carpet, and discarded in a shady corner happily rooted and began spreading in the new site, *not* what I had in mind.

Geophytes (= Bulbs, Corms, and Tubers)

Where it is possible to supply adequate moisture in the spring, a fair number of geophytes—bulbous, cormous, and tuberous perennials—will grow, bloom, and then go dormant as the deciduous trees leaf out. These early harbingers of spring—glory-of-the-snow, *Chionodoxa luciliae* with its sprightly clear blue flowers; mauve *Crocus tomasinianus*; electric blue *Scilla sibirica*; fuchsia-pink, spring-flowering *Cyclamen coum*—even seem to prefer dry summer conditions. They are discussed in the chapter Geophytes, beginning on page 165.

Hardy Geraniums, *Geranium* Species and Cultivars

Hardy geraniums, also called cranesbill, are quite different from the South African plants used for summer bedding. Though most are sun lovers suitable for the rock garden or herbaceous border, a couple are suitable for the lightly shaded woodland garden, even for dry shade. *Geranium macrorrhizum* is a nice solution for a dry shady place. Plants have fleshy underground rhizomes and thick stems that root down, forming dense mats as much as 1 foot or 1½ feet across. They flower in the early summer, a somewhat flat magenta color in the species. More desirable color forms are available as cultivars: `Album' is white with the faintest flush of pink; `Bevan's Variety' is deep magenta; `Ingwersen's Variety' is soft pink; and the plant sold as `Spessart' is also pink. Most cultivars, except

for cream-splashed 'Variegatum', have exceptionally long-lasting, more or less evergreen foliage that also displays seasonal color change in the fall and winter. If winter weather is more severe, plants are not even semi-evergreen; however, new leaves emerge very early in the year, and the dense mats of rhizomes keep down weeds. For best results, first improve the soil with the addition of compost or manure before planting. An occasional sprinkling of slow-release fertilizer in subsequent seasons is also a good idea. I use it as a link between groups of lungworts, *Pulmonaria saccharata*, and Siberian bugloss, *Brunnera macrophylla*. These perennials both have largish, simple, rather blocky leaves that also persist late into the winter. The smaller, somewhat rounded, broadly lobed leaves of the geraniums make a nice foil, and the early summer flowers of the geraniums extend the blooming season, since lungworts and bugloss are both spring-flowering plants.

Hellebores, *Helleborus* Species

Hellebores are among the most handsome of foliage plants to grow in moderate to deep shade, but different species of hellebores

At the gardens of Winterthur (in Delaware) in the dry shade beneath mature beech trees, glory-of-the-snow make a blue carpet in March.

have different growth habits, and dry shade can be stressful for some; for example, Christmas rose, *H. niger*, is not suitable for dry shade. They need ample water from spring through midsummer, and want dry conditions only in the late summer. On the other hand, a couple of species will accept dry, deciduous shade.

Lenten Rose, *Helleborus x orientalis*
As cultivated in gardens, Lenten rose is a mixed bag of variable forms, with semievergreen to evergreen palmate leathery leaves and apple green, white, pink, or purple flowers in the early spring, either unspotted or charmingly freckled inside. The true species requires a moist site in the wild but the various forms available at nurseries are fine plants for drought and shade under trees. Hardy to USDA zone 5, plants even happily self-sow as long as the leaf litter is not too deep.

Bear's Foot Hellebore or Stinking Hellebore, *Helleborus foetidus*
This hellebore grows naturally on dry, calcareous soil in deciduous woodlands and thickets. Its unusual habit of growth produces leafy green stems in the summer that, with the flower buds, persist through the winter, and bloom in the spring. After flowering, these stems produce seed and then die, to be replaced by a new set of stems from the thick rootstock. The effect is evergreen, with handsome, very deeply lobed, very dark, almost black-green leaves, and terminal panicles of numerous small, cup-shaped apple green flowers with purple rims in the early spring. They self-sow freely in my garden. One attractive variant is *H. foetidus* 'Westerfliske', which has deep mahogany red stems. If kept isolated, about 70 percent of the seedlings will display the same handsome stem color.

Both Lenten rose and bear's foot hellebore are discussed more thoroughly in Perennials, beginning on page 125.

Deep green, fine textured evergreen leaves make bear's foot hellebore, *Helleborus foetidus*, a welcome addition to the winter garden.

Aaron's Beard, *Hypericum calycinum*
Suitable even for sandy soils as well as loamy ones, Aaron's beard is a somewhat shrubby ground cover with spreading roots and arching, trailing branches that root at their tips. This growth habit and its ability to quickly cover large areas makes Aaron's beard suitable for steep slopes. An annual trimming in the early spring encourages new growth and keeps plants at their most attractive (tricky work on a steep slope). In sheltered locations or in milder climates plants keep their 3- to 4-inch-long, blue-green leaves year-round. Bright golden yellow flowers with a central boss of long stamens scatter themselves over the plants from July to September.

Stinking Iris or Gladwyn Iris, *Iris foetidissima*

Subdued is a kind description of gladwyn iris' flowers—dull, dingy beige veined with purple, and a malodorous scent to boot. Rather, stinking iris is valued for its fall interest, when seed pods burst and gape open to reveal glowing red-orange seeds that hold for many weeks. Hardy to zone 7, stinking iris thrives in the driest, darkest corners, its dense, spreading habit of growth producing attractive clumps of swordlike, evergreen leaves that also smell foul when crushed. Drought is not required, merely tolerated. There are two yellow-flowered forms: var. *citrina* has yellow flowers veined with mauve, and the even handsomer var. *lutescens*, with unmarked, pale yellow flowers the frosty color of lemon sorbet; `Fructoalba' has white seeds, but having never seen it I don't know if this is an improvement over the typical red-orange or not; the somewhat more tender `Variegata' has cream-striped leaves, quite sprightly and attractive.

Dead Nettle, Yellow Archangel, *Lamium galeobdolon*

Yellow archangel is definitely *not* a plant to mix with other perennials, though fine with large geophytes such as daffodils. It races over ground, covering large areas in a short time. It is the ideal plant for those difficult, dark, dry corners where all you want is something for cover. *Lamium* (= *Lamiastrum*) *galeobdolon* itself is rarely planted; rather, various handsomely silver-splotched forms are cultivated: `Variegatum' and `Type Ronsdorf' both have smaller, more rounded, mottled leaves and are more moderately vigorous in growth; `Silberteppich' (= `Silver Carpet') is even slower-growing, with conspicuous, green-veined, intensely silver leaves. It is

Various species of lamium and lamiastrum with silver-splashed foliage and pleasant flowers make good ground covers in shady situations.

unfortunately less easily established than its more invasive cousins. Most popular is `Florentinum' with 12-inch-tall upright stems of large, silver-splashed leaves that take on reddish hues in the winter. Hardy to zone 4, the 2-foot-long, ground-hugging stems of yellow archangels root down and resprout to cover yards, making a handsome green and silver carpet that flows up hill, down dale, and leaps across small ditches. Yellow flowers in the spring are also attractive.

There is a well-behaved cultivar of *Lamiastrum galeobdolon*, named `Hermann's Pride'. Upright, 12-inch-tall stems of silver-netted leaves make a tidy clump, enhanced with soft yellow flowers in May. Plants grow well in heavily shaded areas where their attractive foliage is especially welcome. Easily propagated from tip cuttings taken in the spring, plants make an appealing edging to a path or bed, especially charming in combination with glaucous, blue-leaved hosta.

Honesty, *Lunaria annua*

Described in Annuals, Biennials, and Tender

Perennials, beginning on page 187, biennial honesty, in both its mauve and white-flowered forms, will naturalize and form self-perpetuating colonies in dry woods.

Nippon Lily, *Rohdea japonica*

Gardeners in the Southeast and Deep South find Nippon lily a mainstay of shady gardens with dry, poor soil. Their landscape is so filled with pine trees that they are taken for granted, and the ground beneath is arid and infertile. With lustrous, dark green leaves looking fresh and elegant through the worst summer drought, you can see why Nippon lily is popularly grown for its foliage. Recently, one summer in Georgia was so dry that farmers only cut hay once, rather than the customary four or five times. Nippon lily, without any irrigation, looked as good as ever. While leaves are the primary reason to grow this Japanese plant, the coblike clusters of bright red fruits in the fall are also showy. Flowers are of little ornamental value, an odd, tightly packed spike of creamy, pale yellow flowers tucked down in the center of the leaf cluster in May or June. Though many reference books suggest Nippon lily is only hardy to zone 7, it grows just fine without any extra winter protection in my zone 6 garden, and thrives at the Arnold Arboretum in Boston. Obviously it is hardier than the first cautious estimates suggest.

Large-flowered Comfrey, *Symphytum grandiflorum*

Once classed among the lungworts, large-flowered comfrey is an adaptable plant that is drought- and shade-tolerant, and also grows well in damp soils. Rhizomes spread just below the soil surface, quickly produce numerous unbranched, scabrous (rough, hairy) stems that rapidly create large, ground-covering colonies. Nonflowering stems clothed in dark green, semievergreen foliage trail on the ground, pointing up at the tip. Pale, unobtrusive, creamy, yellowish white tubular flowers appear over a three-to four-week period in the spring, in few-flowered clusters at the tip of flowering stems. This plant's greatest value is its ability to create a summer ground cover in dry shade, vigorous and dense enough to crowd out weeds before they become established.

Vancouveria, *Vancouveria* Species

A West Coast counterpart of epimedium, vancouveria has flowers with six petals, sepals, and stamens, while epimedium flowers are four-parted. Slender, creeping rhizomes make quick-spreading, weed-suppressing colonies of wiry stems with attractive, open foliage. The compound leaves are divided two or three times into threes, creating a pleasing, fine-textured carpet. Each leaflet is not so acutely pointed as epimedium, nor toothed along their margins. There are two evergreen species hardy to zone 7. *Vancouveria chrysantha* grows about 12 inches tall, has more or less evergreen leaves, and yellow flowers. Somewhat slower-growing *V. planipetala* reaches 12 to 18 inches tall, with white or lavender-tinted flowers.

Deciduous, *Vancouveria hexandra* grows 18 inches tall, usually less, with white flowers in the late spring, and is hardy to zone 5. Especially in difficult, dry sites, attention to watering while the plants are becoming established is important. Hot, dry summers are difficult. Open, cold, snowless winters are also hard on vancouveria, especially its first year in a new site. The evergreen species especially should be mulched with pine boughs for protection.

Plants for Shady Sites with Moist to Wet Soil

There are shade-tolerant plants that actually prefer moist soil, but first you need to understand the constraints and limitations that poor drainage imposes. Generally speaking, the majority of familiar garden plants prefer adequate moisture that moves through the soil, rather than continually wet conditions.

Constantly saturated soils can cause root rot, even in sunny sites where plants utilize water more efficiently and air circulation is better. In shade, susceptible plants come down with fungal leaf diseases such as mildew. Select plants adapted to the condition, rather than try to change the site.

Recognize that moisture-tolerant plants do not grow in water. Where there is open water, plants need to have their crown raised above water on a hummock or berm, with their roots extending down into wet soil. Often water levels fluctuate and a very wet site in the spring is considerably drier in mid-summer. Plants naturally adapted to wet woodlands can frequently, but not always, adjust to these variations. Many moisture-tolerant plants are equally useful in average conditions. Those that demand moisture are so noted. When reading a nursery catalog or gardening book, look for phrases such as "thriving in moist or even boggy ground," as one book characterizes astilbes, or "essentially trouble-free, given a favorable site with some shade and at least moderately moist soil," as another describes spicebush, *Lindera benzoin*.

An excellent choice for moist soil, shadblow is an beautiful flowering tree.

Trees and Shrubs

Swamp Maple, *Acer rubrum*

Swamp maple, often the dominant tree in wet lowlands, is itself shade-tolerant. Hardy in zones 3 to 9, it is serviceable not only in poorly drained sites with occasional standing water, but even accepts those difficult now wet, now dry, situations. Trees have clusters of red flowers in the spring before the leaves appear, individually small, but rather showy en masse. Leaves turn a wonderful bright scarlet, orange, or yellow in the fall. I especially like the appearance of the red leaves fallen onto the yellow fronds of cinnamon or interrupted ferns beneath the tree. Both trunk and branches are clad in silver gray bark, lending winter interest to the landscape. Little maintenance is required, perhaps some pruning if winter ice storms damage the branches. Several cultivars are available, chosen for a more columnar or more compact form, or exceptional fall color.

River Birch, *Betula nigra*

The common name of river birch suggests its adaptability to wet soils. Attractive medium-green leaves turn yellowish in the fall before dropping. The bark is an outstanding feature—reddish amber and peeling off in decorative thin curls. `Heritage' is a clone with especially showy bark. Native to the eastern half of the United States, river birch is hardy in zones 4 to 9; however, local material should be chosen at the extremes of their range. This is pest-resistant birch, seldom affected by bronze birch borers, and little troubled by leaf miners. River birch accepts only light shade; more will affect its growth.

Summersweet, *Clethra alnifolia*

A native shrub that has won a permanent

place in nursery catalogs, summersweet has, as its name suggests, fragrant summer flowers. Native to the eastern United States and hardy in zones 5 to 9, summersweet requires moist soils if it is to do well. Insect pests, particularly mites, are a problem in dry situations. A pretty thing, plants grow about 9 feet tall, somewhat leggy and straggly, but can be kept more compact with a little judicious pruning. The same method controls its modest suckering habit should underground stems spread beyond their allotted space. Tight spikes of fragrant white or pinkish flowers appear from mid- to late summer. `Rosea' is an especially well-colored pink form. Summersweets thrive in moderately dense shade, remaining healthy and vigorous.

Summer-flowering, sweetly fragrant, shade-tolerant, summersweet is a fine contribution to gardeners from North America's native flora.

Tatarian Dogwood, *Cornus alba*
Tatarian dogwood is an adaptable, easily satisfied shrub that happily grows in a variety of soils, moisture levels, and light conditions, hence its suitability for a moderately shaded site with wet soil. Probably the most popular cultivar is `Elegantissima', with white-edged leaves that add a fresh touch to the shady garden. Underplanting with white-flowered impatiens enhances the effect. Tatarian dogwood is also useful for winter interest. Though younger stems are green in the early summer, the bark takes on progressively reddish tones through the late fall, becoming bright red in the winter. Native to chilly Siberia, Manchuria, northern China, and North Korea, tatarian dogwood is hardy in zones 3 to 8.

Inkberry, *Ilex glabra*
Inkberry is a workhorse shrub that grows in shady wet places, remaining healthy and vigorous even in moderately dense shade. Salt-tolerant, inkberry can even grow in coastal situations or where winter deicing salt is used on adjacent roadways. It has small, 1- to 2-inch-long glossy, evergreen leaves. Though the shrub grows 9 feet tall it can readily be sheared into a hedge or

clipped to encourage more fullness if it is used for screening. Leggy plants can be rejuvenated by cutting back hard in the early spring. There is a dense, slower-growing female cultivar, `Compacta', which can readily be kept below 5 feet tall. Hollies being dioecious, each shrub separately sexed male or female, only female hollies bear fruit. Hardy in zones 5 to 9, inkberry's flowers and fruit are insignificant—the former small and white, the latter small and black. `Ivory Queen' is a white-fruited cultivar that does give a better display.

Spicebush, *Lindera benzoin*
Spicebush is a charming shrub native to the northeastern United States, growing as far south and west as Florida and Texas. It grows in wet swales together with skunk cabbage and ferns, enhancing wet woodlands in early spring, with masses of small, fragrant, chartreuse yellow flowers on bare branches before it leafs out. Large, pointed, oval, medium-green leaves have an aromatic fragrance

when crushed. Spicebush is dioecious, and female plants have bright red berries similar in appearance to those of flowering dogwood, attractive against the clear yellow fall color of the leaves. Hardy in zones 5 to 9, spicebush needs a shady site with moist to wet soil and thrives even in densely shaded sites. Smooth hydrangea, mapleleaf viburnum, and inkberry would also grow well and look attractive in combination with spicebush. It is the larval food plant for spicebush swallowtail butterflies.

Sweetbay, *Magnolia virginiana*
Sweetbay is an excellent choice for a small tree to grow in moderately dense shade, especially on sites with moist soil. Its strikingly fragrant, creamy white, 3-inch-diame-

ter flowers perfume the garden in the late spring and early summer. Handsome 5-inch-long, glossy leaves are bright green above and silvery white beneath, very attractive when swaying in a breeze. Foliage is semievergreen to evergreen, especially in var. *australis*, from the southern coastal plains. `Henry Hicks' is a selection that is not only hardy in the warmer portions of zone 5, but remains evergreen even in the Boston area.

Rosebay Rhododendron, *Rhododendron maximum*
At a potential 20 to 35 feet tall, rosebay rhododendron is more of a small understory tree than a typical shrub. Where it grows wild in the Appalachian Mountains, multiple trunks form thickets of intertwining branches,

In a close-up, the flowers of spicebush reveal their simple detail.

making impenetrable tangles that are hellish to hike through. Fortunately, rosebay rhododendron is better behaved in the garden, growing 10 to 15 feet tall with coarse, 4- to 8-inch-long, leathery, evergreen leaves making an effective screen. Large clusters of attractive white to rose pink flowers appear in early to midsummer, partially obscured by new leaves. Under average soil moisture, rosebay rhododendron combines well with flowering dogwood and mountain laurel. Deer eat the leaves, but if they can be protected until the plants grow taller than the deer can browse, rosebay rhododendron can outgrow their depredations. Tolerant of both moderately dense shade and moisture, rosebay rhododendron does not like hot summers. It grows best in zones 5 and 6, in cooler summer portions of zone 7, and in the more sheltered regions of zone 4.

Swamp Azalea, *Rhododendron viscosum*

Swamp azalea is an excellent deciduous rhododendron that naturally grows in swamps throughout the eastern United States, from Maine to Georgia and Alabama. Useful for its tolerance of moderate shade and moist sites, swamp azalea should also be grown for its richly perfumed white flowers in early to midsummer. They are so fragrant that, at the right time of year, I can find them in the wild by their very spicy, clovelike scent before I ever see them. Hardy in zones 4 to 9, plants grow 7 to 12 feet tall, and spread as wide, with an open habit. Leaves are light green when they emerge in the spring, turning darker green as they mature. Fall color is yellowish orange to maroon-purple, providing another season of interest. Hardy in zones 4 to 9, swamp azalea must have a moist to wet site. In the wild it grows on hummocks where the roots can reach constant moisture but the crown is not submerged. Red maple and summersweet are natural associations that would also work well in gardens.

Perennials

Jack-in-the-pulpit, *Arisaema triphyllum*

Jack-in-the-pulpit is an excellent native plant more appreciated abroad than at home. It is discussed in Geophytes, beginning on page 165.

Astilbe, *Astilbe* Species and Cultivars

All astilbes, the cultivars as well as wild species, prefer a damp to moist, fertile soil. They are discussed in Perennials, beginning on page 125.

Shield-leaf, *Astilboides tabularis*

It takes a large garden to provide room for a mass planting of shield-leaf, *Astilboides tabularis* (= *Rodgersia tabularis*), as this is an imposing plant. Often growing over a yard high and wide, plants need moist soil, perhaps along a woodland stream, to achieve this bulk. In damp sites, perhaps planted under deep-rooted trees, plants will be somewhat reduced in scale. The bold, slightly lobed, platelike leaves seem to balance on the leaf stem, for the petiole is centered on the leaf. Leaves may reach 3 feet across, providing a bold accent in a planting of ferns. A tall plume of cream-white flowers appears in June, resembling that of an astilbe on steroids. Almost 5 feet tall, it reaches well above the leaves. While the foliage combination of shield-leaf and astilbe would look good, I think the similarity of flowers precludes using the two together. They are in zones 5 to 7. Usually, American catalogs still label shield-leaf as a *Rodgersia*.

Goatsbeard, *Aruncus dioicus*

Goatsbeard is a handsome plant, a colossus with broad, fernlike leaves that are attractive from spring to fall. Best in moist soil, where plants form 4- to 6½-foot-tall mounds of 2- to 3-foot-long pinnately compound leaves, each leaflet is saw-toothed along the edges. Then, in the late spring, plants produce enormous branched panicles (again, like an astilbe) of creamy white flowers. Goatsbeard is dioecious, with individual plants bearing male or female flowers. Female plants have drooping plumes and, where happy, they provide numerous self-sown seedlings. These can be difficult to accommodate if space is limited. Male plants have more erect, rather feathery, flower plumes that some find more attractive (and that avoids the difficulty of unwanted offspring). Though hardy from zones 3 to 7, goatsbeard really does not tolerate summer heat and performs poorly in southern gardens. Very large hosta would be excellent companions, and shield-leaf would work since the flowering times do not overlap.

Marsh Marigold, *Caltha palustris*

Marsh marigold is among the first native plants to begin growing in the spring. Vivid against the brown carpet of fallen leaves, rich green leaves and bright yellow flowers enliven a swamp. If you have a shaded wet site, turn to nature as a teacher and welcome this plant into your garden.

A site with bright to moderate shade and moist soil is most suitable while the marsh marigold is in active growth. The sunnier the

A marvelous combination for late summer: the stately bulk of goatsbeard, *Aruncus dioicus*, in seed, together with the bold foliage of *Hosta sieboldiana* 'Elegans'.

site, the higher the moisture level should be. Because marsh marigold is summer dormant (not only has it finished flowering, but leaves are also absent) drier conditions in summer are acceptable.

Bugbanes, *Cimicifuga* Species and Cultivars

All the bugbanes, *Cimicifuga* species, prefer moist to damp conditions. Their leaves resemble those of goatsbeard, astilbe, and doll's eyes, so for best results combine bugbane with bolder-leaved plants and others with a linear texture. The self-supporting flower spikes resemble tall white or cream-colored, narrow-diameter bottlebrushes. Different species bloom in the early or late summer, or the fall, offering several options for effective combinations. All have dark green leaves, pinnately compound to a greater or lesser extent. Bugbane grows best in an edge of woodland situation, with rich, acid soil and moist shade. It is more refined in growth than goatsbeard, and takes up relatively little room. All species are hardy from zones 3 to 8.

American Bugbane, *Cimicifuga americana*

Late-summer-blooming American bugbane has flower spikes almost 6 feet tall, and each leaf has three leaflets, each of which is again divided two or three times.

Snakeroot or Cohosh, *C. racemosa*

This bugbane is also native to eastern North America, and flowers earlier in the summer, with 6- to 8-foot-tall spires of white flowers that never need staking. (I've seen trucks barrel down a road beside which plants are growing wild; flowering stems flail around in the slipstream and return upright.) If sufficient moisture is lacking, or if plants are grown in a sunny site, they will be stunted and leaves first brown along the margin, then fall off.

Kamchatka bugbane, *C. simplex*
This bugbane flowers in the late fall, with 3- to 4-foot-tall wands of white flowers. One popular cultivar is `White Pearl'. Consider Kamchatka bugbane as a partner for the maple-leafed, yellow bell-flowered kirengeshoma, which flowers about the same time. In my Connecticut garden, plants bloom in mid-October, and frost may arrive before the flowers, but there is always next year. Another September to October-blooming species, *C. ramosa*, is unfortunately difficult to find at nurseries. Growing to 7 feet tall, the tall spikes of creamy white flowers remain in good condition for a long time. There is a very dark-leaved cultivar, `Brunette', which grows only 3 to 4 feet tall. This cultivar has deeply bronzed leaves and purple stems, against which the white flowers make a handsome display.

Umbrella Leaf, *Diphylleia cymosa*
Umbrella leaf requires moist, woodland soils high in organic matter. It grows best in lightly shaded sites where new leaves can have the necessary protection from late spring frosts. With a common name of umbrella leaf, you might anticipate a plant with bold foliage; indeed, a child could pluck one of the foot-wide leaves for suitable shelter in a downpour. Each leaf is deeply notched, with the two segments again incised into several pointed lobes. The small white flowers in May aren't anything much but quickly fall, to be followed by dramatic, indigo-blue berries. The combination of umbrella leaf's blue berries with the slender white candles of late-blooming bugbanes is an elegant one. Astilbes also furnish excellent foliage contrast. Unfortunately, the leaves of umbrella leaf are subject to slug damage, and precautionary measures are essential. Local wisdom may prescribe saucers of beer in which the mollusks can drown themselves, night patrols armed with bamboo shish-kabob

As bright as pirate's gold, marsh marigold has a treasure chest of flowers.

In early spring the bright yellow flowers and rich green leaves of marsh marigold light up a severe brown landscape.

skewers, a band of diatomaceous earth, or even more ruthless measures.

Ferns
Though we associate ferns with wet, shady places, not all ferns insist on such conditions. Those that grow best with really moist to wet soil, ideally suited for that damp swale or ditch where less tolerant perennials get root rot, are discussed here.

Ostrich or Shuttlecock Fern, *Matteuccia struthiopteris*
Commonly named ostrich fern, for the feathery appearance of fertile fronds, or shuttlecock fern for the striking resemblance of the clustered sterile fronds to an enlarged badminton shuttlecock, ostrich fern is a large, bold, handsome plant for a moist, shady site

in zones 2 to 8. Though these ferns look as if the clusters of 3- to 5-foot-tall, plumelike sterile fronds, wider at the top and tapering gradually toward the base, arise from individual plants, the crowns are all connected underground by a network of spreading rhizomes. This growth habit and invasive tendencies suggest ostrich ferns' suitability for larger sites rather than confined spaces. Native to stream banks, where they grow in large groups, these ferns need a constantly moist site, for they will yellow and go dormant early in drier places. I like to combine ostrich fern with mayapple, allowing the two plants to intermingle freely, or with *Hosta* `Krossa Regal', which has a similar vaselike shape. The woody fertile fronds persist through the winter, lending interest through the dormant season.

Sensitive Fern, *Onoclea sensibilis*

This fern has no tender feelings, and is easily bruised. Sterile fronds turn yellow to russet brown with the first frost. In the wild these ferns are found in damp wooded hollows and swales, and in sunny wet meadows. Like ostrich fern, this is a dimorphic species, with noticeably different appearance in fertile and sterile fronds. Sterile fronds have a coarse, somewhat tropical appearance that contrasts nicely with other perennials such as rodgersia or medium to large hosta for foliage contrast. Sensitive fern also romps around the garden, but at 12 to 30 inches tall, it is smaller in scale. The attractive, dark brown, winter-persistent fertile fronds resemble clusters of beads on stiff stems. They are an elegant addition to dried flower arrangements. Sensitive fern also grows with average soil moisture, and is hardy in zones 2 to 10.

Osmunda Ferns

The three species of osmunda ferns typify "fern" in many minds—large clumps of fronds arise from substantial, tangled, wiry rhizomes that form tussocks above the slow-moving water of a swamp. These ferns definitely need moist soil, for dry conditions first send them dormant, then kill the plants. Hardy from zones 3 to 10, they make excellent, statuesque, well-behaved additions to the garden.

The slender white wands of bugbane, *Cimicifuga racemosa*, are far more elegant than the common name suggests.

Cinnamon fern, *Osmunda cinammomea*, grows 2 to 4 feet tall. Tawny-haired fiddle-heads develop in the fall, creating an eggs-in-a-nest look through the winter. They uncoil in the spring to form a vaselike clump of dark green sterile fronds. Fertile fronds arise from the middle, turning from green to a handsome cinnamon brown as spores mature. These wither away in the early summer, leaving the sterile fronds that remain in good condition until the fall, when they turn from green to gold or russet before dying down.

Similar in size and overall form, the well-named interrupted fern, *O. claytonia*, has one important difference: both have fertile, spore-bearing pinnae, and sterile pinnae, on the same frond. Their arrangement, with green, sterile portions above and below the congested, brown, fertile segment, provides the interruption when the latter fall off after the spores are released in the summer.

Royal fern, *O. regalis*, displays still a different arrangement. This elegant fern has un-fernlike sterile pinnae that more closely resemble compound leaves. Congested, beadlike spore cases on the fertile pinnae cluster at the upper third of the frond, giving a decidedly flowerlike appearance. Fronds grow 2 to 5 feet tall from a compact crown. This fern needs constant moisture, even wet soil, rich in organic matter. With sufficient moisture, royal fern will do well in sunny sites but is most satisfactory in shade.

Marsh Ferns, *Thelypteris palustris*

This fern is easily cultivated with creeping rhizomes that produce scattered, individual 18- to 30-inch-long fronds. Native to wet meadows and swamps, marsh fern can grow in full sun if the soil is very wet. Where it can be given room to roam, it performs admirably in shady gardens with merely moist soil. The delicate, finely textured fronds are a pretty, bluish green color, combining nicely with glaucous, blue-leaved hosta. It is hardy in zones 2 to 10.

The fertile fronds of cinnamon fern have a rusty color and distinctive appearance, quite different from the typical green fronds.

Netted Chain Fern, *Woodwardia aureolata*
This fern is definitely hardy in zones 5 to 9, with some authorities suggesting it is even more cold-tolerant. Certainly you'd want to try netted chain fern, with 1- to 2-foot-tall fronds similar to those of sensitive fern, either singly or in loose clusters along the creeping, quickly spreading, branching rhizomes. The sterile fronds, reddish green when they first appear in the spring and maturing to a glossy dark green, all have netted veins. Fertile fronds have very narrow, linear pinnae with chains of spore cases packing the underside. Native to swampy sites, netted chain fern requires constantly moist to wet soil, high in organic matter. Give it suitably sturdy companion plants, such as rodgersia and drooping sedge, *Carex pendula*.

Virginia Chain Fern, *W. virginica*
This fern is also deciduous, with erect fronds 18 to 24 inches long. The widely spreading rhizomes are often actually submerged in water, indicative of this fern's requirement for constant moisture. The aptly named giant chain fern, *W. fimbriata* (= *W. chamissoi*) comes from the moist coastal forests of the northwestern United States and Canada. The lacy-textured, arching, evergreen fronds are 3 to 5 feet long, sometimes double that. Moderately easy to grow, giant chain fern is hardy in zones 8 and 9, making stately fountains of fronds, for the rhizome is more compact. Obviously it needs to be placed with plants of similarly heroic scale and/or bold, coarse foliage, such as the umbrella leaf and umbrella plant.

Grasslike Plants
Grasslike in appearance, several sedges and woodrush add a lovely linear texture to damp, shady sites. Many sedge species in the

genus *Carex* are commonly associated with moist to wet sites, with some actually growing in water. They often grow in woodlands, making them valuable for shady gardens. As interest in ornamental grasses and grasslike plants continues to swell, new arrivals are regularly introduced. Take the time to check them out; while sedges may be slow to quickly spreading clump formers, some are invasive, fast-running types that can be a problem, especially where space is limited. Woodrushes, in the genus *Luzula*, are also plants of damp woodlands. These tend to be plants of quiet charm, rather than wild excitement.

Crimson Seed Sedge, *C. baccans*

A tender species recently introduced from India, it is definitely hardy in zone 9 and probably also hardy in zone 8. Evergreen leaves less than an inch wide and 2 to 3 feet long fountain out in a clump, making it an excellent focal point for moist to wet sites in partial to full shade. Its most notable attribute, in addition to evergreen foliage, are the seeds, copiously produced by greenish flower clusters 6 to 12 inches long and 2 or 3 inches wide. Green at first, the seeds mature to a vivid red-orange. Easily propagated by division, propagation by seed is difficult and plants are not known to naturalize. This sedge would be interesting as a container plant, brought indoors for the winter in regions where its garden survival is not possible.

Bowles Golden Sedge, *Carex elata*

This is a form of tussock sedge, with wonderful, narrow, arching, soft leaves $1/8$ to $1/2$ inch wide, golden yellow with the thinnest of green margins. Semievergreen new growth in the spring has the most vivid coloration, maturing to a chartreuse green in the late summer. To prosper, Bowles golden sedge must be constantly moist, and colors best in light shade in zones 5 to 9. Since it reaches 2 feet tall by 2 feet wide, more under ideal conditions, one plant creates a wonderful focal point. Chartreuse-leafed hosta makes a great companion. Either use just a couple of plants of a large-scale cultivar such as `Piedmont Gold', `Sum and Substance', `Sun Power', or `Zounds', or mass a more modest-sized golden-leaved cultivar such as `Fortunei Aurea' or `Gold Drop'.

Palm Sedge, *Carex muskingumensis*

Palm sedge is a creeping plant that first falls over, then spreads. Effectively, plants are 2 feet tall, though the stems are longer. Leaves look something like miniature palms, with long, narrow leaves, $1/4$ inch wide by 4 to 8 inches long, radiating from the tips of gracefully arching, 2- to 3-foot-long stems. Leaves and stems yellow with the first hard, black frost. Palm sedge sulks if it dries out, preferring constantly moist soil in lightly shaded to sunny areas. It will even grow in shallow water. In sun the leaves become noticeably more yellow. Attractive when planted in small groups, palm sedge make a nice, shade-tolerant ground cover, thanks to its creeping habit, and colonizes nearby space. It is also charming in container plantings. It is hardy in zones 4 to 9.

Drooping Sedge, *Carex pendula*

Drooping sedge is a popular choice for rich, wet soil in light shade, tolerating full sun only if kept constantly moist. With arching stems up to 6 feet long, this is a somewhat coarse plant with long, arching leaves. Though considered evergreen, there may be some frost damage, and where it occurs, stems should be cut to the ground before new growth begins in the spring. Though it grows slowly, drooping sedge does eventually get quite large, and ample room should be provided when first you plant it. Its linear form accents bold, blocky hosta foliage and the more finely cut leaves of astilbe, goatsbeard, and similar foliage plants. Drooping sedge is hardy in zones 5 to 9.

Creeping Variegated Broad-leafed Sedge,
Carex siderostricia 'Variegata'
If I had to choose just one, I think this would be my favorite sedge. Its almost inch-wide, 12- to 18-inch-long leaves are elegantly striped in medium to dark green, and creamy white. The variegation is found as marginal bands and central streaking. In the winter, foliage turns tawny brown, and new growth in the spring is flushed with showy pink. One is nice, more is better, as plants creep only slowly by means of underground stems. Constant moisture, light shade, and humus-rich soil suit this sedge best. It is elegant with silver-fronded Japanese painted fern and smaller-leaved, glaucous blue hosta. Though listed as hardy in zones 7 to 9, it has been a reliable component in my zone 6 garden for several years, and also grows well in zone 5 gardens around Boston, Massachusetts.

Greater Woodrush, *Luzula maxima*
(= *Luzula sylvatica*)
This sedge is a clump-forming evergreen species that flourishes in moist sites with woodland shade, positively thriving in competition with tree roots. The 8- to 10-inch-long leaves are less than an inch wide, and plants make flattened mounds of foliage, less than a foot tall. The bright green new leaves are edged and covered with fine downy hairs that catch the night-fallen dew, giving leaves a bright sparkling appearance in the morning light of early spring. Though it tolerates average moisture, even intermittently drier sites, greater woodrush grows best with ample moisture in light to moderate shade. Hardy from zones 4 to 9, I like to use it in groups of several plants than as an isolated individual. Typically, the linear, straplike leaves combine nicely with smaller hosta, ferns, and astilbe. `Marginata'

has leaves with a thin, nearly imperceptible, golden yellow edge.

Hosta
Hostas are discussed in Perennials, beginning on page 125.

Virginia Bluebell, *Mertensia virginica*
I remember vividly a river-bottom swamp in Missouri I visited the first of May one year, carpeted with Virginia bluebell, *Mertensia virginica*. Elegant, with smooth, glaucous, oval leaves and stems of clear blue flowers like small bells that dangle in small clusters. There is one major drawback—Virginia bluebell is ephemeral, going dormant soon after flowering. This is not much of a problem if you grow only a few, but can be awkward where plants are massed. Mature plants of Virginia bluebell move poorly; however, self-sown seedlings that soon volunteer are easy to transplant. Suitable for moist to average conditions, this charming native is hardy from zones 5 to 8. Choose companion plants such as ferns, whose foliage conceals the bare spaces left by Virginia bluebell summer dormancy. Further add variegated Solomon's seal or white-variegated hosta for an elegant grouping from spring to fall.

Pattern and contrast of leaf shape is the fundamental principle of designing with foliage.

Umbrella Plant, *Darmera pelatata*

Umbrella plant, *Darmera pelatata* (= *Peltiphyllum peltatum*), needs moist or at least constantly damp soils, for in its native haunts in the Pacific Northwest, it grows wild in mountain streams. The plants flower first in April or May, sending up a wide umbrella head of clustered, star-shaped pink flowers on stout, furry, reddish, 3- to 6-foot-tall stems. After these fade and dwindle away, the thick creeping rhizomes produce masses of rounded, 1- to 2-foot-wide leaves with 10 to 15 deep lobes. The leaves are peltate, similar to those of shield plants, with the petiole centered on the leaf. Easy to grow, umbrella plants make a bold foliage accent in semishaded to sunny sites. The sunnier the site, the more water plants require, until plants in full sun need a pond-side site. `Nana' is smaller in all respects, and grows only a foot high.

Mayapple, *Podophyllum peltatum*

Mayapple is a familiar component of wet woodlands of eastern North America. The tough rhizomes run along at or just below the surface of moist, humus-rich sites, in the spring sending up folded leaves furled like a parasol. Though plants are perfectly hardy to zone 4, the new growth is very susceptible to frost damage. Expanding leaves are peltate when they mature, palmate, deeply lobed, and a pleasing fresh green in color. Between each pair of leaves on their stout supporting stem nods a good-sized white flower, followed by a banty-egg-sized greenish-yellow fruit. Leaves tend to yellow and decline as the summer becomes hot and dry, often going dormant in late August. Therefore, though plants quickly spread and form large colonies, they have scant value as a ground cover. Mayapple is handsome in combination with ostrich fern on a wet site.

Painter's Palette, *Polygonum virginianum*

The plain green-leaved form of *Polygonum virginianum* (= *Tovara virginiana*) is generally

Color and variegation provide additional interest to foliage, beyond that of leaf shape.

not grown. Rather, it is the attractively variegated cultivars, either `Painter's Palette' with splashes of gold overlaid with a pinkish brown chevron, or `Variegatum' with its variegated leaves streaked and splashed with ivory and primrose yellow, that are cultivated. Plants will happily grow in damp soil and even spread themselves out into shallow water. Though leaves emerge rather late in the spring, they continue to grow through the summer to make a pleasant, if somewhat tall, ground cover. Tovara can most kindly be described as "a good doer," while some might be so crass as to call it invasive. Keep it away from other plants with more refined growth habits, lest they be overrun, and partner it with other, equally enthusiastic spreaders such as mayapples.

Japanese Primrose, *Primula japonica*

Japanese primrose has a critical need for moisture. Rather than going dormant if the soil dries out in the summer, this primrose dies. Partially shaded sites that remain boggy (though with some movement of the water as stagnant conditions are also harmful) are ideal. Plants will also grow along the banks of a vernal pool, shallowly inundated in the spring but merely muddy in the summer. With adequate moisture, Japanese primrose sends up 12- to 24-inch-tall stems, with from 1 to 6 tiers of flowers. Each whorl has 8 to 12 flowers, individually an inch or more wide, in

Virginia bluebells are charming when their sky-blue bells open in spring.

bright fuchsia pink, soft rose, or white. The two most commonly available cultivars are self-descriptive `Miller's Crimson' and `Postford White'. Hardy in zones 5 to 7, Japanese primrose associates quite happily with moderately sized hosta and ferns, Welsh poppies, *Meconopsis cambrica*, and false hellebore.

Rodgersia, *Rodgersia* Species and Cultivars
Though their flowers are pretty enough, rather like those of a giant astilbe, rodgersias are grown for their elegant foliage. Bold and stately, a foot or more across, the effect is never coarse, for the leaves are pinnately or palmately compound. Whether grown in semishade or sun, plants only thrive if provided with constant moisture, flourishing at pondside and reveling in marshy soil. Rodgersia generally performs best in zone 5 and 6. One rodgersia with masses of Japanese primroses is beautiful. Big ferns, false hellebore, and umbrella leaf (either one) make good companions. Since rodgersias eventually do make sizeable plants, be careful to allow ample room for their mature dimensions. Remember that shield-leaf, *Astilboides tabularis*, has sometimes been classed as a rodgersia.

Fingerleaf Rodgersia, *Rodgersia aesculifolia*
This rodgersia has leaves like those of a horse chestnut, with seven large leaflets palmately arranged on shaggy, brown-haired petioles. Overall, plants reach 4 feet high and slowly, steadily, spread 4 feet wide. Blooming in June or July, the creamy white flowers (individually rather small) are massed together into a 1½- to 2-foot-long flat-topped panicle.

Featherleaf Rodgersia, *R. pinnata*
Featherleaf rodgersia has pinnately compound leaves, with four to eight leaflets arranged in two rows along the main axis, and one more at the end. When leaves first appear in the spring they have an attractive bronze flush, very nice with copper- or deep bronze-leaved astilbes. The branched panicles have a good dense crop of rosy red flowers. Color variations do exist, and if this is important to you, then choose among the named cultivars: `Alba' has creamy white flowers; the creamy white flowers on `Elegans' have tinges of pink; `Rosea' is, well, rose-pink; `Rubra' has deep red flowers. Featherleaf rodgersias grow in zone 5 to 7.

False Hellebore, *Veratrum viride*
It is a pity that false hellebore is not more widely available at nurseries. Perhaps people are put off by the fact that the plants are poisonous, but usually I don't eat plants I'm growing as ornamentals. In the spring, fat, bronze-tinged shoots quickly emerge from the wet soil of a nearby swamp. Expanding briskly, plants unfold leaves like a Japanese fan, fresh green and pleated. These are strung together in the manner of a corn plant, and make 2- to 4-foot-tall plants. If there is not enough moisture, the leaves brown along their edges and assume a discouraged appearance. Though hardy from zone 3 to 7,

hot summers are a problem. The tiny, bell-like flowers are clustered in a dense spike, and are a pleasing chartreuse. Given the deep, moist, fertile soil and moderate shade it prefers, false hellebore is handsome individually, exciting en masse.

Problem Trees

Some trees are just not good neighbors. Perhaps, like beeches and Norway maples, they cast heavy shade and suck up moisture and nutrients. The year-round constant shade under evergreen conifers results in dry conditions. Some trees even use chemical warfare.

Walnuts are notorious for this allelopathic, or growth-inhibiting, property. It is not so much shade as chemicals in their root zone, which might be three to four times the area under the tree's crown. As long ago as A.D. 37, Plinius Secundus wrote that the shadow of a walnut was poisonous to other vegetation. He was referring to the Persian walnut, *Juglans regia*, also known as the English walnut and frequently cultivated in California. Walnuts, in fact all the plants in the *Juglandaceae* or walnut family (including black walnuts, butternuts, hickories, and pecans), display this allelopathic influence to one extent or another. The trees produce a substance called *juglone*, which inhibits the growth of many plants.

Virginia bluebells are dormant in summer; their absence will be disguised by the hosta's vigorous growth.

One report on the allelopathic effects of black walnuts on forest plants suggests that it may take a decade or more for trees to develop toxic properties, so symptoms of allelopathic toxicity are more likely to occur as the trees mature. The effects are noticeable as a general failure to thrive on the part of nearby plants, as a long-term gradual stunting of the affected plants, or, in especially susceptible plants, like tomatoes, as flagging, wilted leaves. If you decide upon a drastic solution to solve your problem, be aware that it takes a full year after the walnut tree is cut down and removed for symptoms to vanish.

The allelopathic effect occurs during contact between walnut roots and the roots of other plants. This is the only means by which damage can occur unless plants are in soil that is poorly drained, and therefore poorly aerated. Highly reactive, in the continued presence of air the toxic material quickly breaks down into harmless substances. There are some things you can do to alleviate conditions if walnut trees are part of your landscape:

• Make sure the site has good drainage, since juglone activity is decreased or inactivated in well-aerated soils. These soils contain certain species of *Pseudomonas* bacteria that feed on juglone, and they are absent in heavy, wet soils with limited oxygen.

• A physical barrier between the walnut roots and shallow-rooted plants can also be effective, protecting the roots of vulnerable plants from contact with those of the black walnut.

• Applying nitrogen to injured plants can partly offset walnut poisoning. This was discovered when problems with cover crops of Persian walnuts in California orchards were corrected with ample nitrogen. This would be a suitable treatment in the spring through early summer, but could cause problems with winter hardiness if applied later in the growing season. Nitrogen encourages new soft growth, but in the late summer new

Problem Shade/PROBLEM TREES

shoots would be left without sufficient time to harden off before cold weather.

Interestingly enough, black walnut leaves, nut hulls, or even the bark used as a mulch are not harmful even to plants known to be sensitive, and do not produce toxic symptoms even if used as a mulch. Apparently it is the juglone produced in live root bark that is the culprit. There is additional evidence that the effects of black walnut accumulate in the environment. This is indicated by observations that the soil around walnut trees is devoid of earthworms. When water in which freshly hulled walnuts have been washed is poured on the ground, it kills earthworms. The worms wriggle to the soil surface within seconds, and die within an hour or less. The same leachate does not injure grass or adversely affect other plants upon which it has been tested.

Some plants are apparently unaffected by juglone. These include understory trees and shrubs such as: Japanese maple, *Acer palmatum*; various euonymus such as *Euonymus europaea*, European spindle tree; pinxterbloom, *Rhododendron periclymoides*; and the Exbury hybrid rhododendrons `Gibraltar' and `Balzac'. Ground covers such as bugleweed, *Ajuga repens*; European ginger, *Asarum europeum*; lily-of-the-valley, *Convallaria majalis*; woodruff, *Galium odoratum*; and English ivy, *Hedera helix,* are not injured. Perennials such as astilbe; bleeding heart, *Dicentra spectabilis*; several hostas such as *Hosta fortunei* `Glauca', *H. lancifolia*, *H. marginata*, *H. undulata* `Variegata'; polyanthus primroses, *Primula* x *polyanthus*; and lungworts, *Pulmonaria* species, are satisfactory when planted under black walnuts, as are native perennials such as wild columbine, *Aquilegia canadensis*; Jack-in-the-pulpit, *Arisaema triphyllum*; wild ginger, *Asarum canadensis*; waterleaf, *Hydrophyllum virginianum*; wild sweet William, *Phlox divaricata*;

giant Solomon's seal, *Polygonatum commutatum*; bloodroot, *Sanguinaria canadensis*; and merrybells, *Uvularia grandiflora*. Violets, such as Canada violet, *Viola canadensis*, and woolly blue violet, *V. sororia*, grow satisfactorily. Ferns such as crested wood fern, *Dryopteris cristata*; sensitive fern, *Onoclea sensibilis*; and cinnamon fern, *Osmunda cinamommea* can be used for foliage effect. A diversity of geophytes—glory-of-the-snow, *Chionodoxa luciliae*; crocus species; wood hyacinth, *Hyacinthoides hispanicus*; winter aconite, *Eranthis hiemalis*; snowdrop, *Galanthus nivalis*; grape hyacinth, *Muscari botryoides*; and Siberian squill, *Scilla sibirica*—will perform well. Even a few annuals will grow—horned violet or bedding pansies, *Viola cornuta* and *V.* x *wittrockiana* can be used for spring color, and fibrous-rooted begonias for summer bedding. Biennial honesty, *Lunaria annua*, also thrives under black walnut trees.

The crystalline white petals of *Narcissus poeticus* are set off by the colors of its narrow cup.

Foliage Effects for the
SHADY GARDEN

Blue and silver team up for a frosty effect when you pair *Hosta* 'Blue Cadet' with *Lamiastrum* 'Hermann's Pride'.

Foliage Effects for the
SHADY GARDEN

The lacy texture and soft green of these fern fronds softens the angularity of a stone water tank and complements the smooth gray tree bark.

Why You Should Consider Foliage When Choosing Plants

Plants have pretty flowers, so why consider their leaves? For a couple of reasons:

• Flowers are transient. In our climate most perennials are in bloom for two to three weeks, their leaves for six or more months.

• Secondly, plants growing in a shady situation tend to concentrate their flower production in the spring when sunlight is most available. If you choose your plants giving the same care and attention to their foliage appearance as you ordinarily give to their flowering display, the garden will be attractive in or out of bloom.

• Foliage displays can fill in the gap left by absent neighbors, dormant plants. Some

plants absent themselves from view, even during the growing season. These *ephemeral* plants last only a short time, flowering early and quickly retreating back underground with summer's approach. These include geophytes such as snowdrops and winter aconites, even fleshy-rooted perennials such as bleeding hearts and Virginia bluebells. Since these ephemeral plants return the following spring, you don't want to plant another perennial—a hosta, for example—right over them. Rather, the gap they leave needs to be disguised by adjacent plants. Perennials with attractive foliage such as ferns, astilbes, and hostas can be planted so their late spring growth conceals bare spots.

• In much of the United States, winter flowers tend to be sparse, to say the least. In the winter, evergreen foliage on herbaceous plants such as liriope, hellebore, and Christmas fern create an attractive display in the absence of flowers. The most effective garden display relies not on flowers or foliage alone, but rather on the use of foliage and flowers in combination to create a beautiful, harmonious garden in all seasons.

Often, foliage pays better rent in the shady garden than flowers. The chaste white flowers of bloodroot drop their petals in a week or less, leaving the leaf to provide the summer display. Consider lungwort, a familiar, shade-tolerant perennial that's been around for generations. Growth and flowering begin in early spring, and leaves remain attractive through summer into the fall, even winter. Their contribution of attractive, silver-spotted leaves far outweighs the spring flowers. With attention to leaf as well as flower, rather than a haphazard shambles, the shady garden will be interesting and attractive in summer, fall,

Bloodroot leaves may be almost round or deeply lobed. They create a good foliage effect when paired with ferns or astilbe.

and winter, as well as in the spring. Choosing plants for attractive foliage as well as for flowers will be more rewarding than if flowers alone are the criteria. Better yet, maintenance is reduced, as leaves do not need the same level of care (disbudding, deadheading, staking, and so on) as flowers require.

Consider the Details

When choosing plants for their leaves you need to examine both practical, cultural details as well as aesthetic matters. A good foliage plant has leaves that are attractive on their own as well as in combination with nearby plants. Leaves must remain in good condition for most of the growing season. Leaves perforated by slugs, disfiguring diseases such as mildew, columbines attacked by leaf miners, hostas eaten to bare stems by deer—these are not attractive foliage plants. Remember, plants whose leaves are subject to diseases and pests are going to require more care than those that do not need preventive maintenance. One, two, or a few plants needing extra attention can fit into the garden successfully. If there are too many finicky plants needing constant upkeep, the garden becomes a chore rather than a pleasure. Reduce maintenance in the planning stages by selecting easy-care plants.

Sometimes plants can be a problem because they do *too* well. Determine whether plants have aggressive, spreading tendencies; if you choose variegated goutweed, *Aegopodium podagraria* 'Variegatum' for its attractive leaves edged and splashed with ivory, be aware that it is a ruthless spreader. Use goutweed near some less assertive plant, and you should not be surprised if it overruns its neighbor. Self-sowing is a sign that plants are established in suitable sites, and some overtake their neighborhood with numerous offspring. Violets, for example, are very easily satisfied, and indicate their contentment with numberless progeny.

Foliage Effects for the SHADY GARDEN

Slug-chewed leaves really don't add to a plant's appearance!

Shape

When we evaluate leaves for their aesthetic qualities, there are two different categories to consider. One is shape, and the other is color. Shape is basic, and should be considered first, before you think about color. Think about the shape and outline of leaves, and the relationship of different forms to each other. Is the leaf long, thin and linear, grasslike, as in liriope or sedges? Perhaps, instead, it has a blocky but still simple shape. Siberian buglosses, *Brunnera macrophylla*, and hostas are examples of plants with this form. Maybe the leaf is made up of smaller leaflets, giving a more complex, fine-textured appearance. Ferns, astilbes, and epimedium have compound leaves that give just such a visual effect. Variations of leaf shape and texture, glossy surface against dull finish, provide interesting possibilities on a fundamental level. Playing shape against shape—simple to bold, plain to complex—uses the most basic aspect of gardening with foliage. You can create a beautiful garden using only green leaves in all their variety, contrasting outline and form.

When you first begin designing with foliage, start by choosing plants with leaves that are quite simple—the thin linear shape of grasses, sedges, rushes, and the grasslike leaves of lilyturf. When look-alike leaf forms are next to each other, they have a blurry similarity rather than an interesting pattern. Repeating a single shape produces an unimaginative, predictable design. For better visual contrast, make your next selection different, and chose a plant with a rounded, heart-shaped leaf such as hosta or Siberian bugloss.

Different plants with similar leaves growing near each other are boring even if the leaf has a complex shape. Astilbes, bugbanes, goatsbeards, and both species of baneberry, *Actaea pachypoda* and *A. rubra*, are examples of plants with comparable foliage that should not be grown side by side. Different cultivars of hostas planted near one another result in a hosta collection, not a garden. Visually, plants are more interesting if their neighbors have dissimilar leaves.

One simple and obvious combination would be a simple, blocky shape with a com-

Simply elegant, Canada ginger, *Asarum canadensis*, and maidenhair fern, *Adiantum pedatum*, create a beautiful combination based on leaf shape and texture.

Gardeners should value Canada ginger, *Asarum canadensis*, more for its leaves than its flowers, since they are generally concealed beneath the foliage.

plex, compound leaf, such as hosta and astilbe. Another combination of fine lacy texture with a blocky shape would be maidenhair fern with European ginger, *Asarum europeum*. The apple green pedatisect fronds of the fern make a lovely foil to the low-growing, dark green, very glossy, rounded ginger leaves. The effect is different when Canada ginger, *Asarum canadensis*, is used as the soft green, heart-shaped leaves of the deciduous ginger create a softer complement to the ferns through their mat finish. One planting I enjoyed in my Connecticut garden paired Canada ginger with doll's eyes, *Actaea pachypoda*, with astilbe-like foliage. Doll's eyes creates a pleasing summer picture as it rises above the carpet of ginger, and then in the fall I have the bonus of beady white berries with a pupil-like black dot. In addition, the same space can be used for early geophytes, whose yellowing foliage will be concealed by the emerging new growth of the perennials.

Linear, strap-leaved liriope can form a different grouping, associating with either fern- or hosta-type foliage, or both. Envision the dark green, evergreen leaves of liriope with evergreen Christmas fern. Now, when you add a hosta, a very happy association results.

How Many to Use

But how many of each plant should you use? One each of a dozen plants will look cluttered and disorganized, collection versus garden. Effective plantings result from grouping several specimens of a few plants rather than one each of many. Suppose in a shady corner there is room for a dozen plants. Part of your decision rests on the size of the various plants, and the space to be filled. More of the smaller plants, fewer of the larger ones gives a good balance to the grouping. If you plant six sedges, three small to medium hostas, and three astilbes, the effect is stronger, better organized, and more attractive than if the sedges were in the minority, hosta the majority.

Size

Relative size is an important consideration when choosing plants for each combination. Any grouping must display a sense of proportion, of relative scale in order to be pleasing. Most of the time you will use smaller plants in greater quantity in order to have sufficient impact in the landscape; for instance, a small grass such as 10-inch-tall Bowle's golden grass, *Milium effusum* 'Aureum', needs to be used in a grouping of several plants if it is to have adequate effectiveness. On the other hand, 3-foot-tall *Astilbe biternata*, even taller when in bloom, need a landscape on an heroic scale to support a massed planting.

The fine, linear shape of liriope's leaves make it a good stand-in for grasses in a shady garden.

Foliage Effects for the SHADY GARDEN

Take the earlier example of hostas, Christmas fern, and liriope. Perhaps there is space for about a dozen plants. Using four of each kind is arbitrary and poor design. Think of the difference in scale between large- and small-leaved hostas. Choose a big hosta—*Hosta* 'Green Piecrust' grows into a very large plant with waxy, dark green leaves—then just one would be enough, with three Christmas fern, and nine liriope. Choose a dwarf hosta—tiny, vigorous *H.* 'Saishu Jima' with narrow, green leaves—and one large clump of Christmas fern, five hosta, and six liriope would balance nicely.

Simple Foliage
Brunnera macrophylla—Siberian bugloss
Hosta species and cultivars—hosta
Linear, Swordlike Foliage
Carex spp.—sedge
Luzula spp.—rush
Liriope spicata—mondo grass
Lacy, Fine-textured Foliage
Aruncus dioicus—goatsbeard
Astilbe x *arendsii*—astilbe
Cimicifuga racemosa—bugbane
Myhrris odorata—sweet ciceley

It might be desirable in a particular situation to select evergreen plants. Especially in colder climates, flowering is not merely sparse in winter; often it is completely absent, as are the leaves of dormant perennials and deciduous trees and shrubs. Therefore, there is all the more reason to consider evergreen foliage, perhaps as a simple ground cover. The three ubiquitous ground covers—ivy, running myrtle, and pachysandra—may seem boring, plain vanilla. Think of the neat,

tidy winter picture presented by a bare dogwood tree, or a trio of ghostly white-trunked birches, carpeted with an ellipse of glossy, dark green, running myrtle, *Vinca minor*. These ground covers also have variegated forms that lend considerable charm to the landscape year-round. Both *Pachysandra* 'White Edge' and *Vinca* 'Sterling Silver' have white-margined leaves, and there are a number of ivies with gold or silver variegated foliage. Any of these can be used to accent a shady garden, not only in winter but in combination with early geophytes: white snowdrops, blue scillas and glory-of-the-snow, or yellow daffodils, and with perennials that follow them.

Evergreen perennials are relatively few in northern and northeastern gardens, more common in mild winter areas. Their leaves may suffer some damage late in the winter, January or early February, in zone 6 and colder. Group plants for winter interest as carefully as any other gathering of plants in the garden. Perhaps the deeply cut, dark green,

Foliage and flowers work together in this partnership of Bowles golden grass, *Millium effusim* 'Aureum', and forget-me-nots.

fingerlike leaves of bear's foot hellebore, *Helleborus foetidus*, would look even better against the polished bark of red-twig dogwood, *Cornus alba*. After a hard freeze, Christmas ferns' fronds weaken at the base and lay down but remain evergreen, attractive against white birch bark. Liriope look good right through the winter, as a ground cover, as an edging for a formal design, as an accent plant. Use evergreens, especially perennials, where they can be enjoyed from within the house rather than at the back of the garden where boots and gloves and warm winter coats are necessary to see them. Avoid filling the garden with conifers and broad-leaved evergreens, lest the space be static and unchanging year-round.

Perennials with Evergreen Leaves
Asarum europeum, European ginger
Helleborus foetidus, bear's foot hellebore
Helleborus niger, Christmas rose
Liriope muscari, lilyturf
Polystichum achrostichoides, Christmas fern
Rohdea japonica, Nippon lily

Color with Foliage

Color is the other feature to consider when thinking about leaves, and not just green. Plants with silver, yellow, purple, blue, even variegated leaves, can introduce color to the shady garden when flowers are sparse. Take the earlier example of hostas with astilbes. Combine astilbes and a large hosta, *H. ventricosa* with glossy, dark green leaves for an attractive, though rather plain, association. However, if the hosta were 'Louisa', with wavy, elongated white-edged green leaves, then there is leaf color as well as pattern. If white-flowered 'Bridal Veil' astilbe is chosen, so much the better; the entire effect is intensified while the astilbe blooms. (Think foliage *and* flowers to create the best effects.)

Perennials and Shrubs with Variegated Leaves
Aegopodium podagraria 'Variegata', bishops goutweed—invasive perennial/ground cover
Caladium x *hortorum*, caladium—geophyte
Carex morowii 'Variegatam' variegated sedge—grasslike
Cornus alba 'Elegantissima', variegated red-twig dogwood—shrub
Euonymus fortunei 'Silver Queen', euonymus—ground cover
Hakonechloa macra 'Aureola', golden Japanese wind-combed grass—grass
Hedera helix, English ivy—vine
Hosta—perennial
Kerria japonica 'Picta'—shrub
Pieris japonica 'Variegata', andromeda or lily-of-the-valley shrub—shrub
Pulmonaria saccharata 'Margery Fish', 'Sissinghurst White', lungwort—perennial
Vinca minor 'Sterling Silver', 'Aureo-marginata', running myrtle—ground cover

In general, use variegated foliage as an accent, a focal point, as a counterpoint to green and glaucous blue leaves. Use a plant with white variegated leaves together with plants that have green leaves and white flowers, or a yellow variegated plant with glaucous blue-leaved plants, or others that have green leaves and yellow flowers. Just as similar leaf shapes should not be used adjacent to one another, similarly variegated leaves should not be neighbors, for example, *Polygonatum japonicum* 'Variegatum' is a lovely woodland plant with paired, white-edged oval leaves on arching stems. In combination with a white-edged hosta, much of the clarity of the variegation is lost. Instead, plain green-leaved hellebores, small ferns, or astilbes would be a better choice. Lungworts such as *Pulmonaria saccharata* 'Mrs. Moon' or 'Margery Fish' are reliable

Foliage Effects for the SHADY GARDEN

denizens of shady gardens, with sturdy, silver-spotted leaves. Together with primroses, epimediums, bloodroot, and brunnera, lungworts provide an attractive, trouble-free display both in bloom and afterwards. Green or glaucous blue leaves can be marked with white, cream, or ivory white, to golden yellow, and those markings can be a margin or band at the edge of the leaf, streaks and spots over the entire leaf surface, or blotches or bands in the leaf center. Where leaves are white they have no pigment capable of photosynthesis. Plants with considerable white areas on their leaves are not as vigorous as nonvariegated forms.

Woody plants, as well as herbaceous perennials, can be selected with an eye to foliage. There are both deciduous and evergreen shrubs with variegated foliage that thrive in shade. The white-margined leaves of *Cornus alba* 'Elegantissima' are attractive in combination with white-flowered astilbes and impatiens and glaucous, blue-leaved hostas for pleasantly frosty-looking results.

Gray and Glaucous Blue Foliage

Silver is a foliage color most often seen in sunny sites. There are, however, a few shade-tolerant plants that provide this cool hue in

It requires a second look to notice that there are two different plants here. The similar leaf shape, and similar variegation, do nothing to distinguish a white-edged hosta from a variegated Solomon's seal.

their leaves. One I find especially useful is Japanese painted fern, *Athyrium nipponicum* 'Pictum'. Deciduous, its dainty, soft gray fronds uncurl in late April or early May. It seems to be an excellent companion for just about every perennial I've paired it with—glossy, green European ginger, gray-green bloodroot, white-variegated hosta, silver-spotted lungwort—everything looks wonderful. Japanese painted fern looks marvelous with blue hostas such as *Hosta* 'Hadspen Heron', 'Halcyon', or 'Blue Cadet', especially when given a crisp accent with white-flowered impatiens. Not completely silver-leaved but with only a narrow green margin, dead nettles, *Lamium* 'Beacon Silver' and 'White Nancy' make cool-looking ground covers for smaller areas. Gray foliage can be used with any flower color, but is especially fine with blue forget-me-nots, or lavender- and violet-flowered impatiens. Cool, frosty results occur when gray leaves are combined with white flowers, a combination especially effective at dusk or early evening, or in the low light conditions of a shady garden. Frosty foliage can be used to tone down hot, vivid colors, Japanese painted ferns with orange flowered impatiens, for example.

Glaucous, blue-leaved hostas have a cool appearance, especially attractive in the summer when frosty blue seems crisp and inviting. There are many possibilities for foliage combinations, beyond the previously mentioned Japanese fern. Tall, elegant, bold, grayish, frosty blue-leaved *Hosta* 'Krossa Regal' associates nicely with ostrich fern, *Matteucia struthiopteris*, both plants having a similar vaselike form. I planted a sweep of *Hosta* 'Blue Cadet' and *Lamiastrum* 'Hermann's Pride' at the periphery of a fringe tree, *Chionanthus virginicus*. Charming

Japanese painted fern and *Lamium* 'Beacon Silver' prefer shade, where they provide a cool and elegant effect.

before the tree blooms, the combination is absolute perfection when the fringe tree is covered with billows of feathery white flowers sweeping near the blue-leaved hostas and silver-netted ground cover. Sweet ciceley, *Myrrhis odorata*, has a grayish, parsley-like leaf, and umbels of white flowers like Queen Anne's lace. It creates a charming, casual effect when allowed to self-sow among small to medium-sized blue-leaved hostas. One bright trio for a shady corner gathers white-leaved, green-veined, *Caladium* 'Candidum' with the August lily, *Hosta plantaginea*, and white impatiens.

Perennials with Silver Leaves
Athyrium nipponicum 'Pictum', Japanese painted fern
Lamium 'Beacon Silver', 'White Nancy'

A superb foliage effect is made with the pairing of *Hosta* 'Halcyon' with Japanese painted fern.

Yellow/Golden/Chartreuse Foliage

Golden foliage provides a sunny note, even more striking in shade than in sunny sites. Some gardeners do not care for this color, saying it makes leaves look chlorotic. Leaves are healthy and photosynthesize using carotene, a different pigment than green chlorophyll. I find golden foliage attractive, especially in shady areas where it lightens and brightens the woodland in the summer. Dark green leaves best emphasize sunny yellow foliage, and yellow leaves nicely accent glaucous blue foliage. A wide selection of hostas are available, everything from cultivars with leaves of pure gold, to green or blue leaves with a golden edge, or with a golden center. Accentuate the effect with dark green liriope. Not only do the colors work, but shape, that other level of designing with foliage, fits our criteria.

Play first with shape, then with color. This stong form of bloodroot foliage is nicely accented by the lacy leaf and silver color of the Japanese painted fern.

Perennials and Shrubs with Golden Foliage
Acer japonicum 'Aureum'—small tree
Carex stricta 'Bowles Golden', Bowle's golden sedge—grasslike
Coleus 'Pineapple Wizard'—annual
Hosta, many cultivars
Milium effusum 'Aureum', Bowle's golden grass—grass

Foliage Effects for the SHADY GARDEN

Copper/Red/Purple Foliage

Dark foliage, like dark flowers, fades into the shadows. This lowered visibility needs to be accented with lighter, brighter flowers and foliage. The popular burgundy-leaved Japanese maples such as *Acer palmatum* 'Bloodgood' are attractive, shade-tolerant, understory trees. Use *Lamium* 'Beacon Silver' as a ground cover, or an underplanting of white-edged hosta such as 'Francee', rather than the omnipresent green pachysandra.

Young foliage in the spring often has the most intense color. Some epimediums have copper-flushed leaves in early spring. Many of the red-flowered astilbes, such as 'Fanal', 'Feur', 'Glut', and 'Red Sentinel' have new leaves that are coppery or red-bronze in the spring, maturing to more typical green. This characteristic can be used in striking contrast to white or yellow flowers such as *Hyacinthoides non-scriptus* 'Alba' or yellow daffodils. Purple-leaved *Viola labradorica* has strongly purple leaves in the spring, a charming contrast to its own lavender flowers. Leaf color later softens to a somber purple-flushed green as understory and canopy trees leaf out. Darkest of all foliage plants, *Ophiopogon planiscapus* 'Ebony Knight' has black, linear leaves that keep their color in shade. A very striking combination pairs 'Ebony Knight' with Japanese painted ferns. I planted them together in a blue-speckled, black-glazed square pot to better display this rather theatrical combination.

Red and purple leaf color is the result of anthocyanin pigments, and usually the strongest color development is found in sunny sites. Plant purple-leaved barberry in shade and its color fades away to green, while the intense purple-red leaf color of *Heuchera* 'Palace Purple' often deteriorates to olive green.

A golden leaved hosta provides a sunny look and effective background for wood hyacinths, *Hyacinthoides hispanica*.

Perennials and Shrubs with Copper or Red Leaves
Acer palmatum atropurpureum 'Bloodgood'—small tree
Ajuga reptans 'Giant Bronze', 'Jungle Bronze', 'Purpurea', bugleweed—ground cover
Begonia x *semperflorens-cultorum* Whiskey series—annual
Cimicifuga ramosa (*C. americana*) 'Brunette', bugbane—perennial
Coleus 'Othello', 'Red Velvet'—annual
Heuchera americana 'Palace Purple'—perennial

The simple linear shape of Japanese forest grass is accentuated by its golden variegation.

Summing Up

The popularity of ornamental grasses, ferns, and hostas demonstrates that plants can be accepted for their foliage. With attention to some simple principles, leaves offer attractive results with reduced maintenance. Especially in shady gardens, plants with attractive foliage provide continuing beauty after flowering has its seasonal decline.

A combination that works on two levels, the basic one of shape and the overlay of color: Japanese forest grass with *Hosta* 'Frances Williams'.

Foliage Effects for the SHADY GARDEN

Remember that we achieve the most satisfactory results when we choose plants with an eye to their overall appearance.

Aesthetic choices are personal and individual, but for competent plant selection these preferences should be based on certain standards that include foliage texture, shape, and color. A garden needs pattern and balance. Leaves exist in all sizes and shapes, as well as complexity of form. Some large-scale perennials have bold architectural form. Ferns, even large ferns such as the 5-foot-tall cinnamon fern, *Osmunda cinammomea*, retain a daintiness through their lacy texture that offsets their stature. The fine linear texture of sedges, grasses, and liriopes provides gracefulness no matter what the scale of an individual species. Some combinations are obviously appropriate. Anyone can place a fern near a hosta and enjoy the results, but more thought and effort are required when working with leaf patterns on a broader scale.

The rosy flush that decorates epimedium leaves in spring soon fades to green as the foliage matures.

Enchantment and appeal is built upon the creative combinations of plants. Rather than emphasize either flowers *or* foliage, to the disadvantage of both, the two must be chosen to complement each other. Making use of leaves and flowers, color and shape, establishes a beguiling picture that is attractive not merely at the moment of bloom but before and after flowering, reason enough for gardeners to consider the leaf, for additional pleasure from their garden.

The bold blocky form and seersucker texture of *Hosta* 'Frances Williams' is further embellished with a golden edge to the leaf.

Second Interlude:
GARDEN MAINTENANCE

Even a simple carpet of moss needs maintenance—sweeping away fallen leaves and weeding.

I'd like to think that even gardeners with some experience will find useful information here, but if you are an experienced gardener who knows more than "green side up," and want to skip over this section, feel free to do so. Those new to this business of digging in the dirt will find this information very helpful. Use it as a stand-in for the knowledgeable aunt or neighbor over the back fence who answers some basic garden questions.

Planting

Planting is more than a matter of stuffing a plant into a hole and walking away. Time of year, size of hole, alterations to the basic soil, follow-up care—all affect how well, or how poorly, the transplanted tree, shrub, or perennial establishes in its new location.

Time of Year
Spring is traditionally regarded as the best time of year for planting, but how about fall? After all, geophytes (= bulbs, corms, and tubers) are planted then, so why not other herbaceous perennials, or trees and shrubs for that matter? The advantage to you as a gardener is that fall planting adds a second window of opportunity. Actually, fall is just as good in many places, and even better than spring in areas with mild winters and hot summers; but fall planting should be viewed

59

Second Interlude: GARDEN MAINTENANCE

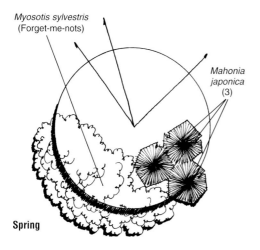

Myosotis sylvestris
(Forget-me-nots)

Mahonia
japonica
(3)

Spring

with caution if plants are borderline hardy. Say you live in zone 6 in New Jersey; you may want to try heavenly bamboo, *Nandina domestica*, which is suggested for your zone only in protected sites. Spring planting allows more time for the shrub to establish itself before winter freeze-up, the more stressful season for borderline hardy plants. Carry that a step further, and recognize that fall planting is risky in regions with harsh winters, such as northern New England and the northern tier of states. One group of plants that are better off when planted in the spring are those small trees with tender, easily damaged bark that oozes sap for a long time when bruised or cut. This category includes beeches, birches, small maples, magnolias, holly, and dogwoods. Ideally, these should be planted as early as possible in the spring, before they leaf out.

Spring or fall, the best time of year to plant is when there will be at least six weeks before the onset of difficult weather conditions, either consistent winter cold or constant summer heat. Extreme weather conditions add to the stress level for plants, especially so for those recently transplanted. Your goal is

to give the plant time to settle in. In the spring, plants are busy making new leaves, and transplants must reestablish roots at the same time. Adequate water is especially critical, not just in the spring but continuing through the summer. Fall planting allows plants to establish their roots in the new site without the need to produce or support leaves. Many deciduous trees and shrubs settle in even better in the cooler conditions of fall, and rainfall is often more reliable too.

Planting Site

The old adage, "Put a one-dollar plant in a five-dollar hole" indicates the relative value between plant and planting site. You want to dig a nice big hole, one that will give the roots ample room to spread out in a natural manner. Don't make an undersized hole and wedge the plant in, or twirl it around like a forkful of spaghetti. Before you even start to dig, remove any competing weeds, roots and all. Remove any rocks you find as you are digging. In sites with sandy or loamy soil, use a shovel for trees, shrubs, or large perennials, a trowel for small perennials and annuals. My current garden in New Jersey

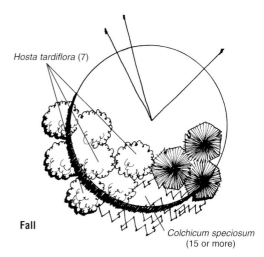

Hosta tardiflora (7)

Fall

Colchicum speciosum
(15 or more)

60

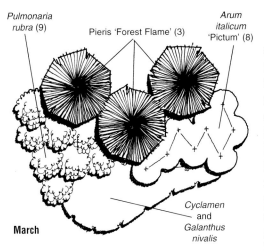

Pulmonaria
rubra (9)

Pieris 'Forest Flame' (3)

Arum
italicum
'Pictum' (8)

Cyclamen
and
Galanthus
nivalis

March

has clay soil that is laced with rocks. My preferred digging tool is a mattock, which has a pick on one end of the head and a broader blade on the other. I can use the pick to pry rocks out, while the broader portion easily chops through the heavy soil. A spading fork or hand fork, with tines rather than a solid blade, is used to mix amendments with the existing soil.

Soil Amendments

Unless you have that holy grail of gardeners, a loamy soil high in organic matter, moist but well drained, you'll need to amend your dirt. In nature, organic matter is constantly replenished as the seasons turn: herbaceous plants die back to the ground in the fall, trees and shrubs drop their leaves, and there is a continual renewal. The neater and more orderly your garden, the more important your restoration of this vital ingredient for a healthy soil. Organic matter improves drainage in heavy soils, helps retain moisture in sandy ones, and provides suitable conditions for the microorganisms that live in the soil and help plants in their uptake of nutrients. These amendments are the roughage in your plants' diet. The easiest time to make this addition is when you are preparing a new planting bed or digging an individual planting hole for larger plants such as trees and shrubs.

Incorporate a layer a couple of inches thick, and till it in a foot deep. In woodlands it is not really necessary to double-dig, and prepare the soil two feet deep. If you've ever seen a road cut or new construction site in a forested area, the changing color of the soil indicates that the uppermost, organically enhanced layer is rather shallow. Many perennials root in this top layer. Trees and shrubs extend their roots into the mineral soil beneath. It is the prairies of the American Midwest, where topsoil extends 8 or 10 feet or more that perennials are comparably deep-rooted. You should keep adding compost right through the life of your gardening. Adding compost or other organic matter when you first plant is only a good beginning. Organic matter in the soil is constantly being used up and depleted, and needs to be replaced on a regular basis.

Many soil amendments are commercially available, neatly bagged and easily brought home. Especially for city gardeners, they are the most available. Your local nursery, garden center, even discount stores such as K-Mart and Home Depot sell dried manures in several flavors: bucolic cow, sheep, chicken, or exotic "zoodoo." They all have one thing in common: They are waste products of herbivores, plant-eating animals. So if you have guinea pigs, gerbils, or hamsters, parakeets or canaries, you can add their cage droppings to the garden. This is not so for carnivores, so don't empty the kitty litter tray into the compost heap!

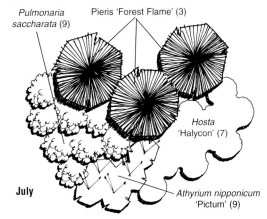

Pulmonaria
saccharata (9)

Pieris 'Forest Flame' (3)

Hosta
'Halycon' (7)

July

Athyrium nipponicum
'Pictum' (9)

Second Interlude: GARDEN MAINTENANCE

Composting

Compost is great stuff for the garden, and the process of composting is a usefully pragmatic way to deal with garden debris. All non-diseased plant waste—weeds, dead flowers, grass clippings (if you did not apply a weed killer to the lawn), spent perennials at the end of the growing season (excepting peonies, phlox, and beebalms which are prone to mildew, a leaf disease), even potato and carrot peelings, and coffee grounds—can be heaped up in an out-of-the-way part of the garden. You don't need an estate-sized property—my sister composts in a trash can on her apartment balcony, so it is possible to compost in the smallest garden. Don't bother with purchased

Proper planting and appropriate maintenance are both necessary if plants are to thrive in your garden.

compost amendments to get high performance from your compost heap. With a mix of green (= nitrogenous) leafy stuff or fresh manure, and brown (= carbonaceous) material such as dried leaves, wood shavings, wood chips, or shredded newspaper, your compost heap will cook along just fine. Green stuff from the garden, kitchen waste (except dairy, meat, bones, or fat), and fresh manure is tossed together with brown stuff such as fall leaves, wood shavings (the kind sold as animal bedding, not workshop waste that might contain chemically treated wood), even shredded black-and-white newspaper. Jumble it all up, add a shovel or two of good soil to start things cooking, keep it just moist, and go away. When the material you piled up is brown, smells rather like mushrooms, and you can't really tell what you started with, it's ready to use.

You may have access to lots of fall leaves, like my two friends in Swarthmore, Pennsylvania. In the fall the two women drive slowly down the street with a pickup truck, collecting bags of leaves from the curb. When composted separately, the end product is sometimes called leaf mold. The process moves along more quickly if the dry leaves are broken into smaller pieces; you can run the leaves through a shredder. For moderate quantities fill a sturdy trash can half full of leaves and plunge your string trimmer into the leaves. Agitate the trimmer up and down, up and down. As leaves are chopped up, dump the contents and do it again with a fresh batch. Contain the leaves, chopped or not, in a cylinder of fencing wire. Since dry leaves are brown stuff, and you need both brown and green for more rapid results, add some nitrogen fertilizer. Don't forget the necessary shovelful of soil. And keep things barely damp, like a wrung-out sponge.

Peat moss is not as useful in the garden as compost or dried manure. It doesn't contain the

A simple bench in spring woods.

same microflora that is necessary for healthy soil. Dry peat moss is hard to wet, and can actually take moisture away from plant roots when it is first incorporated with the soil. There are also concerns over the destruction of peat bogs, a unique, slow-to-recover habitat, for garden use.

Fertilizers

If soil amendments are roughage in a plant's diet, then fertilizers are nutrients. The three major plant nutrients are nitrogen, phosphorus, and potash. You've probably seen relative proportions, represented as N-P-K, on a bag or container of fertilizer. Some common percentages are 5-10-5, 10-6-4, 20-20-20. What do these elements mean, what are they good for, where do they come from?

Nitrogen
Nitrogen is the fertilizer element most directly connected with leaf growth, so it is especially important in the spring. It is quickly used up—too much, and plants have weak, floppy stems and lush, pest- and disease-attracting leaves. Overfertilization with nitrogen makes plants attractive to insects and other pests such as rabbits and deer. Spring is a good time to apply a fertilizer higher in nitrogen, as this is when plants maximize leaf growth. It is equally important to reduce the application of nitrogen, or cease using it altogether after the first week in July. This keeps plants from making soft leafy growth late in the season, which is easily damaged when frosts arrive.

Phosphorus and Potash
Simplistically put, phosphorus and potash are important for overall growth, disease resistance, winter hardiness, flower and fruit production, and root growth. They tend to bind in the soil, so it is important to add them when planting. This gets the nutrients down in the root zone, rather than on the soil's surface where they will only slowly leach down to root level. There are a number of other micronutrients such as boron, magnesium, and calcium, but they are generally available in adequate amounts.

Second Interlude: GARDEN MAINTENANCE

Organic Versus Inorganic

Fertilizers are available from organic, once-living sources, or inorganic, laboratory-produced formulations. By the time microorganisms in the soil have reduced fertilizer to the point where plants can make use of it, there's no difference, especially as far as the plants are concerned. The discussion of organic verses inorganic is more a matter of human concern. If using organic fertilizers pleases you, then that's what you should use. I'm careful to add organic amendments such as compost, leaf mold, and manure, and maintain organic mulches, but mostly, I use inorganic fertilizers. The soil in my garden is healthy and plants grow well; therefore, inorganic fertilizers are fine. If someone "can't be bothered with all that organic stuff," then inorganic fertilizers (which tend to be quicker-acting) can be harmful. Having said all that, let me add that organic fertilizers usually contain more trace elements, are more slowly available to plants, and are more expensive. Inorganic fertilizers are chemical salts that, if they come in direct contact with the plants, can harm them, burning leaves and roots just as road salt does.

Organic sources of nitrogen include dried blood and cottonseed meal. Inorganic sources are ammonium nitrate and urea. Rock phosphate, a naturally occurring mineral, is considered an organic source of phosphorus. Inorganic sources include superphosphate, which is rock phosphate treated with sulfuric acid to make it more soluble, and ammonium phosphates that also supply nitrogen. Green sand, mined from the ocean's floor, is the organic source of potash, while potassium chloride, called muriate of potash, is the most common inorganic source.

These granular fertilizers are mixed with the soil. They are more readily available when the ground is moist. In most instances, it is better to use a complete fertilizer, one containing N-P-K, than a single element. As well as granular fertilizers, you'll find liquid formulations, either crystals or liquids that are diluted for use. They are quick-acting and of short duration. This makes them valuable when transplanting, or pushing, seedlings along. They are also useful for fertilizing bulbs, corms, and tubers in the spring when the soil is cool and microorganisms are not very active.

Steps for Planting

You've picked the time and place, dug a hole, amended the soil and incorporated fertilizer. Now you're ready to plant:

• A gray, overcast day is better than a sunny, breezy one. Given a choice, planting late in the day is better than morning as the next few hours won't be sunny and the new plant can settle in more easily.

• Tree, shrub, perennial, or annual, the plant should be set at the same height it was at in the container or field.

• If in a container, the ball is tightly webbed with roots, tease them apart so they can be spread out in the hole. Or, if too dense, use a knife to cut four or five vertical slits. This also encourages the roots to grow out and away into fresh soil.

• Unless it is raining as you plant, it is very important to water. Water as you plant, one by one, and soak the soil thoroughly. (If you're planting annuals, then it is OK to water a six-pack at a time.) If the weather is dry in the spring and summer, new plants have priority for watering. Consider them "new" for a year.

Maintenance is simplified if plants requiring similar conditions are grouped together.

Mulching

The hole is dug, the soil amended and fertilized; the plant's in place and watered. Are you finished? Not quite. Next comes mulching. Forget what you may have read about mulching to prevent weed growth. If the mulch was applied heavily enough to keep unwanted plants from growing, it wouldn't do much good for those you want to encourage. Keeping the ground covered will reduce germination of those weed seeds that need light to sprout, but that's about all mulch does for weeds. What it does do is shade the soil, keeping it cooler in hot weather, and reducing evaporative water loss. That's practical. Aesthetically, a mulch is the finishing touch, providing a neat and tidy appearance to the garden.

What can you use as a mulch? Whatever is available in sufficient quantity to do the job that also looks good to you. I really like chopped leaves as a mulch in the woodland garden. They look very appropriate and, as they break down, return organic matter to the soil. Remember, in a woodland the natural cycle covers the forest floor with a layer of leaves and small branches, to the tune of a ton and a half per acre per year in deciduous forests. Shredded leaves pack more tightly than whole leaves, so use a couple of inches if shredded; double that if whole. Oak leaves are ideal even when whole, as they remain crisp and airy. Norway maple leaves are unusable; they pack too tightly and can smother herbaceous plants. If you have pine trees on your property, go ahead and use the needles. They will have little effect on the pH of the soil. Pine needles, called pine straw in the southeastern states, make a great mulch— slow to decay so long-lasting, light and airy. Available in the Southeast as baled needles, there is some growing concern that commercial collection may prove harmful in the long term to the forests from which it is removed.

Pine bark also makes a fine mulch. If it is commercially purchased, select the smaller sized mulch or mini-chip grade. It makes better mulch cover than the coarser nuggets that leave too many air pockets. Wood chips from chipping branches also make a good mulch, with a couple of caveats: When leafy branches are shredded, the resulting material has a good carbon:nitrogen mix for rapid decay, which can result in heat damage to growing plants if applied fresh. If you compost the leaf/wood chip material for a couple of months until the initial burst of decay is over, it will be fine. If bare branches are chipped, there can be a problem during the growing season. While microorganisms are active and as they break down the wood chips, they need nitrogen that they'll take from the soil. This may leave too little nitrogen available for healthy plant growth. (The nitrogen becomes available later on, after the wood is all broken down.) A light scattering of a nitrogen

Second Interlude: GARDEN MAINTENANCE

A group of well-tended candelabra primroses form an attractive planting.

fertilizer such as dried blood or cottonseed meal over the wood chips takes care of this situation.

Consider using a living mulch, one or another of the ground covers discussed in Ground Covers and Vines, beginning on page 111, in a shrub border or an established planting bed. Be careful to use a ground cover of appropriate vigor for the plants it will be growing with. Evergreen creeping phlox, *Phlox stolonifera*, gets along with just about anything. Pachysandra can swallow small hostas, and even vine up into azaleas.

What wouldn't you use? I don't like gravel as a woodland mulch, it just makes more work, trying to keep it clear of leaf and twig litter. And I'm not in favor of plastic mulch, even the water-permeable landscape fabrics. I like to be able to change my mind about what's growing where and move things around, and since the plastics must be covered with another mulch material to keep it from breaking down, what do you gain? The various organic mulches are much preferable.

These basic steps are just as sound for tomatoes in the vegetable garden as a hosta in the perennial border or Japanese maple to enhance the woodland understory. Do it right, and the plants will thrive. Do it carelessly, and you've thrown away your time and effort as well as the cost of the plant.

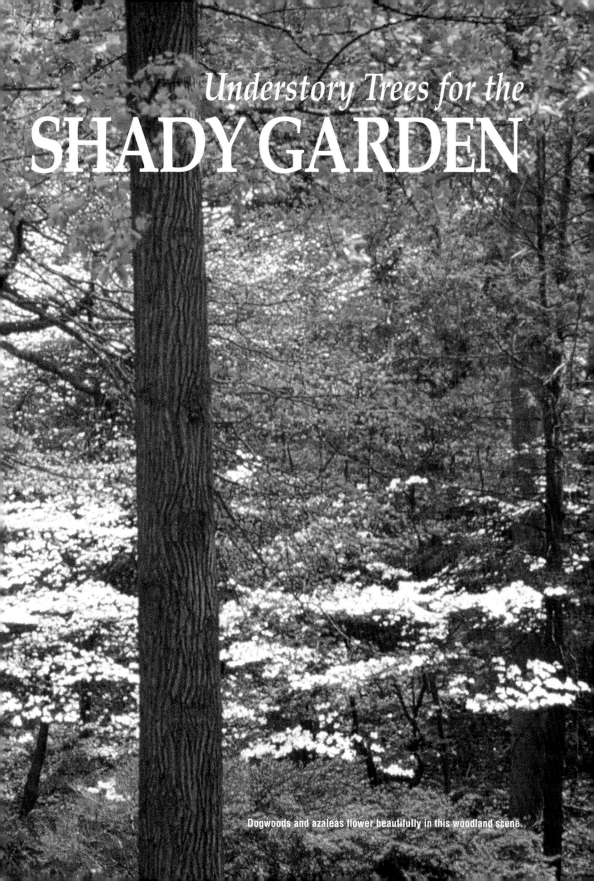

Understory Trees for the
SHADY GARDEN

Dogwoods and azaleas flower beautifully in this woodland scene.

Understory Trees for the
SHADY GARDEN

Attractive in its homeland, Japanese maple is equally beautiful abroad.

Living as they do in the shadows of larger trees, smaller understory trees cannot survive unless they have the ability to grow when at least 50 percent of the sky is obstructed by the leafy crown of canopy trees. All shade is not equal; all canopy trees are not identical in their effect. An oak/hickory forest has a more open branch and leaf pattern, allowing more light to reach the ground plane, thus supporting the growth of less shade-tolerant plants and providing the gardener with a wider palette of plants from which to choose. Maples and lindens have a denser canopy providing heavier shade,

restricting selection to the more shade-tolerant species of small trees, shrubs, and perennials. You can also work with the edge effect, planting less shade-tolerant plants close to the boundary between sun and shade. Though stronger at the forest's edge, this influence exists at the boundary of a glade opening, even beneath a single specimen tree in your garden.

Add several understory trees, introduce some shrubs, and the garden is even shadier than when you began. After you've planted that nice flowering dogwood for spring flowers, a Japanese maple for fall color, an

American holly for evergreen leaves and winter berries, your perennial options are reduced. Heavy shade provided by canopy and understory trees and a shrub layer means choosing among the most shade-tolerant group of perennials and ground covers. As my friend Ed Leimseider of Westport, Connecticut, is fond of saying, "A garden can be overshrubbed." Consider the garden in its totality, rather than falling in love with some attractive tree at the nursery and shoe-horning it in without suitable deliberation.

While large shrubs may be used as small trees in gardens with modest proportions, in this chapter only woody plants over 15 feet tall will be considered. Another characteristic specific to trees—they usually have a single trunk, providing a more commanding presence than that multistemmed shrub. Consider carefully when choosing small trees, whether for the woodland understory or to enhance a shady city garden. Take time to think why you want to add a tree. Determine which season's aspect is most important in order to enhance your garden's overall appearance:

• Should the tree be selected because it provides spring bloom, fall color, or fruiting interest?

• Does the tree of your choice have a second period of interest at another time of year?

• Will an evergreen add sufficient winter interest to justify its addition for that reason alone, or would the garden have a static feel in the spring and summer?

• Consider how rapidly a tree grows, if it is a "good neighbor" to nearby plants, or if there are pest or disease problems that increase necessary maintenance.

These are important considerations for *any* plant you choose, but trees, being larger than perennials, are more obvious. Be certain you choose the best trees and shrubs for your garden, rather than merely accepting anything that grows in the shade.

Types of Understory Trees

Maples, *Acer* Species

There are any number of small maples that are useful and attractive either growing on their own on smaller properties, or as understory trees beneath larger trees. Maples all provide a pleasing form, handsome branching pattern, attractive bark, tidy foliage, and, in sunnier situations, good fall color. Especially in the colder portion of their range, these small maples are better when planted before they leaf out, in the early spring. In mild winter regions, fall planting is also satisfactory. Maples prefer a moist but well-drained soil, and are intolerant of constant, standing water. These smaller maples have a fibrous root system, and prefer a loose, open, friable soil. At planting time amend the soil with organic matter in the form of compost or leaf mold, and maintain a constant mulch of leaf litter.

Japanese Maple, *Acer palmatum*

Beyond a doubt the most familiar of the small maples is the Japanese maple. These tidy trees have muscular gray bark stretched over the numerous branches that divide into fine, twiggy growth. The finely serrate, palmately lobed leaves, (5- to 7-, up to 11-parted), may be red in the spring and turn green by the summer, or remain garnet to burgundy red right through the growing season. There are numerous named forms available. In the fall trees become living bonfires, taking on a lovely clear scarlet hue. Hardy in zones 6 to 9, give Japanese maple room to grow; though slow about it, they eventually become wider than they are high, reaching 20 feet tall and 30 feet wide. Cutleaf forms of Japanese maples, *Acer palmatum dissectum*, are half that size and spread at maturity. Underplanting with a ground cover is better than grass, for the thin bark of Japanese maples is easily damaged by string trimmers or collision with

Understory Trees for the SHADY GARDEN

a mower. Create an oval, somewhat egg-shaped bed with the tree off center toward the wider end. This looks better than a perfect circle with the tree plunk in the center like an illustration in a geometry text. Try ajugas as a ground cover, selecting a cultivar with coppery bronze leaves, accented in the summer with red impatiens. Or, use old-fashioned *Hosta undulata* var. *univitata*, which has mid-sized green leaves with an attractive central creamy blotch, undulating edges, and an unusual, somewhat spirally twisted shape.

As understory trees, Japanese maples can be planted in the shade of massive oaks. A whole grove would be wonderful as a small forest on their own, with broad-leaved evergreen shrubs such as skimmia, leucothoe, pieris, or mountain laurel to keep them company. Japanese maples create an elegant fall landscape when they are displayed against an evergreen background of pine. Consider accentuating that effect with shade tolerant perennials selected for fall interest.

Full Moon Maple, *Acer japonicum*

Perhaps we'd better stay with full moon maple as the common name for *Acer japonicum*, which is sometimes confusingly called

Combine plants and decorative accessories in your garden for attractive results.

Japanese maple. This species grows 30 feet tall, and the leaves are quite rounded in outline, with 7 to 11 lobes neatly spaced along the edge. Hardy from zones 5 to 8, full moon maples are an interesting alternative to their more widely planted relative. Very slow-growing, 'Aureum' has the most delicious golden yellow leaves, and would create an elegant focus in a bed of yellow hosta, variegated liriope, and dark green Christmas fern. 'Aconitifolium' has deeply cut leaves like some intricately scissored snippery.

Vine Maple, *Acer circinatum*

Vine maple is similar to full moon maple but the species is native to the Pacific Northwest rather than Japan. Hardy in zones 6 to 8, vine maple is even more shade-tolerant than Japanese maples, forming a densely branched shrub or small tree sometimes reaching 30 feet tall. Coarse, rounded leaves have 7 to 9 regularly spaced lobes. When grown at the edge of woodland, in the fall the sun-struck leaves turn an extremely brilliant red-orange.

Trident or Three-toothed Maple,
Acer buergerianum

Trident or three-toothed maple is another small Japanese maple, growing 35 feet tall. Hardy in zones 6 to 8, trident maple has interesting, 3-lobed, glossy, dark green leaves, paler on the underside, often drooping or pendulous. Exfoliating bark flakes off, revealing multicolor patches of olive-yellow to gray-brown color, adding winter interest.

Paperbark Maple, *Acer griseum*

Paperbark maple is another maple with exfoliating bark. This maple has thin, papery curls of cinnamon red bark that peel off the trunk and larger branches. Since branching

Start small—a full-grown tree can't be wedged in a crevice!

begins low on the trunk, judicious pruning reveals the flaking bark to better advantage. Trees slowly reach 20 feet tall. In the spring, the new, three-parted leaves are a soft coppery color, maturing to soft green. Fall color is variable, some years a good red or orange-yellow; some years the leaves barely change color before they fall. Hardy in zones 6 and 7, some paperbark maples are reported to have survived in sheltered locations in zone 5. In one garden I paired a paperbark maple with a red-flowered azalea for a charming spring combination of copper-hued leaves and red flowers.

Moosewood or Striped Maple,
Acer pennsylvaticum
Moosewood or striped maple is the best choice for cold climates since it is hardy from zones 3 to 7. The coarse, dull green, three-lobed leaves turn bright golden yellow in the fall. The beauty of this species is also in its bark, which is extraordinarily striated with rather wide white stripes on the branches. Often growing as wide as they are high, these multitrunked maples can reach 35 feet tall. Moosewood can be trained as a standard, to a single trunk. If left to its own, it might be considered either a treelike shrub or a shrub-like tree.

Buckeye, *Aesculus* Species

Ohio Buckeye, *Aesculus glabra*
Ohio buckeye is an understory tree for moist sites. Growing 20 to 40 feet high and wide, rounded in habit, it offers greenish yellow flowers in upright, 4- to 7-inch-long clusters in midspring, which blend into coarse, palmately compound dark green leaves. Unfortunately, the leaves are prone to mildew and leaf blight, sometimes spoiling their summer appearance (though not so severe as horse chestnut, *A. hippocastanum*). In the fall, smooth husks split to reveal the glossy brown buckeyes for which the tree is named. Though similar in appearance, these are not the edible chestnuts of the market-place. It is more a matter of preserving trees growing wild in central midwestern United States from Pennsylvania to Alabama and west to Kansas, than planting new ones—which are difficult to transplant—in gardens.

Red Buckeye, *Aesculus pavia*
This is another native understory tree. Especially suitable for light shade, rich red flowers gathered in 3- to 6-inch upright pan-icles open in April and May. They make a handsome display against the glossy dark green, palmately compound leaves. In the fall, one or two inedible, glossy brown buck-eyes are contained within each smooth husk. I have raised trees from seed, collected promptly to outwit the squirrels and sown immediately for best germination. It will take a few years before they flower, but in gardens there is always next year. Growing 15 to 20 feet high and wide, red buckeye needs some shade and moist soil in order to thrive. Native from Virginia to Florida, westward to Texas, this handsome buckeye is well worth planting in gardens from zone 4 to 8.

Shadblow, *Amelanchier* Species
Call it what you will—shadblow, downy ser-viceberry, or shadbush—*Amelanchier arborea*

Understory Trees for the SHADY GARDEN

Shadblow makes an elegant understory addition to the woodland garden.

At the extremes of its range it is better to select trees of local origin; they are more likely to be heat-tolerant or cold-hardy than a random choice. Trees grow 15 to 25 feet tall. Shadbush thrives in moist to average soils. Plant them at the edge of woodland for best flowering.

Shadblow Serviceberry, *Amelanchier canadensis*

This is often confused with the previous species. The true plant is a multistemmed shrubby plant growing 6 to 20 feet tall. Found wild in wet places along the coast from Maine to North Carolina, it is hardy from zones 3 to 7. Under cultivation it will thrive with average soil moisture, but should be on the "A" list for lightly shaded pond banks or along woodland streams.

Allegheny Serviceberry, *A. laevis*

This serviceberry is similar in form, flower, and fruit to shadblow, with purple to bronze on unfolding new leaves the most obvious difference.

Apple Serviceberry, *A.* x *grandiflora*

This is a naturally occurring hybrid of *A. arborea* and *A. laevis*. It grows 20 to 25 feet tall with equal spread, and is useful in zones 5 to 8.

Camellia, *Camellia sasanqua*

Sasanqua camellia is a treasure and delight in southern gardens. Unfortunately for northerners, these small evergreen trees from China and Japan are hardy only in zones 7 to 9. Flowering will be best with some sun during the growing season. Trees I saw growing in woodland at the Atlanta Botanical Garden one fall were putting on a good show with their exquisite white, pink, or crimson flowers, for not only do camellias have

is a wonderful small tree with seasonal interest in the spring, summer, fall, and winter. In the spring, numerous white flowers in 2- to 4-inch clusters briefly cover the branches with a lacy shawl of blossoms. In June the berries ripen from red to deep purple-blue, delicious eaten fresh from the tree or made into preserves, but you'll need to be quick if you want to pick them before the birds. Fall leaf color is apricot, red-veined orange, or dusty red, resulting in a warm, glowing display. Darker markings on the trunk and main branches subtly enhance the handsome silver gray bark, especially attractive in the winter when trees are bare. Native to the eastern United States into Canada, across to the Midwest, and south to northern Georgia and Louisiana, shadblow is hardy in zones 4 to 8.

handsome, glossy, dark green leaves, effective year round, they flower over a two- or three-month period in the fall. Since the small, 18- to 20-foot-tall trees are shallow-rooted, mulching is important, as well as watering during periods of drought. They prefer an acid soil, and protection from wind and sun in the winter to prevent leaf damage. Their only drawback is that camellias have no scent. Compensate for this minor deficiency by pairing them with skimmia or some other shrub that flowers at the same time and is fragrant.

American Hornbeam, *Carpinus caroliniana*

American hornbeam or ironwood is a superlative, underutilized understory native tree. Tolerant of dense shade, ironwood grows 20 to 30 feet tall, with a graceful branching pattern and muscular ridged trunk and branches covered with smooth gray bark. Light green leaves are oval, tapering to a point and serrate edged, turning yellow to orange in the fall before they drop. Hardy in zones 3 to 9, for some reason it is rarely available at nurseries. Where occuring naturally on your property, cherish them.

Redbud, *Cercis canadensis*

When in bloom, eastern redbud is certain to invite comment, with small, pealike, vivid magenta pink flowers studded in clusters not only on the twigs but even on large branches and directly on the trunk. Large, coarse leaves emerge as flowering finishes, heart-shaped, light green at first and then turning dark green in summer. Fall leaf color is bright yellow. 'Alba' is a cultivar with white flowers, while 'Forest Pansy' has leaves that are bright crimson as they first unfold, turning deep purple-red at maturity. This leaf coloration is strongest with some sun, and leaves on shade-grown trees are green only washed with purple. Hardy in zones 6 to 9, the selection of northern stock yields redbuds that can grow in zone 5 gardens. The flower color is a hard, bluish pink that clashes with other pink flowers, so choose companions carefully. One of the nicest uses I ever saw of this shade-tolerant tree was in Linc and Timmy Foster's garden in Falls Village, Connecticut, where redbuds and white flowering dogwoods mingled in the woodland.

Fringetree, *Chionanthus virginicus*

Slow to leaf out, quick to drop its leaves in the fall...who cares, when fringetree envelops itself in a shawl of fragrant white flowers in May. Individually, each flower is nothing much, four or five straplike petals; however, they cluster in 6- to 8-inch-long panicles borne on the previous year's growth, completely covering the tree. Trees begin flowering at only two or three years from seed. Fringetree is dioecious; only female trees will bear attractive clusters of blue fruits in September. Glossy, medium to dark green leaves, 3 to 8 inches long, mature after flowering is over, turning yellow to yellow-brown before falling. Multistemmed, fringe trees grow 12 to 20 feet tall with an even wider spread. To date, the only means of propagation is from seed, so each tree is somewhat different and individual from the others. Native from southern New Jersey to Florida and westward to Texas, fringetree is hardy in zones 4 to 9. Wonderful as understory trees, fringetree performs well as a specimen but because of its late leafing out, I wouldn't give them the most conspicuous location. I underplanted with small, blue-leaved *Hosta* 'Halcyon', and *Lamiastrum* 'Hermann's Pride', which has silver-netted foliage and yellow flowers in the spring. The spring effect was as fine as could be wished, and summer's was quietly pleasing.

Dogwood, *Cornus* Species

Flowering Dogwood, *Cornus florida*
If you need a template, a paradigm for choosing an understory story tree, then look no

Understory Trees for the SHADY GARDEN

Close-up, the spring flowers of shadblow are handsome with the small tree's coppery new leaves.

further than flowering dogwood. Though it will grow in full sun in northeastern gardens, I find those trees naturally growing in woodland have a more pleasing appearance. They have an open appearance rather than a solid parasol of flowers and foliage, permitting a greater diversity of ground plane plants to grow. Tolerant of a range of conditions, flowering dogwood must have some shade in southeastern gardens. Overall form is attractive; in the spring the small inconspicuous flowers are surrounded by very showy white bracts, fall color is a handsome red, and scarlet berries look great until the migrating robins strip the tree in an afternoon on their way south. Dogwoods are best planted in the spring, preferring a light to moderately shaded site with moist but well-drained soil. Watering during periods of drought, and regular fertilization will help with the overall

health of the trees. Storm damage is not a problem as wood is so dense that it was used for shuttles in southern fabric mills. Anthracnose, a leaf disease, and bark bores are more serious concerns. Weather is the greatest influence on anthracnose, and all we can do about weather is discuss it. Flowering dogwood is hardy from zones 6 to 8, and in sheltered locations in zone 5.

Crosses between *Cornus florida* and *C. kousa* have recently been developed by Dr. Orton at Rutgers University in New Jersey. These hybrid dogwoods are intermediate in appearance between the parent species, and are more resistant to anthracnose than their flowering dogwood parent. Rutgers hybrids making their way into the nursery trade include the registered cultivars Aurora®, Celestial®, Constellation®, Ruth Ellen®, Star Dust®, and Stellar Pink®.

Japanese Dogwood, *Cornus kousa*

Japanese dogwood is an Asian relative of our native flowering dogwood, resistant to pests and diseases, and hardy in zones 5 to 7. It flowers a few weeks later, and the bracts are pointed rather than rounded at the tip. When flowering is heavy one season, the following year is likely to see sparse bloom. Light shade to full sun is necessary for best flower production. The fruits of Japanese dogwood resembles warty, dull red, oversized raspberries, edible but unexciting.

American Holly, *Ilex opaca*

American holly is a useful alternative to English holly as it is more shade-tolerant and cold-hardier, growing in zones 6 to 9. The leaves of American holly are typically spiny, olive green to green, and evergreen, with different cultivars displaying dull or glossy surface. Dr. Orton at Rutgers University in New Jersey has also worked with American hollies for decades, selecting plants for disease resistance, landscape use, flower, form, and foliage. There are over 300 different American holly cultivars, with the majority female plants with heavy fruiting, yellow rather than red berries, or fastigiate or pendulous form. Trees grow well in light to half shade, with heaviest fruiting and most compact growth resulting in light shade. Winter shade protects against leaf damage such as sun scald and winter burn. American hollies can be used for screening, sheared for a hedge, or grown as individual specimens.

Magnolia, *Magnolia* Species

Star Magnolia, *Magnolia stellata*

Star magnolia is best suited for an edge of woodland situation, for this popular, widely available small, 18-foot-tall, Japanese tree needs some sun if it is to flower well. It blossoms early in the spring before leaves appear, producing fragrant white, pink-flushed, or rose pink flowers. The 12 to 18 ribbonlike tepals (petals and petal-like sepals) that make up the flower are damaged by moderate frosts, so choose a protected site. Star magnolia has more the character of a

Summer fruit of shadblow is tasty, if you get it before the birds do!

Understory Trees for the SHADY GARDEN

Worthwhile in several seasons, shadblow has lovely fall color.

large shrub, since it produces several trunks that branch from ground level. The smooth, silver gray bark lends winter interest, as do the fat, fur-coated flower buds, especially charming when they wear a "hat" of snow. Select a site with moist but well-drained soil, high in organic matter. Use a ground cover or mulch to protect the shallow roots and prevent inadvertent damage when digging in the area.

Kobus Magnolia, *Magnolia kobus*
Similar in appearance, kobus magnolia is rarely planted today. We do not have the patience of the previous generation of gardeners, who would wait the 20 or 30 years until a seedling reached flowering size. Maturing at 30 to 40 feet, and rounded with

age, kobus magnolia has somewhat fragrant white flowers, six- to nine-tepaled and 3 to 4 inches across. They open in March or April, before the dark green, 3- to 6-inch-long leaves appear. Fall color is a warm, yellow-brown, and in the winter the silver gray bark accentuates the stately form of this species. It is useful in zones 5 to 8.

Loebner Magnolia, *M.* x *loebneri*
Kobus magnolia's greatest garden value has been as parent (along with star magnolia) to Loebner magnolia, *M.* x *loebneri*. The hybrid exhibits the best characteristics of both parents, developing quickly into a densely branched rounded tree 20 to 30 feet tall with fragrant, commonly white flowers of 12 to 15 tepals, opening in April. Loebner magnolia

heavily shades the ground beneath, the result of their branching habit and a dense cover of medium to dark green leaves 3 to 5 inches long, which turn yellow-brown before dropping in the fall. Useful in zones 5 to 8 (zone 4 with protection), they provide a lightly shaded situation, and a moist yet freely draining site, with acid pH, high in organic matter, protected from wind and lightly shaded. Transplant in the early spring and keep watered—drying of the roots of newly transplanted trees is the most common cause of failure. There are several cultivars available. 'Ballerina' has pure white, long-lasting flowers, very full with 30 tepals; 'Leonard Messel' has 12 to 15 tepalled flowers flushed purplish pink on the outside, and forms a smaller, 15- to 20-foot-tall tree at maturity; 'Merrill' is commonly available, at 30 to 40 feet the tallest cultivar, bearing a profuse display 3 to 3 ½ inches in diameter, with 15 tepalled flowers; 'Spring Snow' grows 25 feet high and equally wide, and has fragrant, long-lasting flowers somewhat later in the season, composed of 12 to 15 broad white tepals.

Sweetbay, *Magnolia virginiana*, is discussed in the chapter Problem Shade/Problem Trees, beginning on page 21, as a tree for moist, shady sites.

Hop Hornbeam, *Ostrya virginiana*
Hop hornbeam or ironwood is very tolerant of shade, but dislikes wet feet or any level of contact with road deicing salt. Birchlike leaves, finely saw-toothed and medium to dark green, make a dense canopy in the late spring and summer. Slow-growing and difficult to transplant, select small, container-grown trees and be patient. On the plus side, hop hornbeam is pest-free and disease-resistant, needing little or no maintenance. Extremely strong, durable, dense wood protects branches against wind or storm damage. Hardy from zones 4 to 9, this small native tree, 35 feet tall and two-thirds as wide, deserves wider use for their simple interest and ease of upkeep.

Sourwood, *Oxydendron arboreum*
Marvelous native tree with summer flowers

Showy in fruit, dogwood berries make excellent food for birds, attracting them to your garden.

Understory Trees for the SHADY GARDEN

Elegant in flower, dogwoods create a natural effect in the shade of large oak trees.

and superlative fall color, sourwood is only grumpy about moving. Small, containerized specimens are easier to transplant than large, balled and burlapped-size trees. The overall shape of mature trees is pyramidal, with alligator-blocky bark on trunk and main branches, smooth olive green to red on young growth. Trees reach 25 to 30 feet tall, and 20 feet wide, and can grow even larger. Long oval leaves, 3 to 8 inches long, are vivid green when they first unfold, turning a lustrous dark green by the summer, then red to maroon in the fall. Young trees color at summer's end, earlier than mature trees. Fragrant white bell-like flowers in trailing clusters 4 to 10 inches long at the tips of the branches open over a three- to four-week period in June and July. Sourwood honey is a delicacy produced in the southeastern United States where trees are native.

They are followed by persistent, gray-brown seed capsules that remain through the winter, lending a decorative aspect to the bare branches. Though suitable for sunny sites, sourwood also grows and flowers well in part shade, preferring an infertile, acid soil in zones 5 to 9.

Persian Parrotia, *Parrotia persica*
You don't see Persian parrotia in gardens very often; more's the pity, for a well-grown specimen is an absolute delight in the fall and winter. Brilliant yellow to vivid orange-scarlet fall color turn the tree into a vividly glowing garden asset. In the winter the trunk and stiffly spreading bare branches are enhanced by exfoliating bark in a gray, green, creamy white, and brown display. Persian parrotia branches low to the ground, creating a full appearance. The gardener's choice then, is to

American holly is one of the few winter-hardy, broad-leaved evergreens that are shade-tolerant, and it is beautiful too!

accept this naturally graceful look, or, over time and as the tree grows, gradually remove the lower branches to better reveal the handsome bark. The tree was in flower when I visited Willowwood Arboretum in New Jersey in early January of 1998. Even though they flower in the winter, an exciting time of year for anything in bloom, the flowers of Persian parrotia are nothing to write home about: round, brown, half pea-sized, with ruby red stamens showing on those close enough to peer at. I had much better flowering plants to see that day, such as witch hazels and mahonias. In the spring new leaves are bronze to reddish purple, maturing to $2\frac{1}{2}$ to 5 inches long and lustrous dark green in color. Though native to Iran, Persian parrotia is hardier than you might expect, useful in zones 6 to 9, even the warmer portion of

zone 5 in a protected site. Growing 20 to 40 feet tall and 15 to 30 feet wide, this is a choice specimen for a lightly shaded site with moist yet free-draining soil. Transplant in the early spring as containerized or balled and burlapped material.

Common Hop Tree, *Ptelea trifoliata*
Common hop tree is another of those native trees deserving wider use, not because it is native but because it is such a nice, trouble-free, shade-tolerant small tree. Usually growing 20 feet tall, common hop tree grows in forests and forest edges, even open sunny areas, in moist to dry soils. The slender crooked trunk is crowned with short, twisting branches, clad in three-parted, palmately compound leaves that have an aromatic, orange-peel fragrance when crushed. Leaves are an attractive pale lime green when they first appear in the spring, maturing to dark green in the summer, then turning pale yellow before they drop in mid-fall. The winged, waferlike fruits persist through the winter. Hardy in zones 4 to 9, perhaps the best use for common hop tree is a naturalistic design incorporating with viburnums and inkberries.

Yew Podocarpus, *Podocarpus macrophyllus*
Yew podocarpus is another of those great plants from Japan that have become important in American gardens. This tender conifer can be considered a tree in zone 9, where it reaches 30 feet tall, but should be classed as a shrub in zone 8 where 6 to 12 feet tall is typical. It is marginally hardy in zone 7. The glossy, evergreen, needlelike leaves, 4 inches long and ¼ inch wide, are dark green on their upper surface and paler light green on the underside. Leaves grow densely on the branchlets. Partial shade is necessary to keep leaves from scorching, both in the summer and winter. Yew podocarpus is useful as a specimen or an accent plant, and can be clipped to create a formal hedge or topiary.

Understory Trees for the SHADY GARDEN

Stewartia, *Stewartia* Species
Because they flower from mid- to late summer when few woody plants are in bloom, stewartias are possibly my favorite understory trees. Unable to move my Japanese stewartia from Connecticut (it had been in the garden for over 10 years), I bought two to replace it in my present garden in New Jersey. Stewartias are easy to grow if you pay attention to their likes and dislikes. They like the same kind of soil as mountain laurel and rhododendrons, humus-rich and acidic. Add ample organic matter for a loose, open, moisture-retentive root run, and mulch for the same reasons. Stewartias want a moist site, but it is important that it be one with a free-draining soil. Not soggy, but not dust dry, just right (plan on watering during periods of drought). At Willowwood Arboretum in Far Hills, New Jersey, stewartias self-sow along a little stream. Morning sun is fine, but shade in the heat of midday is appreciated. Transplant small trees in the early spring before they leaf out. In mild winter areas where the ground doesn't freeze, I'd even consider transplanting in the late winter. These are such magnificent small trees that you must be certain to give them a place of honor in the garden that allows you and your guests to appreciate their superb flowers.

Japanese Stewartia, *Stewartia pseudocamellia*
Japanese stewartia is a choice small tree for any shaded garden where it might be grown.

Exquisite white flowers, 2 or more inches across, look like elegant single camellias (to which stewartias are related). Well-displayed against the green leaves, each flower has a central boss of golden stamens. All flowers do not open at once, so the period of bloom is extensive. Hardy in zones 5 to 8, these small trees are best transplanted as smaller,

container-grown material, spring-planted in zones 5 and 6. Smooth bark that flakes away in rounded, irregular patches on the trunk and main branches adds an attractive appearance when the trees are bare in the winter. Partial shade results in better flowering performance as blossoms are protected from hot summer sun. Good drainage is also important, but avoid dry situations. A tree I planted in the shelter of a mature white oak with a simple carpet of epimedium and ferns did well year after year, creating a charming vignette through the seasons.

Korean Stewartia, *S. koreana,*
S. pseudocamellia var. *koreana*
Whatever the taxonomists call them, Korean stewartia, *S. koreana*, *S. pseudocamellia* var. *koreana*, or *S. pseudocamellia* 'Korean Splendor', we're talking about a superior understory tree. Larger, 3-inch-diameter, white flowers with an extended period of bloom, more vivid golden to orange-red fall color make these choice trees for zones 6 to 8 gardens, zone 5 with protection. Tolerant of heat and humidity, Korean stewartia prefers edge of woodland conditions in light shade, with moist yet freely draining, acid loam. Multicolored bark flakes off in irregular patches to reveal gray, olive greenish, cinnamon red patterning. Fall color is excellent.

Japanese stewartia is the most attractive, and readily available species in this genus; still, should you come across tall stewartia, *Stewartia monadelpha*, or Chinese stewartia, *S. sinensi*, by all means add them to your garden.

Tall Stewartia, *S. monadelpha*
Tall stewartia grows 20 to 30 feet high and wide. Suitable for zones 6 to 8, zone 5 with protection from severe weather, this species is more tolerant of summer heat and drier con-

ditions than Japanese stewartia. Not as showy in bloom, the white flowers are smaller, 1 to 1½ inches in diameter, and open in late June or early July. Stamens are a lovely violet, rather than the golden stamens of the other species. Multitrunked specimens are common, though some naturally develop a single trunk. Tall stewartia also has exfoliating bark in a handsome pattern of gray, brown, and cinnamon red. Fall color is inconsistent, some years turning a gorgeous deep red color and other years not, depending on the weather.

Chinese Stewartia, *S. sinensis*
Chinese stewartia grows 15 to 25 feet tall. Suitable for zones 5 to 7, it should have a protected site in colder portions of its range. Fall color is unexceptional; fragrant white flowers are 1½ to 2 inches across and open over an extended period. Smooth gray-brown bark, mottled like snakeskin, enhances the main trunk. This species is more commonly seen in British gardens than in those of the United States.

Silky Camellia, *S. malacodendron*
Silky camellia is an American species native to the southeastern states. Hardy from zones 7 to 9, I first saw this species in flower at Biltmore House and Gardens in North Carolina. Growing as large shrubs or small trees, silky camellia has large flowers almost 3½ inches across and stamens even darker than those of tall stewartia, a deep violet-purple that appears black against the white petals. It flowers from the late summer into the early fall.

Snowbell, *Styrax* Species

Japanese Snowbell, *Styrax japonicus*
Japanese snowbell is a charming tree for gardens with room to let it spread. The vertical dimension—20 to 30 feet high—is not as awkward as the equally wide spread, which can be cumbersome on a terrace or patio. Where space allows, such use is delightful, especially when the bell-shaped, somewhat fragrant white flowers dangle on 1- to 1½-inch-long stalks in May and June. Place a bench beneath the spreading branches so you can lean back and gaze upward at the canopy. Since the dark green leaves are on the top of the branches, and flowers dangle beneath, the blossoms are very visible and

Azaleas along a wooded path.

Understory Trees for the SHADY GARDEN

create a pretty picture. The smooth gray bark on the trunk and sinuous main branches are handsome in the winter, especially when set off by an evergreen background. Grow in partial shade in a site with acid, moist, but freely draining soil with ample organic matter, and protected from late spring frosts. Transplant in the spring, and select younger, smaller-size material, as styrax is slow to adjust to transplanting. Native to China and Japan, Japanese snowbell is useful in zones 5 to 8.

Fragrant Snowbell, *Styrax obassia*
Fragrant snowbell also grows 20 to 30 feet tall, not quite as wide. Somewhat hardier than Japanese snowbell, fragrant snowbell can be grown in a protected site in zone 4. It has 4- to 8-inch-long trailing clusters of fragrant white flowers, and the largest leaves of any of the snowbells, up to 8 inches long and 4 inches across. More upright in growth than the previous species, fragrant snowbell is elegant as an individual, specimen tree. Provide a partially shaded site high in organic matter, moist but freely draining with an acid pH.

American Snowbell, *Styrax americanus*

Bigleaf Snowbell, *S. grandifolius*
There are two native species, shrubby American snowbell, *Styrax americanus*, and the more treelike bigleaf snowbell, *S. grandifolius*. Both are found in the southeastern United States, from Virginia to Florida, and are useful in zones 7 to 9, perhaps the warmer portion of zone 6 in a sheltered site. Neither is widely available but are definitely worth preserving on sites where they occur naturally.

A rustic bench in fall woods.

SHRUBS

Azaleas reflecting in the still waters of a pond create a tranquil scene in the rock garden of the New York Botanical Garden.

SHRUBS

Perhaps the gold-variegated forms are better known, but I think of green-leaved aucuba as subtle rather than plain.

Both practical and aesthetic considerations influence our choice of shrubs for the shady garden. Such factors as site conditions (amount of shade, soil type, availability of moisture, winter low and summer high temperatures) and compatibility with neighboring plants are pragmatic. Appearance is also a major consideration. What makes the shrub attractive? Flowers, flowering time, foliage and fruit, and how these combine with nearby plants. Personal taste, unique and individual for every gardener, guides the aesthetic component.

In a small garden, large shrubs can serve as small trees. The upper size limit for shrubs discussed in this chapter is set under 15 feet tall, and it may be assumed they are multi-stemmed unless deliberately cultivated as a single-trunked standard. Shrubs may be deciduous or evergreen, and evergreens can be coniferous or broad-leaved. They are the furniture in a room delineated by trees.

Coniferous Shrubs

The majority of *coniferous* (= needled evergreen) shrubs and trees need full sun in order to grow satisfactorily. Fortunately for gardeners, there are a small handful of shrubs that thrive in shady sites. They are valuable for winter interest when deciduous trees and shrubs are bare, and in the growing season their delicate linear needles provide a handsome contrast to the leafy textures of other plants. The strongest effect is provided by varied textures. In a botanical garden, where we go to learn about different plants, planting a yew next to a Japanese plum yew may be fine. It gives us an easy comparison of the appearances between the two. In a garden however, the effect is bland. Evergreens make good year-round screens or hedges. Use taller coniferous shrubs as a background for deciduous flowering shrubs, or those with radiant fall foliage. Prostrate or low-growing coniferous shrubs help blend taller trees and shrubs into the landscape, smoothing the visual transition from ground to canopy.

Japanese Plum Yew, *Cephalotaxus harringtonia*

If for no other reason than their resistance to browsing by deer, Japanese plum yew would be cherished by gardeners. Were both Japanese plum yew and Japanese yew, *Taxus cuspidata*, grown side by side in deer country, Japanese yew would be completely denuded, Japanese plum yew absolutely untouched. The straight species type of Japanese plum yew grows 15 feet tall, but is less often grown than selected cultivars. 'Fastigiata' is an upright, slow-growing form, eventually reaching 10 feet tall and 7 feet wide, excellent as a focal point and accent, or, more formally, in pairs to delineate the beginning of a woodland path; 'Duke Gardens', a sport of 'Fastigiata', grows 2 to 3 feet tall but will spread 4 to 5 feet wide, charming near a reflective pool or as carpet to a piece of statuary; 'Prostrata' is a low-spreading form with no upright leader, which will, over time, also reach 2 to 3 feet tall by as much wide, making it more suitable for small-scale settings. Hardy from zones 6 to 9, somewhat slow-growing, shade-tolerant Japanese plum yew forms a loose, open, spreading shrub. Rich, dark green glossy needles, with grayish bands on the underside, are longer and broader than those of Japanese yew, and have a bitter odor when crushed. Plants are dioecious, each being either male or female, with olive green fruits an inch or so in diameter on female plants. Transplant container-grown plants in the spring in northern gardens, in the fall where summers are hot. Keep well watered until established. Though able to grow in sunny sites, needle color is better, deeper green, in partial shade, in a site with moist yet freely draining loamy soil.

Russian Cypress, *Microbiota decussata*

Discovered near Vladivostok in eastern Siberia in 1921, and unknown in Western gardens until the 1960s, Russian cypress is slowly finding its way into the nursery trade. Another of the limited selection of coniferous shrubs that tolerate shade, this attractive, low-growing, wide-spreading conifer is sure to become popular as it becomes better known. The dense, wide-spreading branches are clothed with aromatic, scalelike needles that grow in flat, downward-facing sprays. Bright green during the growing season, in partial shade they develop a pleasing bronze to purplish brown hue in the winter. In heavily shaded sites they remain green year round. Russian cypress does poorly in full sun. The needles have a pungent, piney scent when crushed. Generally available only in smaller sizes, it is important to remember how broad Russian cypress will spread at maturity. Growing less

Excellent for good looks and shade tolerance, Japanese plum yew is especially esteemed by gardeners who must cope with deer.

SHRUBS

Russian cypress is an attractive conifer for the shady garden.

than a foot tall, in time each shrub will spread into tidy flattened, rounded saucers 6½ feet wide, sometimes as much as double that spread. A specimen at the Arboretum Trompenburg in Rotterdam, where my friend Gert Fortgens is curator, reached 13 feet across in 10 years, though remaining under a foot tall. Much as junipers serve in sunny sites, Russian cypress can function as a ground cover in partially shaded sites. They are an attractive foil to small to medium-size broad-leaved evergreen shrubs such as leucothoe and some rhododendrons. Native to southeastern Siberia, Russian cypress is cold-hardy to zone 3. The one thing Russian cypress will not tolerate is wet soil, so be sure you plant it on a site with open, well-drained soil. I planted three on a shaded gently sloping site. Slow the first year, now that they are settled in, they are beginning to stretch their limbs and grow.

Yew, *Taxus* Species and Cultivars

The different species of yew—English yew, *Taxus baccata*; Japanese yew, *T. cuspidata*; and their hybrid, intermediate yew, *T. x media*—are basic landscape plants. Most shade-tolerant of all conifers, very tolerant of pruning,

yews are grown in foundation plantings, used for hedges, or clipped topiary specimens. Though rarely considered for such use, they are excellent as understory shrubs in less formal gardens.

English Yew, *Taxus baccata*

English yew is typically at its best only in zones 6 and 7. Growing 40 to 60 feet tall when unpruned (as in an English graveyard), plants may be maintained at any desired height, readily controlled by clipping and shearing. This chore, though simple, adds to the regular maintenance necessary in the garden. Creeping English yew, *Taxus baccata* 'Repandens', a prostrate form, is somewhat cold-hardier than the species and may be used as a dark, somber green, nicely textured ground cover. Growing 2 to 4 feet high and spreading 12 to 15 feet wide, it is an excellent choice for this purpose, but only where deer are not a problem. Creeping English yew is a finer embellishment than ivy or pachysandra. Consider it as carpeting beneath a pin oak, *Quercus palustris*, with its drooping branches and rich fall color, or, as I saw it used in a library courtyard, beneath a shadbush with delicate spring flowers and blazing fall foliage. In both instances creeping English yew is especially handsome in its evergreen winter aspect.

Japanese Yew, *Taxus cuspidata*

More cold-hardy than its English relative, Japanese yew is hardy in zones 4 to 7. Generally, the various cultivars of the hybrid, *T. x media*, hardy in zones 5 to 7, are most frequently available at nurseries. 'Brownii' is especially cold-hardy and can be grown in zone 4; 'Densiformis' is a compact, quick-growing shrub reaching 5 feet tall and half again as wide; 'Hatfieldii' is an upright, nonfruiting shrub when young, becoming spreading with age; 'Hicksii' is a fruiting female clone with an upright, columnar habit.

Yews are important; their value is their dense, rich, dark green needles. Plants dislike poorly drained sites but neither do they tolerate drought. Moist but well-drained situations are best, with shade a preference in regions with hot summers, and as protection from sun scald and wind damage in the winter. Yews are poisonous to domestic livestock such as cattle, but they are preferred food for white-tailed deer that cause severe damage to ornamental plantings in the Northeast. The bright red fruits on female plants can be quite showy in the winter, and are popular food for a number of birds. The black seed enclosed within the fleshy pulp is highly poisonous.

Broad-Leaved Evergreen Shrubs

Broad-leaved evergreen shrubs add their singular qualities and textural interest to the winter garden, quite different from the finer needles of conifers. More common in regions with mild winters, in places with cold weather their leaves are subject to winter burn and sun scald, especially if sited where sunlight reaches them first thing in the morning. Leaf edges turn brown and dry, dying as moisture is lost and cannot be replaced from frozen soil. In all gardens, the visually pleasing pattern play of broad-leaved shrubs against conifer and deciduous shrubs and trees is elegant. In northern gardens a woodland setting where the overhead canopy of bare branches offers a surprising degree of protection alleviates these problems of sun scorch and winter burn.

Ardisia, *Ardisia* Species
Coral ardisia, *Ardisia crenata*, and Chinese ardisia, *A. crispa*, are so similar in appearance that they are frequently confused with each other. Since they can be used interchangeably in the landscape, there seems little to worry about. Just allow the botanists and taxonomists their entertainment in looking at the new growth to see if it is slightly hairy (the Chinese species) or not (coral ardisia). The leaf margins are also different in the two species, coral ardisias having crisped or undulate edges. Hardy only in the Deep South, in zones 9 and 10, ardisia makes open colonies of upright, 4- to 6-foot-high stems, spreading from underground shoots. Lustrous, leathery, dark green evergreen leaves, up to 3 inches long, make an attractive background where plants are used in a mass planting in an informal, naturalistic setting. The drooping clusters of waxy, scarlet red fruits are elegant as they dangle beneath the glossy tufts of foliage, providing long-lasting winter interest. Both species also have white-berried forms, both called 'Alba'. Plant in light shade to sun in sites with average to moist but free-draining soil.

Aucuba or Japanese Laurel, *Aucuba japonica*
Aucuba needs shade to the point where its leaves turn yellow and burn, especially in the winter, if the site is sunny. Dark corners are a preferred habitat for aucuba, the shadier the better. Hardy in zones 7 to 9, this shrub will function as a perennial in protected portions of zone 6, dying to the ground in the winter, then coming up again in the spring. Aucuba usually grows 4 to 6 feet tall, and spread 3 to 4 feet wide. The 4- to 8-inch-long, glossy, leathery leaves may be simple dark green, but are often splashed, speckled, or blotched with yellow. Soil should be moist to wet, but with adequate drainage. A heavy, clay-loam soil is better than a sandy one. Aucuba is an easily grown, familiar shrub in the Southeast, frequently used as a foundation plant, planted in groups for screening, even in containers.

Boxwood, *Buxus sempervirens*
Boxwoods are dense evergreen shrubs, rather

SHRUBS

Variegated aucuba is a workhorse, with gold-splashed leaves to lighten a shady corner.

quickly growing 3 to 6 feet tall and 3 to 4 feet wide. They can be left alone with only an occasional light trimming to keep shrubs more compact, or they can be ruthlessly shaped into a highly geometric hedge or parterre enclosure. The lustrous dark green leaves are at their best in zones 6 to 8, though in exposed sites in zone 6 winter burn can be a problem. Protection in the form of burlap wrapping or plywood covers are frequently employed. Plants need soil with a high organic content, moist but well drained, to protect the shallow root system from drying out. A year-round mulch is helpful. Tolerant of partial to full shade or sun, boxwoods are

elegant formal shrubs suitable for the most dignified of settings. Their only drawback is that freshly pruned shrubs have an odor that reminds some people of a cat's uncleaned litter box. Native to Yugoslavia, 'Varder Valley' is cold-hardy to zone 5, and has been known to withstand –23°F; slow-growing at 1 to 4 inches a year, it eventually reaches 6 feet high by 10 feet wide; 'Glencoe', a *Buxus sinica* x *B. sempervirens* cross selected at the Chicago Botanic Garden, tolerates –22°F with no damage, maintains good winter color, and tolerates full shade but grows better in partial shade; 'Green Mountain' is a hybrid between *Buxus sempervirens* 'Suffruticosa' and a different species, *B. microphylla* var. *koreana*; growing in part shade to full sun, just about any soil except heavy clay or rocky sites, 'Green Mountain' is very winter-hardy. It maintains good green color even in zone 5 winters when other boxwoods either die or turn bronze. Two sibling shrubs from the same cross include slow-growing, darker green, rounded/mounded 'Green Gem' and vigorous, rounded 'Green Velvet'.

Wintercreeper, *Euonymus fortunei*
Wintercreeper is a plant with many disguises. It can grow as an evergreen vine, ground cover, or shrub. Climbing, vinelike types can grow 3 to 6 feet high, and spread 2 to 4 feet wide as they cling to tree trunks or masonry walls. Tidy evergreen foliage makes handsome ground covers of the appropriate cultivars, and shrubby types can be used in foundation plantings. Wintercreeper prefers moderately moist, moderately well-drained sites, not soggy hollows nor dry sandy soils in moderate to full shade or sun. 'Vegetatus' is one cultivar often grown as a shrub. It has rounded, medium green, coarsely toothed leaves, and attractive orange-red fruit. Two other shrubby forms, growing about 5 feet high, are 'Emerald Gaiety' with white-variegated leaves, but no fruiting interest, and 'Emerald 'n Gold', which has yellow variegated leaves. Not only can these three cultivars be grown as a 3- to 4-foot-high shrub in foundation plantings, with some pruning they can also be used as a low hedge. Wintercreepers are hardy in zones 5 to 9. They are subject to scale insects, especially in zones 8 and 9.

Burning bush, *Euonymus alatus*, is a native deciduous shrub discussed later in this chapter.

Bush Ivy, x *Fatshedera lizei*
Bush ivy is a horticultural rarity, a cross between two different genera of plants: Japanese fatsia, *Fatsia japonica*, and Irish ivy,

Hedera hibernica. Used as houseplants in colder climates, bush ivy is hardy from the warmer part of zones 7 to 9. It may be grown in cooler portions of zone 7 if a suitable protected site can be provided. From its ivy parents it gets a rapidly spreading, vinelike habit of growth, and needs support in the form of a wall or trellis to which it can cling. Unsupported, it grows erect to about eye level, flops over, then starts growing upward again; longer shoots, therefore, sag and need tieing in. Alternatively, prune to keep a more shrublike lower form. Tolerant of medium to low moisture, moderate fertility, and part to full shade, bush ivy is an excellent choice for that wretchedly narrow shady strip of ground between a wall and a sidewalk. The lustrous, dark green evergreen leaves, up to 10 inches in diameter, have five palmate lobes. There are some showy variegated cultivars with yellow or creamy white markings.

Japanese Fatsia, *Fatsia japonica*
Japanese fatsia is a bold, coarse-textured, evergreen foliage plant suitable for protected,

With male and female flowers on separate shrubs, *Acuba's* berries only appear when both sexes are planted in the garden.

SHRUBS

deeply shaded sites. The glossy, palmately lobed leaves reach 14 inches long, equally wide, sometimes even larger, and can be damaged by wind. Plants need little care, only some light fertilization in the spring and summer. When allowed to grow unchecked as a small tree, Japanese fatsia can reach 12 feet tall. This shrub can be kept at 6 to 8 feet tall with a light pruning in the spring, also removing any winter-damaged leaves. In zones 7 and 8, Japanese fatsia needs some protection, especially in the form of more winter shade. It is hardiest in zone 9. In May 1995 I saw Japanese fatsia in fruit outdoors at Wisley in England. Tall shrubs were well decorated with clusters of small, blue-black fruits. Casual conversation with one of the staff revealed that this is unusual, and attributable to the preceding mild winter.

Inkberry, *Ilex glabra*
Inkberry was discussed in Problem Shade/Problem Trees, beginning on page 21, as a shrub for moist soil and shade.

Anise Tree, *Illicium* Species
A major difference between the two more commonly grown anise trees is that Florida anise tree, *Illicium floridanum*, begins displaying its showy, fragrant, white to yellow or maroon flowers at an earlier age than Japanese anise tree, *I. anisatum*. Related to magnolias, these two tender evergreen shrubs grow in zones 8 and 9.

Florida Anise Tree, *Illicium floridanum*
Florida anise tree grows 5 to 10 feet tall, and spreads 5 to 8 feet wide. The licorice-scented leaves, 2 to 6 inches long and 1 to 3 inches wide, are dark glossy green above and paler beneath, most aromatic when crushed. Leaf color is better, a richer green, in more shaded sites. Leaves droop when temperatures fall below freezing. Flowers are 1 to 2 inches across, with 20 or so narrow petals. They open in March to April. Florida anise tree is native to Florida and Louisiana, where it grows wild in wet ravines and wooded areas. It requires partial shade and moist yet freely draining soil high in organic matter.

Japanese Anise Tree, *Illicium anisatum*
Japanese anise tree also is hardy in zones 8 and 9. Native to Japan, China, and Taiwan, it was introduced to western gardens over 200 years ago. Pale whitish to greenish yellow flowers an inch across, with 30 or so narrow petals, are borne profusely in March or April but have no fragrance.

Japanese anise tree grows 6 to 12, sometimes 15 feet tall, rather pyramidal in form. The glossy, medium green leaves are 2 to 4 inches long and an inch wide.

Note: To some people the flowers smell like rotting fish. I'd find a plant in bloom and check out personal reaction before deciding to add this species to the garden.

Both species are moderate in growth, little troubled with pests or diseases and prefer a moist soil with good drainage. Florida anise tree has been known to grow in wet, mucky soils. Choose a site with moderately fertile soil high in organic matter and part to full shade. Their attractive form suggests groupings several plants in an informal naturalistic shrub border. A conifer with dark needles, such as Japanese plum yew, or yew podocarpus, would make an effective foliage contrast.

Small Anise Tree, *Illicium parviflorum*
Toot Fineberg-Buchner, my friend who lives in Memphis, Tennessee, appreciates her small anise tree, *Illicium parviflorum*. At 8 feet tall, the three shrubs growing under a

mature oak tree in her front garden provide the screening from the street for which she chose them. And, as Toot wrote me, their fragrant foliage also provides "aromatherapy when you brush against them while working in the garden." Native to Florida and southern Georgia, small anise tree is hardy in zones 8 and 9. Under cultivation it is generally intermediate in size between Japanese anise tree and Florida anise tree, reaching 10 feet tall. Foliage appears very full, as the olive green leaves are carried partly erect at a narrow angle from the stem. Pale greenish yellow, starlike flowers with 5 to 12 petals open in May or June, and established plants often produce a few flowers intermittently in the fall. In the trade small anise tree is often confused with Florida anise tree, *I. floridanum*.

Mountain Laurel, *Kalmia latifolia*

Mountain laurel ia an excellent evergreen shrub with engagingly attractive flowers in the late spring to early summer. Hardy from zones 5 to 9, in the warmer end of its range mountain laurel demands a shaded site with protection from summer heat. Either sun or shade is acceptable at the cooler end of their range. Since flowering is reduced in moderately to heavily shaded sites, plant mountain laurel at the woodland's edge or in a gladelike opening where there will be sufficient sun to encourage better bloom. An acid soil, high in organic matter, moist but well drained is the best site for this member of the heath family. It has a fibrous root system, which makes it easy to transplant and suggests the use of a year-round mulch to maintain healthy growth. While mountain

Mountain laurel is one of the finest North American broad-leaved evergreen shrubs for any garden.

SHRUBS

laurel can be pruned to keep it dense, compact, and lower than its potential 10-foot height at maturity, I like the look of older plants allowed to follow their natural habits. The dark bark on the gnarled trunks contrast beautifully with the glossy dark green leaves, accented by the frothy mass of white to pale pink flowers in late spring. Mountain laurel combines beautifully with a ground cover of ferns or running myrtle.

A number of cultivars have been developed by Dr. Richard Jayne at his Broken Arrow Nursery in Hamden, Connecticut. Some of these have deeper-colored flowers in both bud and bloom. 'Bay State' is coral red; 'Heart of Fire' has red buds and deep pink flowers; 'Olympic Fire' has deep pink buds and light but bright pink flowers; 'Ostbo Red' has bright red buds and softer, deep pink flowers; and 'Raspberry Glow' has burgundy red buds and raspberry pink flowers. Other cultivars, such as 'Carousel' and 'Pinwheel' have a band of deeper, cinnamon color on white flowers.

Drooping Leucothoe, *Leucothoe catesbei*

Drooping leucothoe flourishes in dense shade. Like mountain laurel, drooping leucothoe is a member of the heath family and prefers similar conditions of acid soil, high in organic matter, moist but well drained, with a year-round mulch to protect the shallow, fibrous mat of roots. The glossy, dark green, leathery, acutely pointed leaves are arranged in a tidy double row on the arching branches. Hardy from zones 5 to 9, this evergreen shrub needs protection from early morning winter sun and drying winds to prevent winter burn and sun scald damage. Where plants are exposed to some direct sun in winter, leaves turn an attractive, deep plum purple. Drooping trusses of white, bell-like flowers appear in the late spring, dripping from the

tips of the branches. Maintenance is minimal—simply the occasional pruning of older stems at ground level, to be replaced by new shoots from the suckering roots. With its arching habit and modest height (5 to 6 feet at maturity), drooping leucothoe is excellent for foundation plantings, in a naturalistic planting in combination with larger rhododendrons or mature mountain laurel, or even as an occasional specimen at the edge of a woodland path. Deer do not eat drooping leucothoe.

Holly-grape, *Mahonia* Species

There are several holly-grapes that are worthwhile additions to the shady garden for several reasons. They have elegant, leathery, lustrous foliage, pinnately compound, each leaflet pointed and prickly like a holly leaf. In the spring holly-grapes have clusters of bright yellow, bell-shaped flowers, followed in the late summer by blue, pea-sized berries in grapelike clusters. The berries are attractively dusted with a mealy white coating, like very fresh blueberries. The plants are excellent for specimen use or grouped in a more naturalistic manner. There are several different species, of varying hardiness.

The rich purple winter color of Oregon holly-grape enlivens the winter landscape.

Oregon Holly-grape, *Mahonia aquifolium*

Most commonly available is Oregon holly-grape which grows wild in coniferous forests of the Pacific Northwest. Hardy from zones 5 to 9, Oregon holly-grape is susceptible to winter burn in exposed sites, especially in zones 5 and 6. Plants grow 6 feet tall with multiple stems, and spread widely. There is a lower-growing form, 'Compacta', which only grows 3 or 4 feet tall.

Leatherleaf Mahonia, *M. bealei*

Leatherleaf mahonia has large, lustrous, 18-inch-long compound leaves, and upright spikes of deliciously fragrant, pale to lemon yellow flowers. Hardy from zones 6 to 9, especially in zone 6, leatherleaf mahonia needs a protected site, where the leaves will be protected from sun scorch and drying winds. It will grow in full sun but prefers light to partial shade. Plants tend to get leggy over time, but can be kept reasonably full at the base through judicious pruning.

Japanese Mahonia, *M. japonica*

This is the species I grew in Connecticut. It is scarcely mentioned in reference books, with one suggesting it is known only in cultivation in Japan, and is confused with *M. bealei*. The glossy dark green hollylike foliage is handsome, even more so when the long racemes of flower buds open in the late winter. Even a half dozen of the soft sulphur yellow flowers, opening in early January, have the most delectable floral perfume. As more flowers open, it is enough just to walk near the shrub to enjoy its sweet fragrance. Shelter from winter winds and sun scorch is necessary. It is clearly hardy to zone 6.

Chinese Mahonia, *M. lomariifolia*

More tender, Chinese mahonia is only useful in zones 8 and 9. The glossy, leathery leaves can reach 24 inches, with 25 or more leaflets, producing an elegant foliage display. In the early spring, plants produce numerous 4- to 8-inch-long spikes of fragrant flowers, followed in the early summer by large, somewhat trailing clusters of fruit.

Creeping mahonia, *Mahonia repens*, is discussed in Ground Covers and Vines, beginning on page 111.

Heavenly Bamboo, *Nandina domestica*

Heavenly bamboo is a popular garden plant in the southern and southeastern states. Hardy from zones 7 to 9, heavenly bamboo grows in protected sites in zone 6 gardens where it is not exposed to winter sun or wind. Typically growing 8 feet tall, heavenly bamboo can be used for informal hedges or screening. In such instances, it needs more maintenance to keep growth full and dense, rather than leggy and open. The canes do not branch very much, giving an overall pattern reminiscent of bamboo. Older canes should be cut to the ground each spring, to encourage the growth of new shoots from the base. Small, sharply pointed, evergreen leaflets in

Eager to flower, this Japanese mahonia opened its first fragrant blossoms in early January.

SHRUBS

Mountain laurel's perky individual flowers display their detail when you look closely at the flower cluster.

pairs or triplets create an open, attractive pattern. New growth in the spring is bronze to red, turning medium green in the summer, then dull reddish purple to vivid red in the fall, depending on the cultivar and the amount of sun the plants receive. Loose clusters of small white flowers in the late spring are followed by large clusters of bright red berries in the fall, which persist right through the winter.

'Harbour Dwarf' grows only 18 inches high and can be used as an edging or ground cover, 'Fire Power' grows 2 feet high and wide, with leaves tinted red in the summer, turning an incandescent red in the winter; both 'Moyer's Red' and 'Umpqua Chief' are taller, and turn brilliant red in the winter,

'San Gabriel' and 'Umpqua Princess' have very fine, fernlike foliage that provides an airy, almost see-through texture.

Pieris, *Pieris* Species
An excellent choice for heavy shade, mountain pieris, *Pieris floribunda*, is a native shrub that is not as widely grown as its Japanese counterpart, Japanese andromeda, *P. japonica*. Both species grow about 6 feet tall with lustrous, evergreen leaves. Buds develop at the tips of branches in the fall, adding some winter interest before opening in the spring. The waxy, white, bell-shaped flowers of mountain pieris are clustered in semierect spikes, 2 to 4 inches long, and appear in early

to midspring, while those of Japanese andromeda develop from pendulous, 5-inch-long clusters of greenish or reddish buds and open in the early spring. Lace bugs and spider mites can be a problem, especially in hot, dry sites. Adequate moisture, a constant, year-round mulch, and a shaded site with an acid soil high in organic matter are best. Plants should be sheltered from winter wind and sun. Japanese andromeda is hardy in zones 6 to 8, zone 5 in sheltered locations. It is a popular shrub for foundation plantings, and makes an attractive contrast to evergreen rhododendrons. Several named cultivars are available: 'Flamingo' has deep rose-red flowers; 'Valley Valentine' has exceptionally deep red flowers. 'Forest Flame', 'Mountain Fire', and 'Valley Fire' have stunning, deep red leaf color on new spring growth. Deer do not eat andromedas.

Japanese Pittosporum, *Pittosporum tobira*

Japanese pittosporum is a popular shrub in the South and Southeast, useful for informal or clipped hedges, screening, or as a specimen. Begin training when plants are young if you want a sheared hedge. The branching pattern of Japanese pittosporum is similar to that of flowering dogwood, with the terminal bud producing flowers and new branches arising from successive secondary side buds. The result is a stiff, bushy shrub 8 to 10 feet

As vivid as any flowers, the new growth on andromeda makes a fiery display in Amsterdam University's botanic garden.

tall and billowing out 6 to 9 feet wide. The dark green, leathery, rounded leaves are 4 inches long in heavy shade, less in partially shaded situations. Half-inch- to inch-wide white or ivory flowers appear in midspring, deliciously scented, like orange blossoms. Plants are variable in growth from moderate to rapidly reaching their mature size when given moderately fertile soil with average moisture and good drainage in partial to full shade. Cottony cushion scale and aphids may occasionally be a problem. Hardy in zones 8 and 9, Japanese pittosporum can be grown in the milder portions of zone 7 if given a protected, sheltered location. Plants are salt-tolerant, making them useful for seaside gardens. Road salt is not a consideration, as, where snow and ice occur, Japanese pittosporum must be grown as a houseplant. 'Variegata' is more popular for container use, even in southern states, where its gray-green leaves, attractively edged in creamy white, can be effectively displayed. It is slower-growing than the typical form, which also makes 'Variegata' more suitable for containers, and eventually reaches 5 feet tall.

Rhododendron, *Rhododendron* Species and Cultivars

Species and varieties of rhododendrons and azaleas exist in such diversity that entire books are written about them. First some basic information: Azaleas belong in the genus *Rhododendron*. There are evergreen and deciduous azaleas, the same as rhododendrons. All have shallow, fibrous root systems, prefer a loose open soil with acid pH, high in organic matter, moist but well drained. There are rhododendrons native to the United States, Europe, and Asia. Sizes range from dwarf-creeping species to others easily mistaken for a small tree. Some are exceptionally cold-hardy; Lapland rhododendron, *Rhododendron lapponicum*, for example, is hardy in zone 1. Others are rather tender. Oconee or sweet azalea, *R. flammea*, is only hardy in zones 7 and 8.

SHRUBS

The majority are hardy in the middle range of zone 5 and 6.

Indicum Azalea, *Rhododendron indicum*
Indicum azalea is an evergreen azalea native to southern Japan. Hardy from the warmer portions of zone 6 through the cooler part of zone 9, summer shade is helpful in reducing fading of its red to scarlet flowers. It is parent to numerous hybrids, including the Glenn Dale hybrids developed at the U.S. National Arboretum in the 1930s and 1940s, and the Satsuki hybrids developed in Japan centuries ago. Since several species are involved in the development of hybrids, individual cold-hardiness and adaptability to summer heat will vary from cultivar to cultivar. Glenn Dales that have stood the test of time include: 'Dayspring', whose white flowers have pink borders and a pale chartreuse blotch; 'Geisha', with white flowers with a chartreuse blotch, also flecked and striped with purple; and 'Martha Hitchcock' with striking, 3-inch white flowers rimmed with magenta. Satsukis are low-growing, wide-spreading cultivars with speckled and striped flowers; 'Gumpo' has red-flecked white flowers; 'Red Gumpo' has rose pink flowers; 'Pink Gumpo' has light pink flowers; 'Pink Ice' has frosty pink double flowers occasionally spotted and flecked with purple; 'Rukizon' has salmon orange flowers; and 'Yume' has white flowers with salmon pink to orange-red markings.

Carolina Rhododendron,
Rhododendron carolinianum
This rhododendron is an evergreen species from the southern Appalachian mountains of North Carolina. It is hardy in the warmer portions of zone 5 into those portions of zone 8 where summer temperatures are moderate.

Growing 5 feet tall and wider than high, the mounding form is attractive to more upright shrubs such as pieris and mountain laurels. Though it can grow in heavy shade, flowering is poor so consider Carolina rhododendron for half to lightly shaded sites. Pale pink to rosy purple flowers in clusters of up to 10 open at the tips of branches in mid- to late spring. Var. *album* has pure white flowers. The deep green leaves, 2 to 3 inches long and an inch wide, are attractive. They will curl when cold, or if subject to drought.

Catawba Rhododendron,
Rhododendron catawbiense
Catawba rhododendron comes from further south, Virginia to Georgia. The species is astonishingly hardy from zones 4 to 7; however, the cultivars are less cold-hardy, generally zone 5 or even 6. Lilac purple flowers, 2½ inches across, in clusters of up to 20, open in the late spring just before the new leaves unfold. Var. *album* has pink-flushed buds that open pure white. Cultivars include late-flowering 'Album Elegans' with white flowers, while 'Boule de Neige' means bowl of snow, and with compact growth to 6½ tall and masses of white flowers in mid- to late

Rhododendron yakusimanum.

spring, it is an apt description; 'America' has good red flowers and an unappealing shrub form; you'd be much better off with 'Nova Zembla', which has both good red flower and good form; 'Roseum Elegans' has large, lavender-pink flowers and a good habit of growth. Winter damage occurs in exposed sites where winter sun and drying winds cause leaf scorch. Partial shade is best, both for protection and good flower production. Reaching 12 feet tall, catawba rhododendron can serve as an evergreen screen. Well-grown plants make a dense mass of ever-green foliage, with each leaf 3 to 6 inches long.

Rosebay Rhododendron,
Rhododendron maximum
Big, bigger, biggest; rosebay rhododendron grows 15 to 18 feet tall. Native to the north-eastern United States and nearby Canada, southward in the Appalachian Mountains to Alabama, this big rhododendron is useful from protected sites in zone 4 into moderate summer regions of zone 7.

Note: It is prudent to select plants from the northern portions of their range if you live in the northern tier of states, and vice versa if you garden in the Southeast.

Light to partial shade is important in both the summer and winter. Leathery evergreen leaves, 4 to 8 inches long and 2 inches wide, are subject to scorch. Small rose pink to white flowers, in clusters of 25 or more, appear in early to midsummer. They are partially obscured by new leaves unfolding at the same time. The value of this species is its use as large scale screening. Rosebay rhododen-dron is tolerant of moist soil.

Sweet Box, *Sarcococca hookerana* var. *humilis*
Sweet box is a suckering, low-growing shrub 18 inches to 2 feet tall, hardy from zone 5 to 8, with elegant glossy dark green leaves. The inconspicuous, small, greenish white flowers are exquisitely fragrant. They open quite early in the spring, in the last lingering days of winter. Tolerant of heavy shade and dry soil, this ground-hugging shrub is charming as ground cover, adjacent to a path, or any-where you find a dark corner to embellish. Leaves become scorched in full sun. Use this shrub to face down taller shrubs, decid-uous or evergreen, which also thrive in shady, acid-soil sites. The type species, Himalayan sarcococca, *S. hookerana*, at 4 to 6 feet high, is taller and also more tender, somewhat risky, and surviving only in pro-tected sites in zone 5.

Bamboo, *Sasa*, Various
Bamboo is a catchall term, much like "grass" or "fern." All bamboo are members of *Graminaceae*, the grass family. Some are restrained clump-forming species. These tend to be tender, requiring sites in mild winter regions. The hardier bamboo tend to be run-ners, sometimes aggressively so. Growth is influenced by conditions of the previous year. The first season in the garden, bamboo makes only modest growth. The next year it creeps about, and after that, it leaps in search of new territory. Underground runners seemingly with the consistency of steel hawsers, spread beneath paths, through shrubs, and pop up in unexpected places. Where there is room to run, bamboo is matchless for its beauty in the shaded garden.

Palmate Bamboo, *Sasa palmata*
Among my favorites is palmate bamboo. Native to Sakhalin and the mountains of Japan, it is one of the hardiest bamboos, suit-able for gardens in zones 6 to 8. If snow cover is reliable, I'd try this bamboo in the warmer part of zone 5. Wiry, invasive rhizomes give rise to an impenetrable thicket of arching, purple-streaked stems 2½ to 5 feet long, clothed with large, broad, dark green leaves up to 12 inches long and 3 inches wide. An established colony was lovely, green against the snow one January day, when I visited Willowwood Arboretum in Far Hills, New

SHRUBS

The fruits of heavenly bamboo provide a beautiful display in fall and winter.

Jersey. On the far side of a little stream, the bamboo was shaded by stewartias and Japanese maples on the near side, where I stood. Perhaps this is the best solution to control rampant growth, for bamboo (like vampires) cannot cross running water.

Kuma Bamboo Grass, *Sasa veitchii*
Palmate bamboo has a close relative, Kuma bamboo grass. Some authorities advise it is not hardy below zone 7; others suggest zone 6. I think a site sheltered from exposure to winter wind, and a soil with reasonably good drainage will make the difference. Many plants dislike wet conditions around the roots, especially so when dormant. Growing less than 4 feet tall, the dark green leaves are less than 10 inches long, almost 3 inches wide. Common in Japanese gardens, the appeal of this bamboo is actually the result of winter damage. Leaf edges dry and die back in a very tidy manner, edging the evergreen leaves with a pale, creamy beige margin resembling variegation. This bamboo, and the preceding species, would be useful container plants if protected from freezing over winter.

Other bamboos are discussed in Ground Covers and Vines, beginning on page 111.

Skimmia, *Skimmia japonica*
Skimmia is another of those superlative broad-leaved evergreens that have come to us from the forests of Japan. Shade-tolerant, it is marginally hardy in zone 6, requiring a protected site. Plants are best suited to zones 7 and 8. The 3- to 5-inch-long, leathery, dark green leaves neatly clothe the branches on 4-foot-tall, 3-foot-wide plants. Separately sexed (the fancy word is *dioecious*) each shrub is either male or female. The females have showy, bright red berries in the fall, but only if there is a pollinating male nearby. You'll enjoy the male for his larger, showier flowers that are also more fragrant than those on female plants. Two clones you might want to look for: 'Nymans', selected in England, is a female clone with especially heavy production of large scarlet fruit; 'Rubella' is a male clone with good winter display of showy red leaves on the upper portion of the branches, and deeply colored red flower buds that are very fragrant when they open in the spring. Camellia and skimmia combine well, or use skimmia as an evergreen accent in a mixed shrub border with deciduous trees behind them. Their low rounded shape also suggests their suitability as foundation plants. Plant in partial to densely shaded sites, as leaves become discolored in full sun, and a moist, loamy soil with good drainage.

Deciduous Shrubs

Nothing provides a sense of seasons as clearly as deciduous woody plants. Tender new leaf growth in the spring, sometimes striking fall foliage color, and the tracery of bare branches in the winter place them clearly at the appropriate location in the yearly cycle of renewal and rest. This seasonal cycle of burgeoning growth and slumbering rest is especially appealing in combination with the more static habit of evergreens. It is a gray day in early January as I write this. The view from the window of a group of large-leaved rhododendrons tucked just back of the woodland edge is particularly attractive with their foliage against the upward thrust of oak and maple, and the brown carpet of fallen leaves.

Bottlebrush Buckeye, *Aesculus parviflora*
Bottlebrush buckeye remains healthy and grows and survives in moderately dense shade. Tolerant of average to moist soils, its suckering habit recommends it to naturalistic, informal designs where the early summer candles of fluffy white flowers create a charming display. The colonizing roots and dark-barked branches create a thicket 15 feet across. In the fall the coarse palmate foliage turns a lovely clear yellow, adding a sunny note to the fall woods. The glossy brown conkers, horse chesnuts, produced in the fall are not edible for people but are relished by squirrels and other wildlife. Their span of

viability is brief, so if you wish to raise plants from seed, collect and sow promptly. Use a deep container (I used tomato juice cans with both ends removed) in order to provide the necessary space for the young plants' tap root.

Sweetshrub or Carolina Allspice, *Calycanthus*
Common sweetshrub, *Calycanthus floridus*, has unusual flowers, deep maroon in color, rounded like a little ball, and marvelously fruity fragrant. Once popular, this old-fashioned native shrub fell into disregard, replaced by exotic imports from abroad. With the resurgence of interest in our own flora, it is once again gaining a well-deserved place in gardens. With little need for maintenance and no pests or problems, sweetshrub is a good choice for today's hectic lifestyle. Growing 6 to 10 feet tall and 6 to 12 feet wide, this large, rounded shrub may be grown from zones 5 to 9. The lustrous dark green leaves are also fragrant when crushed. They turn yellowish in the fall before dropping. Where it grows wild along the coastal plain from Virginia to Florida, sweetshrub is found in

Bottlebrush buckeye has wonderful summer flowers.

SHRUBS

The fall becomes a second season for display as bottlebrush buckeye leaves turn a lustrous yellow.

heavy shade on dry slopes. In gardens, performance is better in part to light shade, with good drainage. Seed-raised plants are variable in perfume, so always choose shrubs during the flowering season in April and May. 'Athens' is a sweetly fragrant clone with chartreuse-yellow flowers, and leaves that turn clear yellow in the fall. 'Edith Wilder' is reliably fragrant with typically brown-maroon flowers; and 'Michael Lindsey' also has delightfully fragrant, maroon flowers and more compact form.

Summersweet, *Clethra alnifolia*
Summersweet was discussed in Problem Shade/Problem Trees, beginning on page 21, as a shrub for moist soil and shade. It is a very shade-tolerant native North American shrub, surviving and flourishing in dense shade and moist soils. Flowering in June/July, the clusters of fragrant white flowers are produced at the tips of the branches. Its upright growth

and deciduous habit make a nice accent to lower, more rounded shrub forms, especially evergreens such as skimmia or leucothoe.

Tatarian Dogwood
Tatarian dogwood was discussed in Problem Shade/Problem Trees, beginning on page 21, as a shrub for moist soil and shade.

Disanthus, *Disanthus cercidifolius*
When I moved my garden from Connecticut to New Jersey, disanthus was one of the half dozen large shrubs tucked onto the moving truck, disguised in wardrobe cartons. I couldn't bear to leave behind this graceful member of the witch hazel family, with its redbud-like heart-shaped leathery leaves, 2½ to 4 inches long, bluish green in the summer and turning deep claret red flushed with orange in the fall. It flowers in the fall, but the deep purple flowers are so inconspicuous they come as a surprise. Eventually reaching

6 to 12 feet tall and wide, this Japanese shrub thrives in partial shade and prefers a moist but free-draining acid soil in a site sheltered from wind. Suitable for gardens in zones 6 to 8, perhaps a zone colder, disanthus is easy to transplant. The difficulty is finding it in the first place.

Burning Bush or Winged Euonymus, *Euonymus alatus*

Burning bush is a popular shrub, valued for fall color and winter interest provided by the strong horizontal branching habit on older, unpruned plants. Under this approach it will reach 15 feet tall and as wide. It can be clipped into a boxy hedge. 'Compactus' is a third to half as tall, and 'Rudy Haag' even more compact at 5 feet tall and wide. Native to the United States, burning bush is hardy from zones 4 to 7. Plants grow well in shade or sun, with fall color strongest in open situations. In woodland settings, fall color will be fluorescent to soft pink rather than flaming red. Wet soils or droughty conditions are both stressful.

Witch Hazel, *Hamamelis* Species and Cultivars

Fall-flowering witch hazel, *Hamamelis virginica*, is a large shrub that grows 20 feet tall or more, with a vaselike habit generally wider than it is high. It is welcome for its spice-scented flowers in the fall. The fragrance is crisp and light, not cloying. Fragrance is often the first thing you notice, for fall leaf color is also yellow, and the yellow flowers, with narrow, ribbonlike petals, stand more clearly revealed after leaves fall since the fall leaf color is a clear lemon yellow. Flowers first open in late September and persist through early November. Very shade-tolerant, witch hazel needs at least light shade, especially in the warmer portions of its range, zones 4 to 9.

The first mild spell in January encourages the spring-flowering witch hazel into bloom before winter's end. Its flowers, pale yellow through red in color, have small, ribbonlike petals. They display nicely against a background of evergreen conifers, and invite

Autumn witch hazel flowers seen in close-up reveal their delicate detail.

SHRUBS

Autumn flowers make this North American witch hazel a welcome addition to the shady garden.

close inspection that a dooryard or pathside site provides. Their overall vaselike shape is attractive, and fall foliage color may be yellow through orange to red. Provide a moist yet free-draining soil high in organic matter, in partial shade to full sun. The *Hamamelis japonica* x *H. mollis* crosses are hardy from zones 5 to 8.

The most commonly available cultivar at your neighborhood nurseries will be 'Arnold's Promise', which opens its rich yellow flowers in February or March, and they last for a month. Few gardeners visit nurseries in January, so the impulse buyer is unaware of the existence of the earlier (January) flowering *H*. x *intermedia* cultivars. Look for bronze-red flowered 'Diane', possibly the best of the deeper colored forms that also has good, orange-red fall leaf color; vig-

orous, coppery orange-looking 'Jelena', which on close inspection is actually red to orange to yellow at the tip of the petals, with a lovely apricot orange to red, fall leaf color, very floriferous, very fragrant; soft yellow 'Primavera'; and copper red 'Ruby Glow' with more upright growth habit and orange to scarlet fall foliage.

Chinese Witch Hazel, *Hamamelis mollis*
Chinese witch hazel is among my favorite shrubs. Slow-growing, at maturity it makes rounded, spreading shrubs 10 to 15 feet high and wide. The delicately fragrant pale yellow flowers open in early February. If the weather is too cold to catch their scent, cup your hands around some flowers, breathe on them gently to warm them up a bit, then sniff. Plant in part shade to full sun, in a moist but

free-draining soil high in organic matter. 'Pallida' is a greeny, sulphur yellow, free-flowering cultivar.

Hydrangea, *Hydrangea* Species and Cultivars

Smooth Hydrangea, *Hydrangea arborescens*

This hydrangea is a good choice for your shadiest site. Suitable for use grouped as an informal low hedge, individually as a specimen, or in a mixed border, the shrub makes a rounded mound about 4 feet tall and 6 feet wide. Coarse, dark green leaves 6 inches long, make a fine background to the June flowers. Six-inch-wide flattened clusters of tiny, creamy white sterile flowers are edged with an outer whorl of showier white sterile flowers. Prune spent flower clusters, and the shrub will reward you with a second flush of somewhat smaller flower clusters in August. 'Annabelle' is a much showier cultivar, with symmetrical flower clusters up to twice as large as the wild type, and almost all the flowers are sterile; 'Grandiflora', also known as hills-of-snow hydrangea, has 6-inch, somewhat lumpy-looking globes of sterile flowers. Don't confuse *H. arborescens* 'Grandiflora' with peegee hydrangea, *H. paniculata* 'Grandiflora', which is more sun loving, grows 15 feet tall, and has cone-shaped flower clusters. Provide smooth hydrangea with a site that has moist yet freely draining soil high in organic matter, heavily shaded to full sun. Native to eastern and central United States, smooth hydrangea can grow in zones 3 to 8, even the cooler portions of zone 9. Should harsh winter weather kill it to the ground, this shrub still produces a summer show of flowers, since it blooms on new, current season's growth. In fact, a good hard pruning close to the ground in late winter will keep the shrub nicely shaped, more rounded and mounded. Fertilize when you cut back, to support vigorous new growth.

Oakleaf Hydrangea, *Hydrangea quercifolia*

This hydrangea also grows well in dense shade. It has handsome, interesting lobed leaves up to 8 inches long that turn a deep burgundy purple color in the fall, even in shady places. Foliage holds until late in the fall. Exfoliating bark peels away in thin, papery, cinnamony brown strips, adding winter interest. Oakleaf hydrangea is summer flowering, with cone-shaped flowers clustered up to a foot long on the tips of last year's growth. The 1½-inch-wide showy sterile flowers intermingle with small fertile flowers for a nice display. White when they open, sterile flowers age to an attractive purple-pink, and remain for a long time. They can be cut for dried arrangements. The shrub grows 4 to 6 feet tall, even 8 feet high in the southern edge of its range, and spreads by suckers as wide or wider than tall. Native from Georgia to Florida and Mississippi, oakleaf hydrangea can be grown in zones 5 to 9. At the colder end of its range branches may die back to the ground. Wait

Oakleaf hydrangea is valuable for its summer flowers, a time when few other shrubs will bloom in shade.

103

SHRUBS

until buds begin to swell in the spring to decide how far back to prune. If there is winter damage or if deer browse on the shoots, flowering will be reduced. Site oakleaf hydrangea at the edge of woodland in a site with adequate moisture and fertile soil high in organic matter. Use individually or in groups. 'Snowflake' is an elegantly tidy double-flowered form whose 12- to 15-inch flower clusters are heavy enough to pull the branch tips into a graceful arch; 'Snow Queen' is also double-flowered, with somewhat shorter, 8-inch-long flower clusters that remain upright. Several other selections are available. Choose 'Pee Wee' if you want a more compact, broadly mounding shrub, with half-size leaves and flowers; 'Alison' is more vigorous, growing 8 or more feet tall, and spreading 10 to 14 feet wide, with commensurately large leaves, excellent fall color, and good-size flower clusters.

Aaron's Beard or St. John's-wort, *Hypericum calycinum*

Aaron's beards or St. John's-worts, *Hypericum calycinum*, was discussed in Problem Shade/Problem Trees, beginning on page 21, as plants for dry soil and shade.

Kerria, *Kerria japonica*

Kerria grows 4 to 6 feet tall and spreads 3 to 5 feet wide, with slender upright stems. It is an old-fashioned shrub most often seen in gardens with abundant, butterscotch yellow, double flowers and plain green leaves. There is also a single-flowered, green-leaved form. I prefer 'Picta', which has white-variegated leaves and single flowers, adding a pleasant touch to my informal garden. It flowers in May and is attractive through the summer. Its plain green stems (like all kerria) add a quiet note to the winter garden. While kerria will grow in sunny sites, the flowers tend to

scorch and fade quickly, so some shade is beneficial, especially at midday. An undemanding shrub, kerria needs a going-over in the spring to remove any winter-killed stems and old branches. It suckers from underground stems and makes small thickets. 'Picta' needs another look after the leaves appear. It sometimes reverts and any plain green, more vigorous shoots should be trimmed off before they out-grow the variegated portions. Hardy in zones 5 to 9, kerria is easily satisfied with moderate moisture, good drainage, medium fertility, and partial shade.

Spicebush, *Lindera benzoin*

Spicebush, *Lindera benzoin*, was discussed in Problem Shade/Problem Trees, beginning on page 21, as plants for moist soil and shade.

Azaleas, *Rhododendron* Species and Hybrids

There is a lovely diversity of deciduous native azaleas and rhododendrons.

Cumberland Azalea, *R. bakeri*

This native deciduous azalea is from the Appalachian Plateau, West Virginia to Alabama. Red, orange-red to yellow flowers in large clusters open in the summer. Hardy in the warmer portions of zone 5 and into zone 8, Cumberland azalea matures at 6 to 7 feet tall. A site at the forest edge encourages the best flower production, and also reduces sun fade in the red-flowered forms. It is an excellent choice to associate with tall pine trees in southern gardens.

Plumleaf Azalea, *R. prunifolia*

This is a similar, slightly taller species. Native to southwestern Georgia and nearby Alabama, it is a little more tender, hardy only to zone 6.

Japan is a fine source of shade-tolerant plants, exemplified by kerria's abundant bloom.

Flame Azalea, *R. calendulacea*

This azalea also has scarlet to orange and yellow flowers that open very late in the spring, and is deciduous like the preceding species. It is found in the mountains of the eastern United States, from Pennsylvania to Georgia, and is hardy from zones 5 through 8. Taller yet, flame azalea reaches 10 feet tall at maturity. It is one of the parents of the Ghent, Knap Hill, and Exbury azaleas, popular deciduous azaleas with large white, yellow, orange, pink or red flowers.

Pinkshell Azalea, *Rhododendron vaseyi*

This deciduous azalea is native to the mountains of North Carolina. It is hardy in zones 5 to 8, where it is useful in light to moderately shaded sites with moist soil. Heavy wet clay soils are not suitable. Light pink, fragrant flowers appear in mid- to late spring just before the new leaves appear. Leaves turn a light red in the fall before dropping, thus providing a second season of interest. Useful for naturalistic plantings, as an individual specimen, or massed for screening, pinkshell azalea is a charming addition to the woodland garden. 'Alba' has white flowers.

Swamp Azalea, *Rhododendron viscosum*

This azalea is another moisture-tolerant native azalea. It is discussed in Problem Shade/Problem Trees, beginning on page 21.

Korean Rhododendron, *Rhododendron mucronulatum*

Korean rhododendron is among the earliest to flower in the spring, flowering at the same time as forsythias. Found, among other places, in northern Japan, this deciduous azalea is hardy in zone 4 if given a sheltered site, through all portions of zone 7. Though plants tolerate full shade, they become scraggly and flower poorly, so a site in partial to light shade is best. Light rosy purple to magenta

SHRUBS

A close-up of kerria reveals the simple yet elegant form of its flowers.

flowers, in clusters of three to six at the tips of bare branches, appear in the early spring, often clashing with clear pink azaleas or a screaming combination with yellow forsythias. 'Cornell Pink' has clear rosy pink flowers that lack the magenta tint. Leaves sometimes turn red, more often pinkish bronze or yellow before dropping in the fall.

Jetbead, *Rhodotypos scandens*

Jetbead is an old-fashioned shrub growing 3 to 6 feet high, and spreading 4 to 9 feet wide, with sharply toothed dark green leaves that have an almost pleated effect produced by the prominent veins. Leaves appear in the early spring and remain until the late fall. White flowers over an inch across, looking like wild roses, appear in the spring, to be followed by clusters of four glossy black fruits about ¼ inch in diameter. These beadlike fruits remain after the leaves drop in the fall, persisting through the winter. Jetbead was introduced from Japan and China. While not wildly exciting, it is a reliable performer, adding quiet winter interest in zone 5 to 9 gardens. Once established it thrives with minimum care, even neglect. Use jetbead in naturalistic shrub borders, as a low screening plant along a woodland walk, or on sloping banks.

Cutleaf Stephanandra, *Stephanandra incisa*

Cutleaf stephanandra can grow in dense, heavy shade, but looks best when grown in moderate shade. Hardy in zones 5 to 8, this unassuming shrub produces thickets of arching, zigzag branches that create a dense yet fine-textured mound of bright green, lobed leaves. Rooting at the branch tips where they sweep the ground, cutleaf stephanandra is an excellent choice for a shady bank where it can root down, spread, and hold the soil in place. The species grows 4 to 7 feet high and wide. Many gardeners prefer the form 'Crispa', which grows a more restrained 3½ feet tall and spreads 6 feet wide, in contrast to the 8-foot height and comparable spread of the species. In 15 years, my shrubs have made little demand for care, staying tidy and healthy. In the early summer they become covered with numerous clusters of pale greenish yellow to creamy white flowers, spaced widely enough to give a lacy appearance. In the winter, the bare reddish brown stems are mildly interesting, more so where an evergreen ground cover is spread before it for contrast. Pruning should basically be avoided as any shearing will spoil the natural arching, moundlike shape of the shrubs. I've never found a way to get in underneath to remove old dead growth so I just allow the new shoots to spread over as a surface layer.

Blueberries, *Vaccinium*

Though they are commonly found in old fields, both lowbush blueberry and highbush blueberry are shade-tolerant, remaining vigorous and healthy in moderately dense shade. Their urnlike, milky white flowers in the spring, and luscious summer berries enhance the garden. Fall leaf color is unlikely to be the vivid red found in more open, sunny sites.

Lowbush Blueberry, *Vaccinium angustifolium*

This shrub is very small, typically growing about 2 feet tall, occasionally 3 feet. Numerous upright shoots form a twiggy tangle clothed in the summer with oval, bluish green leaves. Adaptable, lowbush blueberry grows in moist to dry situations, but always with well-drained soil. In the wild I often find it in those glade openings in a pine woods, with acid soil and an infertile peaty duff, situations where little else seems to grow. Flowering occurs just before or with the leaves, with few flowered clusters of milky white or pinkish bells. Fruit ripens from early July to mid-August, with

Kerria's apple-green bark displays nicely against a winter blanket of snow.

SHRUBS

¼- to ½-inch berries ripening from a bloom-dusted blue to black. Weather strongly controls their palatability, and in a dry season I am content to leave them for the birds. Since blueberries are ericaceous, they require an acid soil and associate well with other such shrubs. Lowbush blueberry would combine nicely with such broad-leaved evergreens as mountain laurel or pieris, serving to face down the larger shrubs. Where it is grown in more formal situations, or to maintain more vigorous, denser growth, cut established plants close to the ground every few years in the spring to encourage renewed production of vigorous new shoots. Lowbush blueberry is extremely cold-hardy, and is useful in zones 2 to 6.

Highbush Blueberry, *V. corymbosum*

This shrub is much taller, growing 6 to 12 feet high, with an equal spread. Numerous upright stems spread widely as they ascend, with dense twiggy branches. The slender twigs are noticeably red-barked in winter, an additional interesting feature to flowers and fruit. Requirements are much the same as for lowbush blueberry, though highbush blueberry will tolerate a wetter situation. The most common problem, in both species, is chlorosis, a yellowing of the leaves that occurs when the soil is not sufficiently acid. Blueberries demand strongly acid to moderately acid soil; pH 4.0 to 6.0 is suitable. Highbush blueberry can be used for screening, in naturalistic or more formal situations. One friend of mine gave up contesting the fruit harvest with birds and turned her blueberry patch into a copse. Pruned high enough to create an overhead canopy, itself in the shade of trees, the ground beneath the shrubs is carpeted with small geophytes, forget-me-nots, lungwort, ferns, and other low-growing herbaceous plants.

Viburnum, *Viburnum plicatum* forma *tomentosum*

Consider doublefile viburnum, with its tiered horizontal branching pattern and numerous showy flower clusters in the spring. Popular and widely available at nurseries, best growth is in sun to light shade. But there's more. Viburnums are a diverse group of shrubs—some are evergreen, others deciduous, with pleasing flowers and attractive fruit. Other species of this underutilized genus also accept lightly shaded sites, and more shade-tolerant species are available, though some are not yet widely available. The exotic introductions bought at nurseries are better known than are the native species. These exceptionally shade-tolerant shrubs are found in forests of the northeastern and southeastern United States. Their limited availability is changing, and several native species are taking their just place in gardens.

North American species of viburnum are deciduous. Their leaves turn red to purplish red in the fall before falling. Numerous small white to creamy white flowers appear in mid- to late spring in flattened clusters 3 to 4 inches across. Flowers are followed by berries that progressively change color, either from pale apple green to yellow-green, then blue-black, or green to red, then blue-black when ripe in early to midfall. The leaf/berry contrast is most handsome, and ripe berries are greedily eaten by birds, making viburnum among the most valuable shrubs for attracting birds to the garden. Some species produce numerous suckers. That is not a problem in an informal setting; thinning and shaping is required in more formal settings.

Mapleleaf Viburnum or Dockmackie, *Viburnum acerifolium*

This shrub grows well in dense shade in preference to sunny sites. It will tolerate dry shade once established. Ivory white flowers add simple interest in the late spring while maplelike leaves turn a highly attractive purplish red in the fall. Hardy from zones 3 to 9, mapleleaf viburnum is a wide-spreading suckering shrub growing 4 to 6 feet tall that is useful for naturalistic plantings or screening.

Hobblebush or Alder-leaved Viburnum, *V. alnifolium*

This remains healthy and vigorous in dense shade, and prefers moist soil. Useful in zones 3 to 6, hot summers are a problem for this northeastern North American species. Rather loose and open in habit, attractive clusters of white flowers in the spring, good rich red fall leaf color and blue-black fruits suggest their use in naturalistic plantings to attract birds.

Witherod, *V. cassinoides*

Witherod remains robust in moderately dense shade. It is useful from zones 3 to 6, with white flowers in early to midsummer, and deep purple to scarlet foliage in the fall. Tolerant of wet soils, witherod is useful in the same situations as spicebush, *Lindera benzoin*. The two shrubs would pair nicely, providing separate bloom times and different fall foliage color.

Smooth Witherod, *V. nudum*

This is a southern counterpart to witherod. Larger in form, flowers, and foliage, it is hardy in zones 6 to 9, perhaps zone 5. 'Winterthur' is a clone from southern Delaware with a more refined habit and compact growth than the type species.

Arrowwood Viburnum, *Viburnum dentatum*

Arrowwood viburnum grows vigorously in moderately dense shade and is useful in gardens from zones 4 to 9, though at the

Quietly beautiful, the simple flower clusters of mapleleaf viburnum decorate the shady garden.

SHRUBS

extremes of its range I'd look for local material; a clone from Minnesota might not like Georgia summers! Growing 6 to 10 feet high and wide, it may be used for screening and also make a good if informal hedge. In the late spring plants produce 3-inch-wide flattened clusters of small, creamy white flowers that display nicely against dark green leaves. Fall color is sometimes, but not always, a bright red. Popular with birds, the blue-black fruits ripen in September and October.

Black Haw, *V. prunifolium*

Black haw has an extensive range across much of the eastern United States, which means it is useful from zones 3 to 9. Stiffly branched and growing 15 feet tall, with some training in the early stages, plants can be grown as standard, treelike specimens. Numerous small white flowers in clusters in the late spring, mildew-resistant medium to dark green lustrous leaves that turn deep purple to scarlet before dropping in mid- to late fall.

Nannyberry, *V. lentago*

This shrub is similar but larger, to 25 feet tall. Soft yellow-green when they first appear in the spring, leaves are a glossy dark green in the summer and sometimes turn purplish red in the fall. Leaves are prone to mildew, so avoid planting in closed-in sites with poor air movement. Three- to 4-inch flower clusters are followed by purplish black mature fruit.

Viburnums are also native to China and Japan. Many of these are evergreen, and somewhat less hardy than our native species.

Siebold's Viburnum, *Viburnum sieboldii*

Hardy from the warmer part of zone 5 through zone 8, Siebold's viburnum is native to Japan. At 20 feet tall, Siebold's viburnum is one of the largest viburnums and is suitable for individual specimen use. Though deciduous, its lustrous, dark green, leathery leaves, 2½ to 5 inches long, look as though they belong to an evergreen species. Leaves hold until the late fall and they drop with little color change. Four-inch-wide clusters of creamy white flowers, profuse enough to hide the foliage, appear in the late spring and are followed in mid- to late summer by rose to red berries that ripen to blue-black. The pedicels or fruit stalks are red, and they remain for nearly a month after the berries are eaten by birds. 'Seneca' is a selection of the U.S. National Arboretum especially valuable for heavy fruiting with berries that remain red for three months in the summer and early fall before completing their color change.

Sandankwa Viburnum, *V. suspensum*

This viburnum is native to southern Japan and is only hardy in zones 8 and 9. Best with summer shade and winter sun, this evergreen species has dense clusters of somewhat fragrant white or pinkish white flowers in the early summer. Berries are inconspicuous until they ripen to bright red.

Close inspection reveals fine detail of mapleleaf viburnum flowers.

GROUND COVERS AND VINES

Vigorous as it is, dwarf running bamboo can't quite conceal this frog. Together statue and ground cover create a stunning effect.

GROUND COVERS AND VINES

Mix and match ground covers: **Hosta ventricosa** *with* **Epimedium youngianum** *'Niveum'.*

Ground Covers

Wgeter my preoccupation with gardening began, I craved choice specimens,
rare perennials, and exotic shrubs. Now that
I am several decades into my horticultural
compulsion, ground covers are revealing
themselves to be the workhorses of the garden. Spreading plants that neatly clothe the
ground have risen in my esteem. Sometimes
they are permanent residents, intended for
long-term occupancy. They may be room-
mates, sharing space with a planting of
herbaceous perennials or covering the
absence of geophytes that are dormant for
part of the year. I also use them as transients,
temporary cover for a bed that has been prepared but not yet planted. If, for whatever
reason, there will be a season's delay or more,
I would rather have plants I chose rather than

a mixed assortment of tenacious weeds that
may be difficult to evict when the time
comes.

Of course, there is a fine line between weed
and ground cover. We want plants that
spread, but they should somehow know
when we want them to stop. Obviously,
human intervention and a sense of proportion are required. Plants described as "vigorous" are not suitable for restricted space, and
are only good neighbors for plants of robust
character. Pachysandra will swallow primroses, yet maidenhair ferns emerge each
spring, looking far too delicate for such vital-
ity. Woodruff runs rampant, but large hostas
are unfazed. Equally, you cannot toss some
epimedium at the hastily scratched-up soil
beneath a Norway maple, then wonder why
it did not take, especially if you never
watered afterwards.

Remember, site preparation is five times as important as what you plant. Digging 50 individual holes for 50 pachysandra plants is not only inefficient and exhausting, it does not give the ground cover the right conditions to spread and fill in. Loosen the soil for the entire planting bed to allow easy root penetration by your chosen ground cover. Add compost, leaf mold, or other organic matter, and fertilizer. Plant, mulch, and water. Consider the source of the shade, and do not expect similar results under the avaricious darkness of a Norway maple as under the benign conditions of an oak. Mulch, to provide the benefits of reduced evaporative losses, gradual replenishment of organic matter, and reduce soil compaction.

For shady sites the popular, nay ubiquitous, three are pachysandra, running myrtle, and ivy. At certain stages in our gardening careers we first purchase these, then remove them and, if we garden long enough, restore them to our favor. If you want to accent specimen trees and shrubs, or protect the ground from unwanted plant invaders, then consider the possibilities provided by these "big three" of the ground cover world.

Pachysandra, *Pachysandra* Species and Cultivars

Whether you call it pachysandra or Japanese spurge, *Pachysandra terminalis* is poorly regarded. Its glossy evergreen leaves positively demand shade, becoming yellow and anemic if grown in the sun. Plants have a tidy appearance, rather deceptive, as once established they spread rapidly. They are often seen as a narrow ring or fringe around a tree in an otherwise grassy lawn, or circling several trees, each with their own, poorly proportioned skimpy tutu. Where trees must be treated as individual units, increase the size of the ground cover's bed to approximate the shadow area or drip line perimeter of the tree. Rather than a geometric circle with the tree at the compass point center, create an

oval. An egg-shaped bed is even better, with the tree planted toward the wider end, about two-thirds along the long dimension. Where the trees are growing near each other, consider uniting them in one large bed. Visually, balance is improved and the trees and pachysandra are perceived as a unit, gaining in importance. There is less edge, reducing maintenance.

An elegantly variegated form, named 'White Edge', is usually sold as individually potted plants, rather than by flats. Massed, 'White Edge' lightens shady areas. Imagine it carpeting the ground beneath ghostly, white-barked trunks of Himalayan birch, *Betula utilis* var. *jacquemontii* in the winter. A few plants of 'White Edge', can be used as perennials, embellished with summer annuals such as white-flowered impatiens and white-leaved caladiums, or accenting the late summer white berries of doll's eyes, *Actaea pachypoda*.

Allegheny Spurge, *Pachysandra procumbens*

Whether or not you prefer native American plants to exotic foreigners, Allegheny spurge is a graceful plant for shady gardens. Evergreen, it came through the bitter

You can add visual interest to a broad sweep of any ground cover with some sculpture, in this case *Pachysandra terminalis* embellished by a statue of a child on a snail.

GROUND COVERS AND VINES

winter of 1993–94 unharmed. Leaves are larger than those of its Japanese cousin, mat-surfaced, and mature from bright apple green to dark forest green with a definite silver mottling or spotting. Remember, pachysandra is among the rather limited palette of plants that deer appear to find unappetizing. They also seem uninterested in the culinary properties of myrtle.

Running Myrtle, *Vinca minor*

Myrtle, Running Myrtle, Lesser Periwinkle, Vinca, *Vinca minor*
This is an elegant ground cover hardy to zone 5. If sufficient care (site preparation, watering) is given to get it established, running myrtle even grows in poor, dry soil. Pairs of oval, polished, dark green evergreen leaves clothe the stems that trail along the ground. This habit of growth, coupled with its ability to root at the nodes, results in the prompt establishment of a good dense carpet. As plants mature they develop a bushier habit as shorter shoots fill in, with the eventual development of a 6-inch covering. In late April the plants have attractive periwinkle-blue flowers. For quick cover, plant running myrtle on a 6-inch center, four plants to an area one foot square. Planting more than 10 to 12 inches apart is usually impractical, needing higher maintenance (weeding) while the plants fill in.

There are several cultivars of running myrtle, with either variegated leaves or variations in flower color. As well as the typical lavender blue form, 'Bowles Variety' has very large, deep lilac blue flowers. There is one with wine red flowers, called 'Puniceas', or 'Burgundy' in England. Here, it is usually a passalong plant, traveling from gardening friend to gardening friend as "the wine red vinca." There are two different white-flowered forms: one,

named 'Alba', is similar in habit and growth to the typical lavender blue form. The other, named 'Miss Jekyll', is smaller-growing and more clumping in habit.

I have one with gold-variegated leaves. Alas, the buttery yellow color appears only on the new shoots in the spring, making a striking contrast to the lavender flowers. When they mature, the leaves turn completely green. 'Sterling Silver' has a crisp, tidy, clean white edge that persists year-round. And a friend gave me starts of a running myrtle with a broader, creamy white edging.

English Ivy, *Hedera helix*

English ivy is such a garden plant in my mind that it is hard to think of it as wild. It was rather disconcerting to see it growing wild in Cheddar Gorge, in England. You should be aware that English ivy has created problems in the United States, wandering out of backyards and escaping to the wild where it swamps woodlands. In gardens deer adore it, standing around with banners of ivy dangling from their mouths while you rant and rave. In zone 6 gardens, about its northern limit of hardiness, plants are less winter-hardy than pachysandra and running myrtle.

English ivy can be grown informally, rambling as it will on the ground and using its

And, if you are bored with Japanese spurge, remember it has an American relative, *Pachysandra procumbens*, with a softer look and more refined habits.

holdfasts to climb trees. Where it serves as an evergreen ground cover in more formal settings, tidy maintenance will require trimming the edges several times during the growing season, for English ivy continues to send out new growth. The contrast of soft green new leaves against the dark green of old foliage is pleasing. The vining form of English ivy is actually the juvenile form. Adult plants have more rounded, rather than lobed leaves. They also flower, with spiky globes of green flowers, followed by black beadlike fruits. Stems are also stiffer and woodier, and plants can be trained as standards, with a single, self-supporting stem.

The two hardiest vining cultivars are 'Baltica' and 'West 254th Street'. These both have somber green leaves with unobtrusive darker markings. Where they are exposed to winter wind and cold temperatures, the leaves often winter-burn, turning brown and dying off. It is easy to determine if the stems are still alive and new leaves will be produced in the spring by gently scraping at the bark with a fingernail. If the stem shows green and is pliable, it is alive. If it shows brown and is stiff, it is dead. Even in such instances, English ivy will often regenerate from the roots. Ivy grows throughout the season, extending vines and producing tender green new leaves that contrast well with the dark older growth. This habit also means it needs clipping back several times each season, where it attempts to blanket paths, walks, and driveways. Self-attaching aerial rootlets fasten ivy to walls and trees, creating a handsome evergreen cover.

The various cultivars with small, narrow, frilly, dissected, white- or yellow-variegated leaves are not as hardy as the plain green cultivars. Gray-green and white variegated 'Glacier' and a soft, buttery yellow-leafed form, both from a discount store's houseplants aisle, grow well in my garden in zone 6. They are, however, in sheltered sites and I allow fallen oak leaves to mulch them in winter.

These three musketeers, pachysandra, myrtle, and ivy, are widely available, sturdy plants that function well in their allotted role, but they are hardly your only option for ground covers in the shade.

Bishop's Goutweed, *Aegopodium podagraria*

Be cautious; the boundary between vigorous ground cover and obnoxiously invasive weed is one this plant often oversteps. Bishop's goutweed, *Aegopodium podagraria* 'Variegatum', is indeed attractive, with lobed, compound leaves of soft, pale green attractively white variegated. From late May to late June it foams with loose flat umbels of Queen Anne's lacelike flowers. Tolerant of any condition short of drought, bishop's goutweed is difficult to evict once you've invited it into your garden. Often listed in nursery catalogs, I'd recommend it for that strip of soil between sidewalk and curb where they can be safely confined.

Ajuga, *Ajuga reptans*

Bugleweed or ajuga, *Ajuga reptans* comes in a

Evergreen English ivy makes a fine backdrop for two small figurines of doves.

115

GROUND COVERS AND VINES

couple of sizes, a variety of leaf color, is close to evergreens, and flowers beautifully in early May. Perhaps because it is such carefree a plant it is underappreciated, considered suitable not for gardeners, but yardeners, those homeowners who tend to their outdoors from necessity rather than preference. I like bugleweed for its ground-covering capability, loose enough to allow other plants to mingle with it. A simple combination of bugleweed's rich blue, 6-inch-tall flower spikes and pure white-flowered violets such as *Viola sororia* 'Albiflora' (or any white violet that crops up in yours or a neighbor's garden without concern for Latin names) for delightful, maintenance-free tapestry of spring color. Another equally effective pairing mixes bugleweed with its shorter spikes of deep, blue-violet flowers with wild sweet Williams, *Phlox divaricata*, which bloom at the same time with taller stems of soft blue flowers. 'Jungle Beauty' has large, outsize green leaves, and tall spikes of deep indigo violet flowers.

Bugleweed is good ground cover for shrubs. The short spikes of deep blue, pink, or white flowers accent azaleas with white, soft pink, lavender, or purple flowers. Later bugleweed's tidy carpet of leaves makes a neat ground cover. There are selected forms of bugleweed with bronze, gray-green, or multicolor leaves. Consider a copper-leafed Japanese maple underplanted with a bronze-leaved bugleweed, such as 'Atropurpurea', 'Bronze Beauty', or 'Gaiety'. All have blue to violet flowers, which add an attractive accent. Follow the spring bloom with a summer accent of annuals: red impatiens or a copper-leafed, red-flowered wax begonia for enhancement of the simple yet effective foliage display. 'Caitlin's Giant' has large bronze leaves, 3½ inches long rather than the usual 2 inches, and 8-inch-high spikes of blue flowers.

'Multicolor' (= 'Tricolor') has dark bronze leaves splashed with pink and ivory. In Holland one September I saw 'Multicolor' used as a ground cover for fall-blooming *Cyclamen hederifolium*, and liked it so well I copied the combination in my own garden, using 'Burgundy Glow', a similar cultivar with white-, pink-, rose-, and green-splashed leaves, turning dark bronze in the winter. The small pink butterfly flowers of the cyclamen apparently have no difficulty wriggling through the mat of bugleweed, whose burgundy-, pink-, and white-splashed leaves are a most effective carpet. 'Silver Carpet' makes a mat of silver foliage; 'Silver Beauty' has silver green and white leaves, and light blue flowers; 'Variegata' makes a dense, tight mat of gray-green leaves edged in pale creamy white.

As well as foliage variants there are bugleweed with different flower colors than the familiar blue-violet. Some have soft, pale lavender or light blue flowers. 'Rosea', 'Pink Spire', and the smaller 'Pink Elf' have pink flowers, and var. *alba* has creamy white flowers.

Should you want more of one of the named cultivars, bugleweed is simple to propagate. In midspring the established rosettes produce 4- to 8-inch-long leafy stolons, which

A good work-horse, ajuga grows well in shade or sun, moist to average soil, and flowers attractively in spring.

root at the tips to produce new plants. Once rooted, the stolon can be cut, and the new plantlets moved to another site. Or dig established rosettes early in spring, transplanted to another location where new plantlets can develop, creating a good cover the first season.

Barrenwort or Epimedium,
Epimedium, Various

Barrenwort, *Epimedium* species and cultivars, are excellent, easily maintained plants that require little care beyond a once-a-year trimming before growth begins in the spring. Once established, *Epimedium alpinum*, *E. peralderianum*, and *E. pinnatum* ssp. *colchicum* tolerate the most unpromising dry sites in heavy shade. These three are discussed in Problem Shade/Problem Trees, beginning on page 21. Other species and cultivars are discussed in Perennials, beginning on page 125.

Bigleaf Wintercreeper, *Euonymus fortunei*

Bigleaf wintercreeper is an evergreen scandent plant—give it a tree trunk, fence, or wall to cling to and up it will go; lacking support, it trails along the ground. Excellent for covering banks, wintercreeper's moderately rapid growth, once established successfully, competes with many weeds. 'Gracilis' (= 'Argenteo-marginata', 'Pictus', 'Tricolor') is a delightful form to use as a ground cover, with white-variegated leaves often tinged with pink, especially in cold weather. Several other readily available cultivars include 'Coloratus' with 1- to 2-inch leaves that turn reddish purple in cold weather, adding interest to a winter-bare landscape; tiny-leaved, slow-growing 'Kewensis' whose ¼-inch leaves make a fine-textured ground cover for small areas; and 'Minimus' whose ½-inch leaves also provide dainty texture. They are discussed in more detail in Shrubs, beginning on page 83.

Ferns
Ferns offer options for evergreen or deciduous ground cover.

Christmas Fern, *Polystichum achrostichoides*
This fern is a good choice for a lacy-textured evergreen carpeting plant. A friend in Westport, Connecticut, wanted an evergreen ground cover, showy flowers not necessary, but something more creative than the typical suburban three of ivy, pachysandra, and running myrtle. Because Christmas fern is clump-forming rather than a running fern, it was planted about 15 to 18 inches apart on center, staggering the rows to develop better cover. Another gardener used Christmas fern at the top of a slope leading to a little brook. In the winter Christmas fern's fronds lay down, creating protective cover for the soil and reducing erosion.

Sensitive Fern or Bead Fern,
Onoclea sensibilis

This fern has coarse fronds and creeping rhizomes that enable it to form spreading colonies that briskly cover a fair amount of ground. Handsome as an accent with hostas, sensitive fern can compete with pachysandra, creating an interesting tapestry of interwoven foliage in the spring and summer. As soon as the first frost arrives, the fern's fronds turn straw color, then droop and collapse. While it does spread, especially in shady sites, sensitive fern does not need annual maintenance since it is not nearly as aggressive as hay-scented fern.

Hay-scented Fern, *Dennstaedtia punctiloba*
How quickly we reveal our horticultural preconceptions and prejudices! Hay-scented fern is often described as a pernicious, running weed. Provided with some moisture, it will make new fronds throughout the growing season, functioning as ground cover in otherwise inhospitable sites. It is discussed in more detail in Problem Shade/Problem Trees, beginning on page 21.

GROUND COVERS AND VINES

Small-leaved evergreen euonymus makes a fine backdrop for this little statue.

Oak Ferns, *Gymnocarpium dryopteris;*
Narrow Beech Ferns, *Theylepteris phegopteris;*
and Broad Beech Ferns, *T. hexagonoptera*
These ferns are sometimes suggested for ground cover use. Their rhizomes are best described as long-creeping, so fronds arise at spaced intervals, rather than in masses. I find them more of a filler than a covering, creating wonderful tapestry effects together with false Solomon's seal, *Smilacina stellata,* wild sweet William, *Phlox divaricata,* and other woodland plants.

Woodruff, *Galium odoratum*
Woodruff presents a dainty, fragile appearance that belies its thuggish, tough-as-nails character. Deciduous, masses of 8-inch-high stems clothed in whorls of fresh green leaves, topped in early May with dainty white flowers, it will tolerate the deepest, driest shade. For further discussion see Problem Shade/Problem Trees, beginning on page 21.

Bigroot Geranium, *Geranium macrorrhizum*
Bigroot geranium can be used to carpet moderate to heavily shaded areas. It is discussed in Perennials, beginning on page 125.

Hosta, *Hosta* Species and Cultivars
Hostas, discussed in more detail in the following chapter, Perennials, may be planted en masse and thus used as a ground cover. Obviously, if you intend a bulk planting of hosta, varieties that spread rapidly on their own and are reasonably priced are your best choice. A few hosta have spreading, stoloniferous roots, and can even hold the soil on a slope. These are the best for use as ground covers: species such as quickly spreading, rhizomatous *H. gracillima* with lanceolate to somewhat rounded green leaves; *H. lancifolia* with green, lance-shaped leaves that overlap to form a tidy mound, quickly reaching mature size; and vigorous, old-fashioned *H. ventricosa* with glossy dark green leaves that reseeds freely for me. A few cultivars to consider for ground covers include: medium-sized, quick-growing 'Francee', with heart-shaped, dark forest green leaves narrowly edged in white; 'Ginko Craig', a small hosta with lance-shaped, white-margined green leaves; 'Golden Tiara', which has small, heart-shaped leaves with a wide, creamy golden margin, and which multiplies well; somewhat stoloniferous and a good multiplier, 'Ground Master', with narrow, lanceolate to somewhat rounded, ruffled, matte-finished, dark green leaves with wide white margins; 'Neat Splash', which is stoloniferous, with lanceolate leaves streaked and splashed with yellow (this type of variegation is unstable, as plants often revert to a yellow-margined form); stoloniferous 'North Hills', which is a rapidly spreading, medium green hosta with white-margined leaves; 'Rock Princess', which makes very low, tight clumps of small, dark green, heart-shaped leaves, and is a strong multiplier; 'Saishu Jima', whose very rapid multiplication make a good ground cover, with very low, ground-

hugging, narrow, dark green, somewhat wavy leaves; 'Serendipity', with medium-small, glaucous, heart-shaped leaves on rapidly multiplying plants; and rapidly multiplying, stoloniferous 'Wogan Gold', with long, narrow, rich golden yellow leaves forming 18-inch-tall plants.

Dead Nettle, Yellow Archangel, *Lamium galeobdolon*

Vigorous, spreading, invasive, all are accurate but there are still places where yellow archangel, *Lamium* (= *Lamiastrum*) *galeobdolon*, is a useful ground cover. Drought-tolerant, it is discussed in Problem Shade/Problem Trees, beginning on page 21.

Lilyturf, *Liriope muscari*

Hardy, evergreen, grasslike lilyturf is discussed in the following chapter, Perennials. *Ophiopogon* species are also mentioned there.

Creeping Mahonia, *Mahonia repens*

Creeping mahonia has bluish green hollylike leaves with a dull, matte finish. They turn bronze-purple in winter. Growing only a foot high, creeping mahonia very slowly spreads to make an attractive ground cover, tolerant of dry sites in zones 5 to 9. The larger growing mahonias are discussed in more detail in Shrubs, beginning on page 83.

Creeping Phlox, *Phlox stolonifera*

Creeping phlox is a marvelous ground cover, rapidly spreading into large, flowering, evergreen mats. It is a mystery to me why it is not more widely used. Pairs of oval, dark green leaves nearly 2 inches long are dense enough to closely cover the ground and prevent the growth of many weeds. These trailing stems, also root at the nodes, heightening the plants ground cover abilities. Blooming in early May, erect, 10-inch-long stems have dense terminal clusters of flowers. Typically, the flowers are a soft blue, sometimes tinted violet. Cultivars include yellow-eyed, white-flowered 'Ariane' and 'Bruce's White', deep heliotrope violet 'Sherwood Purple', which is also intensely fragrant, soft blue 'Blue Ridge', soft pink 'Pink Ridge', and vivid pink 'Home Fires'. Plants thrive in partial to heavy shade, and prefer a loose soil high in organic matter, moist but well drained. Intolerant of humid, hot summer weather, creeping phlox is best in zones 4 to 7. Growth is vigorous enough that only sturdy perennials can successfully compete in an established planting of creeping phlox; others are swamped.

Bamboo, *Pleioblastus* Species

Where they have room to run, low-growing, spreading species of bamboo make handsome ground covers. Keep in mind, though, that one gardener's ground cover is another

Boston ivy is attractive in winter even though its stems are bare.

GROUND COVERS AND VINES

Phlox stolonifera is a superlative ground cover, especially in spring when it conceals its evergreen leaves with a carpet of flowers.

gardener's weed. (At a garden club plant sale I once referred to variegated goutweed as a rampant thug. In some hauteur the woman staffing the booth corrected me, "We call it a good doer.") Bamboo takes a season or two to become established. They then spread, and spread, and spread. Only an impervious barrier, such as water or poured concrete or sheet metal, sunk at least 18 inches into the soil, will stop them. If you are desirous of growing bamboos in a small garden, consider them as candidates for a container, a large one.

In general bamboo are a genus where the taxonomists happily play about with name changes. Though currently valid names are provided, older names are given in case your local nursery or mail order catalog source have not caught up.

Dwarf Fern-leaf Bamboo, *Pleioblastus argenteostriatus (= Arundinaria argenteostriata)*
This is a semi-dwarf variegated bamboo, long popular as a garden plant in Japan and unknown in the wild. It grows 2 to 3 feet tall, with attractively white variegated medium

green leaves. It is easily confused with dwarf white-stripe bamboo, *P. variegatus* (=*A. variegata*), which also has dark green leaves variably striped in a yellowish white like old ivory. This low-growing, compact, wide-spreading bamboo is similarly unknown as a wild plants. Variegation is more variable, with some leaves mostly green, a few leaves entirely white, and the majority handsomely variegated, all on the same plant.

Dwarf Fern-leaf Bamboo, *P. pygmaeus*
Continuing the confusion, there is another plant commonly named dwarf fern-leaf bamboo, *P. pygmaeus* (=*A. pygmaea*). Known as a common wild plant in Japan, this dwarf fern-leaf bamboo has plain green leaves. The same is true for yet another dwarf fern-leaf bamboo, *P. pygmaeus* var. *disticha* (formerly known as *A. disticha*). It may be distinguished from the other dwarf fern-leaf bamboo as its bright green, fine-textured leaves are arranged in a *distichous*, two-ranked, manner on 18-inch to 3-feet tall *culms*, the correct term for bamboo and grass stems.

Gold Stripe Bamboo, *P. auricoma*
If silver does not suit your garden design, there is goldstrip bamboo (also known as *A. viridistriata*, also *Bambusa viridistriata*). Its color is most striking in the spring, when the new leaves, about 5 inches long and an inch wide, are variegated in a brilliant golden yellow/green pattern, turning all green by summer. Maintain the best display by mowing the old growth down in the late winter. Growing 18 to 30 inches high, the new shoots have the best color. I love to gently pull a new leaf between my fingers, for they have a sensuous, velvety feel. There are low-growing bamboo with plain green leaves too.

Other Low-Growing Bamboo

Pleioblastus gramineus (=*A. graminea*), is hardy to zone 7, extremely invasive, and variable in height from 3 to 16 feet. Be careful to select a smaller clone for ground cover use. *P. humilis* (=*A. humilis*) has very slender culms 2 to 3 feet tall that grow upright rather than arching, and has medium green leaves up to 6 inches long and ¾ inch wide. Even more compact, at 1½ to 2 feet tall, *Pleioblastus humilis* var. *pumilis* (=*Arundinaria pumila*, or *Sasa pumila*) has somewhat arching culms and bright green leaves up to 6 inches long and ¾ inch wide.

Keep in mind that low growth has nothing to do with how far, or how fast, these bamboo spread. Some of these dwarf species send their rhizomes shooting along just below or humping along at the soil surface with astonishing speed and persistence.

Sweet Box, *Sarcococca hookeriana* var. *humilis*

Sweet box, *Sarcococca hookeriana humilis*, is discussed in Shrubs, beginning on page 83.

Foamflower, *Tiarella*

Foamflower, *Tiarella cordifolia*, is a rhizomatous, more or less stoloniferous plant, with runners a foot long. Palmately five-lobed leaves, covered with scattered, bristly hairs, are attractive in their own right as well as useful as a ground cover. Individual plants make a pleasing cluster of foliage in April, with sparse, very much reduced leaves scattered on the stolon. Rooting at the nodes, new plantlets also form, making a somewhat open carpet. Loose, humus-rich soil and a mulch of chopped leaves encourages the plants' proliferation. In the winter foamflower is quite attractive, knitting together a loose tapestry of evergreen Christmas fern while in the summer their froth of white flowers accentuates wild sweet William, trilliums, bloodroot, and hostas. Recent selections for leaf shape and color add variety to the shade gardener's palette. 'Laird of Skye' has a robust, trailing habit, and lobed, dark green leaves. Suitable for partial to fully shaded sites, 'Laird of Skye' has larger than usual racemes of white flowers. 'Slickrock', found near Slickrock Creek in North Carolina, has beautiful, deeply lobed, maplelike leaves and light pink flowers. A vigorously spreading plant, 'Slickrock' is a good ground cover for the shady garden.

Vancouveria, *Vancouveria hexandra*

Vancouveria hexandra is a fast-spreading, deciduous, American relative of barrenwort, and may be used in the same manner. It, and its two evergreen cousins, *V. chrysantha* and *V. planipetala*, are discussed in Problem Shade/Problem Trees, beginning on page 21.

Vines

Vines are plants that need some support from their friends. By means of tendrils, holdfasts, or some other type of twining mechanism, they use a nearby tree, shrub, wall, or trellis to get off the ground. Some vines can be a problem to their host. You've no doubt seen a

Like a foamy wave, foamflower, *Tiarella cordifolia*, splashes its white flowers across its ground-covering carpet of leaves.

GROUND COVERS AND VINES

sapling strangled and killed in the fatal embrace of bittersweet or wild grape vine. Vines that climb by coiling are the ones that cause the damage, and young trees are more at risk than mature trees. Naturally, you'll want to give some consideration to relative rates of growth. A quick-growing vine is a poor choice as a companion for a slow-growing tree. One way around this concern is to use a masonry wall, wire fence, or wooden trellis as an inanimate support for an attractive vine. It is a great way to add the effect of a vertical plant where space for a tree or shrub may be lacking, such as a narrow strip between path and building. Vines with holdfasts, such as Boston ivy, Virginia creeper, or climbing hydrangea, are better on a solid wall than a vine that climbs by twining, such as fiveleaf akebia, which does better on a trellis. Lacking any support, vines sprawl, which in some instances allows their use as a ground cover. Vines can be annual or perennial, herbaceous or woody. Those that grow in shady places have above-ground stems that persist from year to year.

Kolomikta Actinidia, *Actinidia kolomikta*

With medium green heart-shaped leaves handsomely blotched pink and white, kolomikta actinidia makes a showy display to brighten partly shaded gardens. Color is brighter on male plants than on females, and in a situation that allows morning sun to reach the vines while providing afternoon shade. Native to Manchuria, Korea, and Japan, this deciduous, hardy relative of the kiwi fruit is useful in the warmer portions of zone 4 to the cooler parts of zone 8. A word of advice: Cats love to chew and roll on plants, much as they do catnip. It's not a problem on established plants; the trick is to protect them until they outgrow the feline depredations.

Fiveleaf Akebia, *Akebia quinata*

Fiveleaf akebia is a vigorous twining vine suitable for part shade to full sun. The fine-textured appearance created by the dark green, palmately compound leaves make an attractive screen, and quick growth of the vines makes fiveleaf akebia suitable for covering chain link fences. The foliage effect is delicate enough for small spaces; vigorous growth means the vine needs some room to run. Pruning may be necessary to keep it within bounds. Native to China, Japan, and Korea, fiveleaf akebia is hardy from the warmer portions of zone 4 to zone 9. In zone 6 and colder it will be deciduous. In the late spring clusters of small chocolate-maroon flowers, with an intense, spicelike fragrance, open at night. In Japan I've seen the surprisingly large, pendant, bluish purple fruits offered for sale in late September. When ripe, they burst open to reveal numerous black seeds and translucent whitish flesh. Both rind and pulp are edible. It is rare for cultivated plants to fruit in American gardens.

Dutchman's Pipe, *Aristochia durior*

Once called porch vine, this coarse-leaved deciduous vine was popular as a summer screen for front porches and arbors. Dutchman's pipe refers to the unusual shape of pipelike, 3-inch-long, greenish yellow flowers in the early summer. Most species of *Aristochia* are tropical, but dutchman's pipe is natives of the eastcentral to midwestern United States, hardy from the warmer portions of zone 4 through zone 7. Growth is vigorous, and, given support, it climbs by twining to 25 feet. It can be pruned back to the desired height in the winter or early spring before growth begins. The dramatic, tropical-looking heart-shaped leaves reach 12 inches long and wide. You may want to trim back a leaf here and there to better reveal the flowers when the vines are in bloom. Vines are the larval food source for pipevine swallowtail butterflies.

Bigleaf Wintercreeper, *Euonymus fortunei*
Bigleaf wintercreeper is discussed earlier in this chapter, in the section discussing ground covers.

English Ivy, *Hedera helix*
English ivy is discussed earlier in this chapter, in the section discussing ground covers.

Golden Hop Vine, *Humulus lupulus* 'Aurea'
Quick-growing golden hop vine is a variously useful plant. In the summer enjoy the screening effect of its golden yellow, three- to five-lobed, coarsely toothed leaves. Additionally, in the spring the young shoots may be eaten; the fruiting vines may be air-dried for dried arrangements, using them in swags and garlands in the fall. Though gardeners in England are advised to grow golden hop vine in full sun, I find the more intense light in the United States greens up the foliage. Half shade results in more golden, chartreuse yellow leaves. Vine stems are bristly and rough, and climb by twining to 20 feet. Though somewhat slow-growing the first year, golden hop vine makes quick cover once established. Scramble it through large open shrubs, give it a rough tripod of poles to cling to, or in more formal gardens provide a sturdy tuteur of metal or wood. In cold climates golden hop vine often dies back to the ground in the winter, then scrambles back up again in the spring.

Climbing Hydrangea,
Hydrangea anomala ssp. *petiolaris*
Climbing hydrangea is a workhorse in both formal and informal shady gardens. This elegant deciduous vine clings to trees and walls by means of holdfasts. Glossy oval leaves, 2 to 4 inches across, are held on secondary stems that extend 1 to 3 feet out from the main trunks, providing a nice depth to the vines' appearance. In mid-June these branchlets bear numerous 6- to 10-inch clusters of white florets, attractive for two months and persisting into winter. Showy sterile flowers ring the flattened clusters around the less conspicuous fertile florets. Cinnamon brown flaking bark becomes most prominent after the leaves drop in the fall. It takes several years to get really lush growth, so be patient for the first four or five years the vine is in your garden. Given the right support, the primary vine trunks can reach 60 feet high or more and it is easy to maintain mature plants at the desired height by pruning as necessary to control their growth. Climbing hydrangea is hardy from zones 5 to 7, the cooler portion of zone 8.

Parthenocissus, Various

Virginia Creeper, *Parthenocissus quinquefolia*
This is also called woodbine, so if you ever wondered what it was ("where the woodbine twineth"), now you know. Native to moist woodlands of eastern North America, this deciduous vine goes rambling through woodlands, clinging to trees and rock cliffs by means of disk-tipped adhesive tendrils. Lacking supports, it scrambles around as a

Detail of Boston ivy, in winter.

GROUND COVERS AND VINES

loose, open ground cover. It has escaped and naturalized in parts of Europe. Not very fussy, Virginia creeper grows well in sites with moist to average soil, in heavy shade to full sun. Palmate compound leaves with five leaflets are pleasant in the summer, and turn an intense red in the fall. Flowers are easily overlooked, not so the dark blue-black fruit that is eaten by a number of birds. Where given adequate space, Virginia creeper is a fine vine for fall interest.

Boston Ivy, *Parthenocissus tricuspidata*

This ivy would more accurately be known by its less frequently used common name of Japanese creeper, as it is an Asian native. Vigorous, growing to 50 feet and more, efficient at clinging to supporting trees, trellises, or walls, Japanese creeper has tooth-edged, glossy, mid-green leaves that vary from jauntily pointed and heart-shaped to 8-inch-long, three-lobed versions, all on the same plant. Its fall colors are crimson, scarlet red, or purple. Suitable for urban, suburban, or rural gardens, Japanese creeper is hardy from zone 4 to zone 8. There are several cultivars, rather hard to find. Two to keep your eye out for are 'Lowii', which has small, three- to seven-lobed leaves an inch across and is smaller-growing overall, while 'Purpurea' has leaves that are reddish purple throughout the growing season.

Silvervein Creeper, *Parthenocissus henryana*

This creeper is the most tender of the three, only useful as year-round garden plants in zones 7 to 9. At the Chicago Botanic Garden, in zone 5, it is considered marginally hardy and best used as a ground cover. Keeping it close to the ground reduces radiant heat loss on cold nights, and a winter comforter of pine boughs would also help. Marco Stuffano of Wave Hill, a fabulous public garden in Riverdale, New York, zone 6, plays it safe and uses it as a container plant. Feeble climbers at best, silvervein creeper has stunning foliage: leaves up to 4 inches across are an attractive bright red when they first open, maturing to a white-veined, velvety-looking dark green in the summer, and a handsome purple underneath. Leaves again turn a clear scarlet red in the fall before they drop. Since best variegation needs heavy shade to develop, consider using silvervein creeper as an unusual tub plant for patio or terrace, or as an accent in the woodland garden. Sheltered winter conditions, perhaps a dark basement where the dormant plant can rest, should carry it through quite nicely until spring.

Japanese Climbing Hydrangea, *Schizophragma hydrangeoides*

A close relative of climbing hydrangea, Japanese climbing hydrangea is distinctive enough to warrant growing both vines in any garden where space permits and conditions allow. The major difference is in the flowers, as the Asian species has only a single, rather large petal to the outer ring of sterile florets, in place of the four or five of our American species. The result is a lacier, rather elegant appearance. Overall, once established, Japanese climbing hydrangea is a larger, showier plant. New branchlets are a downy, light buff brown, and mature to an ashy grayish brown. The leaves are dark green above, paler to an almost silver green on the underside, and most attractive when fluttered by the wind. Slow to establish, the vine will, in time, reach 40 feet and climb by means of short rootlets, the same holdfast system used by climbing hydrangea and poison ivy. I think this may be hardier than its suggested range zones 6 and 7, for they grow quite well at the Arnold Arboretum in Boston.

PERENNIALS

It is the fortunate gardener with the proper shady site who can grow the exquisite Christmas rose, *Helleborus niger.*

PERENNIALS

Perennials add interest to the shady garden at different seasons, depending on which you choose.

In the shade, gardening with perennials is both a delight and a juggling act. Given the limitation of diminishing sunlight imposed by woody plants, herbaceous perennials tend to hurl themselves into growth and bloom rather early. Afterwards, not only are flowers sparse, some plants even call it quits and retreat underground. The thoughtful gardener considers not only flowers but evaluates the time of year they appear and the other, nonflowering aspect of each plant as well.

Dividing the year into its usual four seasons results in a false perspective of when things bloom in shady gardens, giving "spring" the lion's share. I prefer to follow the seven seasons suggested by the great German plantsman, Karl Foerster. In *Garten als*

Zauberschlussel (*The Garden as a Magic Key*), first published in 1934, he suggested that the year be separated into early and late spring, early and high summer, fall and late fall, and winter.

According to Foerster, the gardener's year begins in the early spring, from late February until the end of April. Spring proper lasts from late April until the beginning of June. Early summer is the month of June, while high summer is from the end of June until the end of August. Fall begins in late August and lasts through October until early November. Late fall covers the period from the beginning of November until early December. And winter grips the garden from the beginning of December until the end of February. Early spring usually begins for me in late February, sometimes early March if winter is severe.

This is when *Adonis amurensis*, an ephemeral perennial, starts flowering.

Flowers—Early Spring

Adonis, *Adonis amurensis*

Found in deciduous forests of Japan's northernmost island of Hokkaido, adonis is a harbinger of spring. Growth begins in late February, no later than early March. Finely cut leaves surround a satiny, taffetalike bud that unfurls a glossy yellow flower reminiscent of an enormous buttercup. In cool weather the flowers last for a month or six weeks. Leaves mature to fine linear segments on 9- to 12-inch stems. Adonis is ephemeral, and foliage turns yellow and plants go dormant by mid-June. Quite cold-tolerant, to zone 4, adonis does poorly in mild winter regions and needs at least six weeks of cold weather to initiate growth. This period of *vernalization* (chilling period before growth) is required by various winter-hardy plants, shrubs, and trees as well as perennials and geophytes. A site with loose, woodsy soil high in organic matter, moist but well drained is best. Plants prefer an acid pH, the same as rhododendrons and mountain laurel. Place the dense, woody mass of wiry black roots only a few inches deep. Since adonis does not set seed, division is the only means of increase and may be done in late May or early June as the foliage is just beginning to yellow. Separate established plants into three or four pieces, not more often than every five years or so. You'll need a knife to cut plants apart. Points to remember:

• Adonis flowers so early that early-blooming geophytes such as snowdrops and winter aconites are the most available companions.

• Since adonis goes dormant as summer approaches, plant ferns, hostas, or other foliage plants nearby to conceal the bare space.

Winter's icy grip doesn't hold *Adonis amurensis* back, for here it is in flower in late February.

Hellebores, *Helleborus* Species and Cultivars

Popular in mild winter southeastern gardens, the various hellebores are also well liked in gardens of the colder Northeast and Midwest, because of the effect of their early, handsome flowers, attractive foliage, and increased availability, and the discovery that they are not so hard to grow after all. Long-lived, hellebores add a note of welcome cheer to spring's approach, and a recognition of winter's end.

Though there are over 20 species of hellebores, only three are readily found at nurseries: Christmas rose, *H. niger*, Lenten rose, *H. x orientalis*, and bear's foot or stinking hellebore, *H. foetidus*. Each is quite distinctive and certainly all three could be effectively used in the same garden.

Christmas Rose, *H. niger*

This hellebore has stately, slightly nodding, 2½-inch-wide white flowers, often faintly stained with pink outside, elegant flowers that do not open as early as the common name suggests. The petals surround a central boss of yellow stamens. Evergreen leaves are a handsome feature in their own right, thick, leathery, dark green, and divided into seven to nine palmately arranged segments. Older roots are blackish brown, and this characteristic provided the species name of niger, meaning dull black. Plants are hardy from zones 3 to 8, though in regions with moist, humid weather plants are subject to fungal leaf spot diseases. As new leaves develop in the early spring, treat with a suitable fungicide such as Bordeaux mix, which is also used for botrytis on peonies.

Close up, the flowers are even more beautiful.

Christmas rose needs a site with free-draining, reasonably fertile soil high in organic matter, in deciduous shade or on the north side of buildings. Adequate moisture is especially necessary when new leaves are produced in the spring. Established plants can tolerate drier conditions in the summer. Hellebores are in the family *Ranunculaceae*, and in common with many other members of that plant family, old seed germinates poorly. Sow fresh seed from your own plants as soon as seed is ripe—when capsules turn brown

and crack open. I take a more laissez-faire approach and transplant self-sown seedlings that volunteer in the leaf litter around established plants after they have been in the garden for a few years. Dig and transplant young plants in mid- to late spring.

Combine Christmas rose with early geophytes: winter aconite's golden buttercups or the plump starched petticoat-bells of spring snowflakes, and pair them with pheasant-eye daffodil, *Narcissus poeticus* 'Actaea'. In the summer the apple green, black-stemmed fronds of maidenhair fern make an attractive foliage accent, perhaps with the addition of evergreen greater woodrush. Cultivated since the Romans ruled Europe and the British Isles, Christmas rose grows just as well in modern times.

Lenten Rose, *Helleborus* x *orientalis*
The Lenten rose sold in nurseries is not a true species. The plants we grow are a mixed lot of always attractive hybrids, properly named *Helleborus* x *orientalis*. Blooming in early March, flowers vary from a pale apple green to white through blush pink on to plum and maroon. The paler flowers may be handsomely speckled with maroon and crimson inside, or completely unmarked. Some plants have a hint of green flushed over the flowers both inside and out. Hardy from zones 5 to 8, Lenten roses want partial to full shade as provided by deciduous trees. Provide a soil high in organic matter, and maintain a constant mulch of leaf litter. Though established plants tolerate dry conditions, adequate moisture results in better appearance of the foliage. Leaves are evergreen in warmer regions, deciduous in zone 6 and colder, becoming brown and stiff in January or February. For aesthetics, I usually trim them

away, on one of those mild days that encourage gardeners to believe winter is over before it is truly gone. Lenten roses reseed prolifically. Mixed colors and hues can be very attractive, but you might want to grow seedlings in a nursery area until they flower, then decide where and what to plant them with. I like all colors of Lenten roses, both deeper colors, apple green, and white forms, with blue-flowered geophytes such as scillas and chionodoxa.

Bear's Foot or Stinking Hellebore,
Helleborus foetidus
This perennial has a different growth pattern from the two previous species, producing new shoots in the late summer that overwinter, flower in the spring, then die away after producing seed. Numerous small, cup-shaped, pale green flowers rimmed with wine-purple, open in the early spring. Leaves are an especially dark green, deeply lobed into as many as 11 narrow segments, very handsome in contrast to the flower buds. After seed matures, the old stems die away. Though scary to a first-time grower who is sure the plant is dying, don't rush to dig it up and hide the corpses in the compost heap. New shoots will soon emerge to begin the cycle anew. They are best in zones 6 to 8, or in a sheltered site in zone 5. Soils high in organic matter with good drainage, even dry sites, are fine. Use bear's foot hellebore with tartarian dogwood, *Cornus alba*, elegantly pairing the perennials' dark green finely cut evergreen leaves and early chartreuse flowers with the glossy red-barked branches of the shrub, perhaps with snowdrops and the silver-mottled leaves of *Arum italicum* 'Pictum'. Or, team bear's foot hellebore with one of the white-flowered cyclamineus daffodils with its swept-back crown of petals, such as 'Dove Wings', and purple-leaved, lavender-flowered Labrador violet, *Viola labradorica*. This hellebore reseeds most prolifically of all, and are always welcome.

Lungwort, *Pulmonaria* Species and Cultivars
Impatient to start the season, red-flowered lungwort, *Pulmonaria rubra*, is often in bloom in late February, certainly no later than early March in zone 6, earlier in warmer places. When you consider that plants are still in flower through May, their rent-paying abilities become abundantly clear. Small bell-shaped brick red to warmer, more salmon or coral red flowers open in succession and wither away without any fuss or muss. They do, however, produce copious amounts of seed, and new plants generously volunteer in the path or across the path, working their way around the garden. If you also grow the later blooming spotted-leaved lungwort, *P. saccharata*, rogue these seedlings and pull out any that show even faintly spotted leaves to be certain of a continuing stock with red flowers. Pale green unspotted leaves are softly hairy, very tactile when gently stroked. Evergreen in mild winter areas, leaves are deciduous where cold weather prevails. Hardy in zones 4 to 7, a friend in Atlanta to whom I'd sent plants reported them in bloom

Bear's foot hellebore in seed pairs nicely with the flowers of grape hyacinth.

PERENNIALS

for New Year's! Red-flowered lungwort needs a steady supply of moisture, but not a soggy site. With the extended period, plants can work through several partners in the course of the spring. Daffodils are fine for an early effect, as the smaller geophytes are too petite for the lungwort's 15-inch height. Hosta leaves are more similar than is desirable, so look for plants with compound leaves such as ferns, doll's eyes, red baneberry, and astilbe. Red lungwort can also be used as a ground cover for shrubs.

Flowers—Spring

Bugleweed, *Ajuga reptans*
Life has enough challenges without hard-to-grow plants. It is a pity when gardeners consider themselves too sophisticated for this "common" plant or that "merely ordinary" one, familiar because they are sturdy and reliable. Dependable plants have much to recommend them. Take bugleweed, *Ajuga reptans*. This tidy ground cover prefers partial to moderate shade, and tolerates full sun. Give it suitably attractive companions, and bugleweed becomes a handsome addition to the shade gardener's repertoire. One such practical community in my garden effectively combines bugleweed with violets, wild sweet William, broad beech fern, and *Trillium cuneatum*. Stoloniferous, bugleweed spreads rapidly and should be considered as unifying an area rather than as an individual specimen accent. As such, it is discussed in Ground Covers and Vines, beginning on page 111.

Lady's Mantle, *Alchemilla mollis*
Popular in herb gardens, the adaptable lady's mantle prefers light shade especially in the warmer portions of its zones 4 to 7 range. Dry soil is an anathema, resulting in stunted growth. Plants grow best with constant moisture, humus-rich soils, and light to partial shade. Abundant light green leaves are softly hairy. These small hairs catch raindrops and dewdrops, like small milky moonstones. In hot summer regions, leaf diseases can result if water remains overnight. The shallowly lobed, serrately edged leaves have another magical property. Small pores at each saw-toothed point release excess moisture. Perhaps a visit to your garden first thing on a summer morning will show each lady's mantle leaf necklaced with a tiny bead of water.

Note: The fancy term for this is "water of guttation."

In addition, lady's mantle produces attractive billows of tiny, ¼-inch-wide, petal-less chartreuse flowers, foaming above the 12- to 18-inch-high plants. The pleasing, neutral, yellow-green flowers associate equally well with yellow to cantaloupe orange flowers, and blue to violet flowers. Choose flowers with a more emphatic shape to stand out against lady mantle's scrim of massed, tiny flowers. Siberian bugloss is excellent for foliage, somewhat subtle in flower effect. Leopard's bane's yellow daisies are excellent in a lightly shaded site. Fringed bleeding heart is a suitable foliage partner. Plants may readily be divided in the early spring, before flowering occurs. Sometimes plants self-sow. Vigorous, lady's mantle can sprawl, cover, and smother slower growing neighbors.

Columbines, *Aquilegia* Species and Cultivars
Columbines are among the more transient perennials, with individual plants lasting three or four years. They happily self-sow and remain as self-perpetuating colonies. The thing to watch out for is their promiscuous nature. It

seems that any columbine will provide, or receive, pollen from any other nearby columbine. The offspring, though attractive, will display their mixed ancestry. If particular appearances are important, be sure to grow your columbines well separated. Columbines want edge of woodland situations, or a glade opening, where shade is light. Consider plants that stay within bounds and avoid aggressive neighbors for columbines or they will be overrun. Primroses are suitable; bugleweed is not.

Canada Columbine, *Aquilegia canadensis*

This columbine is a charming native with deep to rosy red sepals and spurs surrounding soft lemon-yellow petals, the combination creating a flower of great charm. It has the usual ferny columbine leaves, and appears less troubled by columbine leaf miner—a noxious insect whose larvae tunnel between the upper and lower leaf surface, leaving silver curlicues as a sign of their presence—than do other species. One plant by itself looks lost, three is a beginning, but Canada columbines are really at their best when used en masse, for their flowers and foliage have an airy grace that does not pall. Consider pairing them with forget-me-nots, whose delicate blue flowers make a charming foil for those of the columbine. 'Corbett' is a cultivar with entirely pale yellow flowers. Canada columbine is hardy from zones 3 to 8. Plants grow 15 to 24 inches tall and spread about 12 inches wide.

Common Columbine, *Aquilegia vulgaris*

Since they readily hybridize, it can be difficult to find plants of the true common columbine, *Aquilegia vulgaris*. Bluish green leaves create a tuffet above which dance short-spurred flowers in a range of colors from dark blue and dark violet, through crimson, plum, pink, and white, for this European species is itself variable. One hallmark is the short, incurved spurs, rather than the elongated, straight-spurred columbines that are popular today.

The flowers of Canada columbine, *Aquilegia canadensis*, appear to hover above the leaves like little butterflies.

No less a garden personage than Gertrude Jekyll was fond of the common columbine, so favoring the white-flowered var. *nivea* (also named 'Nivea') that it is often referred to as Munstead White named after her garden. It has rather gray leaves and pure white flowers, on vigorous plants up to 3 feet tall. It would be elegant with white-flowered foxgloves, or against the glaucous blue leaf of hostas such as *Hosta sieboldiana* 'Elegans'. There are a number of double-flowered forms. Arguably the best known is 'Nora Barlow', with pink and lime green pom-pom fluff-ball flowers, which interestingly seed true regardless of other columbines in the neighborhood. Hardy in zones 3 to 8, common columbine typically grows 24 inches tall and spreads 12 inches wide.

Scrambling among the rocks, the healthy growth and numerous flowers of *Aquilegia flabellata* 'Nana' reveal its sturdy nature.

PERENNIALS

Siberian Bugloss, *Brunnera macrophylla*
Brunnera's older name of *Anchusa mysotidiflo-ra*, paid tribute to the myosotis (the Latin name for forget-me-not) appearance of the flowers. Today's accepted name, *Brunnera macrophylla*, remarks upon the characteristically large heart-shaped leaf that plants develop at maturity. Siberian bugloss is tolerant of a range of soil conditions, prefers some moisture, but needs half to full shade. Then, in late April or early May plants develop 18-inch stems with vivid blue forget-me-not-like flowers, sturdily held above bright green leaves nicely in scale. As flowers fade, the leaves continue to grow, until by June they are 6 inches or more across, and darkening in color. Though not quite evergreen, leaves remain in good condition until quite far into the winter. Mature plants have tenacious, thonglike roots resentful of disturbance. The numerous self-sown seedlings transplant easily in their first year or two. Hardy from zones 3 to 7, Siberian bugloss prefers full shade in the South, and tolerates morning sun in the cooler portion of its range, especially if the site is moist. For a spring-flowering effect, combine the airy blue flowers of Siberian bugloss with yellow and white primroses, or the somewhat lavender-hued blossom of wild sweet William, *Phlox divaricata*. In the summer, its bold leaf looks well with the linear texture of liriope, and the compound form of astilbe.

Corydalis, *Corydalis* Species
With ferny leaves very reminiscent of fringed bleeding heart and wild bleeding heart, the various corydalis make pleasant foliage accents in the shady garden. Add their attractive flowers, and their appeal becomes clear. One caveat: Many are generous about providing more and more volunteers in subsequent years.

Corydalis bulbosa
Corydalis bulbosa properly belongs in the next chapter, Geophytes, since plants have a solid, somewhat flattened tuber an inch across, slightly concave on the upper surface. However when plants are available, they are sold as potted perennials rather than dormant tubers. Each tuber sends up a single 9-inch stem of finely cut, glaucous leaves, with a short, densely packed raceme of 10 to 20 deep rose to purple flowers. For all its delicate appearance, *C. bulbosa* is surprisingly frost-resistant. Plants vanish by midsummer, dormant until the following spring when they return in increased numbers. I find this charming with the intense cerise-pink flowers of Persian violet, *Cyclamen coum*.

Corydalis cheilanthifolia
The leaf rosettes of *Corydalis cheilanthifolia* are striking. Each leaf is 6 to 12 inches long, deeply, pinnately cut to the midrib. Each segment is again cut toward the central vein, beyond fernlike to the point of skeletal, and an unusual brownish green color. The soft yellow flowers appear in May or early June, densely clustered on a 15- to 18-inch stem. My plants thrive in moderate shade, with soil high in organic matter, moist but well drained. Native to western China, this species is said to be hardy to zone 5.

Corydalis lutea
I'm not sure yellow fumitory is as nice a name as this plant deserves. Belying its delicate appearance, *Corydalis lutea* is evergreen. Small leaves develop in the fall, then expand to make bushy, 8- to 16-inch-tall mounds. Plants are never heavy or bulky in appearance, for the fernlike leaves are pinnately compound in a filigree of foliage. I cherish yellow fumitory for its flowers; plants begin

blooming in May, and continue to produce their yellow flowers (like minute bleeding heart blossoms) through September. This is not a plant for a formal garden though, since it merrily flings its seed far and wide. The fleshy roots are not hard to weed out, should plants move into a place where they are not wanted. Hardy in zones 5 to 7, and happiest in a moist, light to partially shaded site, plants naturalize even in heavy shade. Try their fine-textured, leafy filigree and yellow flowers in combination with a hosta that has creamy yellow variegation, or with Dalmatian bellflowers, *Campanula portenschlagia*, which are willingly produces scrambling stems of violet-blue flowers from late spring through midsummer, then rebloom in September after a brief time out.

Bleeding Heart, *Dicentra* Species and Cultivars

Introduced a century and a half ago, bleeding heart, *Dicentra spectabilis*, with its fernlike leaves and rosy red flowers, makes a charming addition to the garden. The long-lived plants make a 30-inch-tall mound of foliage, atop which arching stems of heart-shaped, rosy pink buds open to pink and white heart-shaped flowers. (Pluck a mature flower, turn it upside-down, and gentle pull the skirts aside to see the "lady-in-her-bath.") Mature plants are difficult to move, as the fleshy, thonglike roots resent disturbance. Alas, plants go dormant in midsummer, first yellowing and collapsing on their neighbors, then leaving a gap in the garden. Partial shade and adequate moisture slows, but does not prevent, this decline. The slower-growing, paler green-leafed, pure white flowered form (sold either as 'Alba' or 'Pantaloons') does not go summer dormant. I also prefer white flowers, which stand out more satisfactorily in shade. Bleeding heart is hardy in zones 2 to 9. Provide bold foliage contrast in the form of large-leaved hostas. Glaucous blue-leaved cultivars such as 'Big Mamma', 'Blue Angel', or 'True Blue' are elegant with 'Pantaloons'.

While popular, bleeding heart is not the only dicentra available. Several smaller species (which avoid summer dormancy) are excellent additions to the shade gardener's repertoire.

A close-up look at the flowers reveals just where bleeding heart got its common name.

PERENNIALS

A popular perennial for shady gardens, bleeding heart produces a fine show of spring flowers before going dormant in summer.

Fringed Bleeding Heart, *Dicentra eximia*
This dicentra is a lovely woodland native of forests from New York to Georgia. Hardy from zones 4 to 8, plants have gray-green ferny foliage, and longer, branched racemes of rosy pink flowers. Leaves and flower stems arise directly from the scaly rhizomes, forming compact 10- to 15-inch mounds. Fringed bleeding heart is hardy from zones 4 to 9. Somewhat tolerant of drier sites, fringed bleeding heart suffers in hot, humid summers.

Wild Bleeding Heart, *D. formosa*
Native to British Columbia, the Pacific Northwest, and northern California, wild bleeding heart has creeping rhizomes, rather than the compact habit of fringed bleeding heart, with light green, fernlike leaves and rose-pink, rose-purple, or white flowers.

Confusing the issue, what you will find offered at nurseries are cultivars, and there is debate as to whether these belong to one species or the other or are hybrids. Why worry? Just grow and enjoy. 'Adrian Bloom' is a vigorous, dark green-leaved, floriferous cultivar with large, ruby red flowers; 'Bacchanal' grows 12 inches high and has dark red flowers with peak bloom in the spring, then scattered bloom throughout the summer; 'Bountiful' has abundant, dark rosy pink flowers and finely dissected, silvery gray leaves; 'Luxuriant' (which fails to thrive in zone 8) has cherry red flowers beginning in late April and continues to bear scattered blooms through the summer; and 'Snowdrift' has beautiful pure white flowers and an extended period of bloom. Since all the bleeding hearts have dissected, fernlike leaves, avoid placing them near ferns, astilbe, or other plants with similar foliage. Rather, use Siberian bugloss with its simple, bolder leaf.

Our other native woodland species— Dutchman's breeches, *Dicentra cucullaria*, and squirrel corn, *D. canadensis*—are true bulbs, and are discussed in the following chapter, Geophytes.

Leopard's Bane, *Doronicum* Species and Cultivars

Suitable for lightly shaded sites, leopard's bane, *Doronicum orientale* (= *Doronicum caucasicum*) was originally a wild plant of mountain forests. As such, leopard's bane is eminently suited to a woodland edge situation, bright enough to encourage good flowering, but with light to partial shade. Heart-shaped, saw-toothed leaves often become shabby in the summer. Adequate moisture helps, but especially in the warmer portion of its zones 4 to 7 range, leopard's bane is apt to go dormant. This is easily disguised by nearby astilbes or comparable plants. One of my favorite, more vivid spring combinations is the bright yellow daisies of leopard's bane on their 15-inch stems, adjacent to an astilbe with deep copper to bronze spring foliage. More subdued, try the yellow daisies with chartreuse flowers, perhaps a shade-tolerant euphorbia or lady's mantle. Or, leopard's bane with white-flowered honesty and forget-me-nots. There are several cultivars available, such as 'Finesse', with dense clusters of flowers on 20-inch stems, or large-flowered, 20-inch-tall 'Magnificum'. Both of these cultivars may be raised from seed. Flowering in late April and May, the flowers of leopard's bane make good cut flowers.

Nestled in a shady rock crevice, western bleeding heart, *Dicentra formosa*, creates a delicate display of rosy flowers and fern-like leaves.

Doronicum plantagineum has quite long flower stems, growing 30 inches high. This allows its bright yellow daisies (about the color of New York City taxicabs) to appear in May above the rapidly expanding leaves of a large-leaved golden hosta such as 'August Moon' or 'Shade Master'. This is effective placement in another regard. *D. plantagineum* goes dormant after flowering, and its bare branches can be concealed by the hosta.

Epimedium, *Epimedium* Species and Cultivars

Barrenwort is an unpromising common name for *Epimedium*, a genus of tidy, easily grown plants that is a workhorse in the shady garden. They have twice to thrice compound leaves for a pleasing airy effect. New growth in the spring is often flushed or rimmed with copper or red. Loose clusters of flowers appear just before or as the leaves appear in early to midspring. While plants are in bloom for a brief period, the leaves remain neat and tidy through the summer

PERENNIALS

into the late fall and winter. Once established, the only necessary maintenance is to cut back the old leaves in the late winter or early spring before new growth begins. At this time a quick cut with hedge clippers is most effective. Propagation is easily accomplished, either by division in the spring after the leaves have fully developed, or in the fall when rhizomes can be separated, potted up, and held in a cold frame over the winter for planting out the following spring. Combine epimediums with bold-leaved plants such as hostas, use them with linear-leaved plants like liriopes, or mix them with native woodland perennials such as bloodroot.

So dainty, this plant becomes even more charming: the closer you look, the more attractive it appears.

We tend to lump all epimediums together, but there are some distinctions between the different species, mostly in the amount of moisture they need. Those from the Mediterranean and Caucasus regions—*Epimedium alpinum, E. peralderianum,* and *E. pinnatum* ssp. *colchicum*—are, as might be expected, most tolerant of summer heat and drought. They are discussed in Problem Shade/Problem Trees, beginning on page 21. The Japanese and Chinese species *E. diphyllum, E. grandiflorum,* and their hybrids, prefer cool, moderately moist sites with humus-rich soil. They are hardy in zones 5 to 8.

Daintiest of all epimedium species is 4- to 8-inch-tall *Epimedium diphyllum.* Racemes of four to nine spurless, nodding white flowers appear in the early spring, with paired leaflets on the flower stem. While the species itself is rarely offered, its hybrid offspring with *E. grandiflorum* are popular garden plants. Keeping the delicate appearance of its smaller parent, *E.* x *youngianum* grows 4 to 12 inches tall. Two to nine leaflets make tidy mounds of foliage. The flowering stem has a single leaf, and 3 to 12 flowers; 'Niveum' is white and 'Roseum' is a soft rose pink. I use 'Niveum' at the edge of a path in combination with the purple-leaved Labrador violet, accepting the periodic maintenance of heading it back when it crowds the epimedium.

Epimedium grandiflorum is deservedly popular. Twice- or thrice-divided leaves on stiff, sturdy stems make 12-inch-tall mounds. Planted in a row, this makes a neat edging for a formal design. Equally staggered groupings accent a naturalistic planting. Leaves are copper-bronze when they first appear in the spring, maturing to a soft, light green. Four to 16 flowers appear in mid- to late spring. 'Rose Queen' holds its flowers well above the leaves. White-tipped spurs accentuate the

Soft rose-pink flowers create a springtime display on *Epimedium grandiflorum* 'Rose Queen'.

extra-large, light crimson flowers. 'White Queen' is an all-white counterpart, while forma *violaceum* (= 'Violaceum') has pale violet flowers, and scarce 'Lilafee' has darker, lavender-violet flowers.

Epimedium grandiflorum was crossed with *E. pinnatum* ssp. *colchicum* to produce *E.* x *versicolor*, which is most notable for its yellow flowers. 'Sulphureum' is a particularly nice cultivar, with 8 to 20 yellow flowers, and leaves often conspicuously mottled with red or brown while young. It is hardier than drought-tolerant, yellow-flowered *E. perraldianum* 'Froehnleiten', suitable for zone 5 in sheltered sites.

Geraniums, *Geranium* Species and Cultivars

Hardy geraniums are distinctly different from the tender perennials of the same common name used in window boxes or containers for summer color. Most of the true geraniums, also called cranesbills for the shape of their seed pods, are sun lovers, but a couple of species are good choices for the shady garden.

Wild Geranium or Spotted Cranesbill,
Geranium maculatum
This geranium is a familiar wildflower of eastern North America. Found along the forest edge or somewhat shaded roadsides, plants have broad, somewhat hairy, medium green leaves divided into five to seven lobes. In May, 18- to 24-inch tall-stems are topped with clusters of upward-facing, saucerlike, rosy purple or lavender pink flowers. 'Album' has pure white flowers, and paler green leaves. Suitable for lightly shaded sites, wild geranium combines attractively with fringed bleeding heart and wild bleeding heart, both when in bloom and as a foliage association.

Bigroot Geranium, *Geranium macrorrhizum*
Native to southern Europe, the thickened, creeping rhizome creates a carpet of deeply cut, five- to seven-lobed leaves up to 6 inches across. The leaves have a pungent, rather medicinal smell when crushed. In the fall the older leaves turn red and yellow. Some plants seem practically evergreen, especially in milder portions of their zones 3 to 8 range. Established plants are heat- and drought-tolerant. Bigroot geranium flowers in the late spring, with up to nine slightly nodding, magenta-pink flowers held in red calyces, on 12- to 16-inch stems. There are a number of cultivars available: 'Album' has white flowers and pink calyces; 'Bevan's Variety' has intense deep magenta-pink flowers and deep red calyces; 'Ingwersen's Variety' has soft rose pink flowers. Use bigroot geranium as an

Planted in large sweeps, *Epimedium* 'Snow Queen' makes a lovely, not-quite-evergreen ground cover that brightens a shady area.

137

PERENNIALS

accent plant on its own or massed as a carpet, perhaps with evergreen Christmas fern as an accent.

Crested Iris, *Iris cristata*
Quite different from bearded iris, its better-known border cousin, crested iris is a dainty woodland species. Its slender creeping rhizomes spread over the forest floor, though not as widely as I'd like. These questing runners suggest its preferred conditions, a humus-rich, light open soil, moist but not wet, with an organic mulch of chopped leaves or similar, into which the expanding shoots can easily root. Soft green fans of swordlike leaves continue to grow after flowering, though remaining under a foot tall. One or two sweetly fragrant flowers appear in late April or early May. Their colors range from soft lavender, lilac, violet, and purple to almost true blue, accented by a white blotch crested in cream or yellow on the lower petals. There's even a white one, quite vigorous, which is not the norm for white forms of typically colored flowering plants. With such variation, it is no wonder that some forms have been named: 'Abbys Violet' has violet-flushed lilac flowers; 'Alba' is pure white with a yellow crest; 'Summer Storm' is deep blue. Pair crested iris with dainty oak fern, a small epimedium, primroses, even violets if they are kept within bounds.

Forget-me-not, *Myosotis sylvatica*
Forget-me-nots are a mixed lot of annual, biennial, and perennial species. The spring-blooming species available in garden centers for bedding out with tulips is a biennial. The shade-tolerant, woodland forget-me-not, *Myosotis sylvatica*, is also biennial and is discussed in Annuals, Biennials, and Tender Perennials, beginning on page 187.

An adaptable plant, *Iris cristata* makes a fine transition plant for those tough sites between sun and shade.

Virginia Bluebells, *Mertensia virginica*

Virginia bluebells are one of those North American woodland natives that successfully made its way into the perennial garden. In fact, they have been in gardens for almost two centuries, especially popular as companions to May-blooming tulips. The smooth, grayish green oval leaves, up to 8 inches long and 5 inches wide, make a cool blend with the arching, 2-foot-high stems from which dangle narrow, bell-like, soft sky blue flowers. Virginia bluebells have fleshy, carrotlike roots, resentful of disturbance when they've become established. Self-sown seedlings can easily be moved in their first year or two. Select a semishaded to fully shaded site, with moist soil high in organic matter. A quite wet river bottom in Missouri had a solid carpet of Virginia bluebells in bloom when I was fortunate enough to visit one spring. Alas, the plant is ephemeral and goes dormant shortly after the flowering cycle is complete. While they are present, leaves make a nice contrast to ferns and fernlike plants that, if carefully chosen, fill the empty space.

Note: The typical bleeding heart also goes dormant and would worsen the situation. White-flowered 'Pantaloons' remains in growth through summer and is clearly a better option.

Japanese Woodland Peony,
Paeonia obovata 'Alba'

What would you say to a peony for the shade? Not deep shade mind you, but quite happy in the bright shade under an oak tree, or at the woodland edge. This paragon is Japanese woodland peony. In the early spring, the thong-like root mass sends up shoots of a rich ruby red, overlaid with a hoar-frost, crystalline dusting. Leaves unfold to a soft, somewhat grayish green, on stems about 18 to 24 inches tall. When the plant is mature enough to flower, each shoot produces a single flower. A fat bud emerges swaddled in the folded leaf shoot, enlarging

The pristine white flowers of Japanese woodland peony, *Paeonia obovata* 'Alba', appear to float above the stems.

to a pure white chalice centered with golden stamens.

After pollination the petals drop and seeds begin to swell. Unlike most perennials, which are dead-headed (the spent flowers removed), allow this beauty to complete its reproductive cycle. The seeds are beautiful, a rich metallic blue, about the size of a fat pea. Ovules that were not fertilized are a bright scarlet, and the contrast between the two is striking. Sowing the fresh seed is your best means of increasing this treasure. Patience is necessary, though, as it takes years from seed to blooming plant.

Plant Japanese woodland peony in a well prepared area, making sure that drainage is good and that there is ample organic matter. Choose a fertilizer higher in phosphorus and potash than nitrogen. Set the plant carefully to avoid damaging the roots or the shoot-buds on the crown. While the fall is the traditional time to plant peonies, in this instance *anytime* you can obtain it is the best time.

PERENNIALS

A single row of petals creates a chalice-like appearance for the flowers of Japanese woodland peony.

A look into the flower reveals a cluster of soft yellow stamen, further embellishing the chaste white flower.

Rather scarce in commerce, Japanese woodland peony is slowly becoming available as young, not-quite-ready-to-flower plants.

Wild Sweet William, *Phlox divaricata*

Based on the garden phlox that are a mainstay of the summer border, gardeners tend to think of phlox as sun-loving plants. There are two spring-blooming, woodland species that are excellent choices for the shady garden: Wild sweet William or woodland phlox, *Phlox divaricata*, forms clusters of leafy stems clothed in dark green, 1½- to 2-inch-long leaves. Upright, 12- to 15-inch tall flowering stems have clusters of soft to medium blue flowers. Nonflowering stems are trailing, and root at the nodes. Named forms include dwarfer, extremely floriferous 'Fuller's White' with pure white flowers, and icy, pale blue 'Dirigo Ice'. Discovered by Mrs. J. Norman Henry, noted native expert who used to botanize by chauffeur-driven automobile, purple-eyed, deep violet 'Chattahoochee' is a naturally occurring hybrid with prairie phlox, *P. pilosa*. Such parentage explains its preference for light shade, as wild sweet William and its other cultivars do well in partial to heavy shade. Hardy from zones 4 to 8, wild sweet William is a good filler, blending nicely with violets, primroses, bugleweed, small to mid-sized ferns and trilliums, and small to mid-sized hostas. One of my favorite pairing interplants this phlox with white-flowered *Trillium erectum* var. *album*. Plants grow best with soil high in organic matter, moist but well drained. Though not mentioned in books, I've noticed plants of wild sweet William in my garden take a summer vacation, dormant through the last of July and all of August, then sending up new growth in the fall which remains evergreen through winter.

Creeping phlox, *P. stolonifera*, is a superlative ground cover, and is discussed in Ground Covers and Vines, beginning on page 111.

Primroses, *Primula* Species and Cultivars

Primroses are truly harbingers of spring, their early flowers a welcome indicator of more settled weather. While some primroses are fussy plants better suited to the blandishments of experts, others are remarkably good-natured plants that belong in every shaded garden. One common complaint is that not all the primroses bought as bedding plants in the spring survive zone 6 winters. The Pacific Giant hybrids were bred on the West Coast, and are not as hardy as their progenitors. Developed from several species, including *Primula juliae, P. veris, P. elatior,* and *P. vulgaris*, these are now called Pruhonicensis or polyanthus hybrids. Hardy from zones 4 to 8, they dislike both severe winters lacking snow cover, and hot summers. Spider mites are a problem in hot, dry weather; remember that a miticide, not an insecticide, is the necessary remedy. Slugs also dine on primroses, as do deer. Pruhonicensis hybrid primroses prefer a moist yet well-drained site, with a woodsy soil, in light shade. They have flowers in a rainbow of colors, often with a white or yellow eye, and either have bunched flowers at the top of a relatively stout stalk, or one flower to each slender stem. It seems to me that those plants with smallish, dark green or red-flushed, somewhat wrinkled leaves that resemble more closely those of their *P. juliae* parent, are hardier than those with larger, somewhat thinner-textured, lighter green leaves. (*P. juliae* is a species with roundish leaves and yellow-eyed, mauve to deep magenta flowers.) If you want to search for named forms, then look for 'Garryarde Guinevere' with pink flowers and bronzed leaves; 'Kinlough Beauty' with salmon pink flowers and a yellow eye that extends in a raggedy stripe down each petal; diminutive 'Snow Cushion' with small, pure white flowers; and yellow-eyed, vivid purple-red 'Wanda' with red-flushed leaves. There are literally dozens more. Barnhaven hybrids, with large flowers and diminutive leaves, have been developed in color series—yellows, rusts, oranges, reds, pinks, blues, wines.

I feed my plants with a thin mulch of dry cow manure after they finish flowering. This is also a good time to divide large plants with several growing points. Dug at this time they almost separate on their own, while if dug before they flower, the thickened rhizomes all hold firmly together. The yellow- and white-flowered ones are charming with forget-me-nots. Any color primrose looks great massed with a hellebore or two towering over them. The clumping fringed bleeding heart is another choice, but be careful as its cool, slightly bluish pink flowers can clash with warmer pink-flowered primroses. Solomon's seal, liriope, dwarf hostas, small ferns, are all pleasantly enhanced by primroses.

Siebold's Primrose, *Primula sieboldii*

This is another of the garden treasures that came to us from Japan, its 2- to 4-inch-long leaves on long petioles have a corrugated appearance. Each sturdy stem holds 6 to 10 large flowers, 1 to 1½ inch wide. Color varies from pure white through soft pink to rose or lavender, and some plants are bicolor with different hues on the surface and underside of the petals. The tip of the petal may be rounded or notched. One magnificent combination seen in Harold Epstein's Larchmont, New York, garden paired mauve-flowered Siebold's primroses with the chocolate spathes of a Japanese Jack-in-the-pulpit, *Arisaema sikokianum*. While these primroses do not demand a boggy site, neither do they accept a droughty one. Moist but well drained is the happy medium, with a loose, open soil high in organic matter, in zones 5 to 7. Siebold's primroses flower well in light to moderate, even in relatively heavy shade. One event to be aware of is that plants go dormant in the summer, and remain underground until the following spring. It doesn't mean plants are dead, and they surely do not

PERENNIALS

A closer look reveals the chocolate hood and white interior of this Japanese cousin to our native Jack-in-the-pulpit.

want to be disturbed by inquisitive digging to find out what's going on. Leave the wrinkled rhizomes alone in their slumbers, allowing small deciduous ferns, dwarf hostas, coarse Siberian bugloss, bloodroot, and trillium to provide the summer foliage interest.

Lungwort, *Pulmonaria* Species and Cultivars

Cowslip Lungwort, *Pulmonaria angustifolia*
This lungwort differs from the more familiar spotted lungwort in that the hairy, lanceolate leaves are plain, unspotted, fresh green.

Flowers change to a clear, electric blue as they open, from rose pink buds. 'Munstead Blue' is a vigorous, 12-inch-tall cultivar with pale blue flowers; while 'Johnson's Blue' has gentian blue flowers on plants only 8 inches high; 'Mawson's Blue' has bright blue-violet flowers. Tolerant of root competition with trees and shrubs, cowslip lungwort could be used as a ground cover. Though hardy in zones 3 to 8, cowslip lungwort wilts in hot weather, making it more suitable in the cooler portion of its range. Consider a pairing with white bleeding heart, *Dicentra spectabilis* 'Pantaloons', using at least seven to ten

142

cowslip lungwort to each bleeding heart. With their downy-textured leaf and fresh green hue, cowslip lungwort would stand out nicely in contrast to the glossy, dark green leaf of European ginger.

Violets, *Viola* Species

It is a pity that violets are so often considered a pest, "just another weed." If weeds are plants growing in the wrong place, then violets, too, can be considered beautiful wildflowers. Found across the United States and abroad, growing in sun or shade, their dainty flowers and rugged nature suggest placement where plants have room to romp, yet can be regarded close up, perhaps along a path in a less refined area of the garden, perhaps mixed with equally sturdy plants such as ajuga. Caterpillars, the larval stage of several different fritilary butterflies, feed on violet leaves, great spangled and meadow fritilary among others. The butterflies are orange with black checkering on their wings.

Violets manage their prolific self-seeding as the consequence of hidden *cleistogamous* flowers that never open fully but self-pollinate in the bud. Additionally, violets may form *stolons,* underground stems that send up new plantlets near the original plant, or surface runners that root along the stem and form new plants at the end. Often, individual plants increase nicely and gardeners who want more can simply pull the clump apart into smaller divisions.

There are two basic forms of violets, stemmed and stemless. Some have stems from which leaves and flowers branch and grow. Many are stemless; that is, the leaves and flowers come up from the ground each on their own stalk. If you think of violets as violet (or lavender, blue, or purple), think again. There are white-flowered violets, yellow ones, pink, or red, even bicolored kinds. Violets grow in open fields, dry deserts, high mountains, fields, and forests. It is these shade lovers that I recommend to you.

Canada Violet, *Viola canadensis*

A white-flowered stemmed violet found across the United States, this is an easily cultivated woodland species that thrives in part shade and prefers an open, free-draining soil. Canada violet has a long period of bloom, right through the summer into the fall if conditions are suitable.

Dog Violet, *Viola conspersa*

This is a stemmed violet with quite lovely light blue flowers with just a hint of lavender. One of the most common species of the northeastern and central United States, you may be excused for thinking it is stemless, especially in the early spring when new growth is just expanding from the forest floor.

Siebold's primrose's rich mauve makes a fine background to snow-ricecake plant, *Arisaema sikokianaum.* Both plants make an elegant addition to gardens far from their native home in Japan.

PERENNIALS

Spear-Leaved Violet, *Viola hastata*
This violet has halberd-shaped leaves, gently rounded at the base.

Labrador Violet, *Viola labradorica*
This is one you'd want to grow even if it never flowered. New leaves in spring have a rich purple hue, which softens in the summer to a purple-flushed green. This is a stemmed violet that spreads around a bit, making it useful as a ground cover for modest areas. In the spring, lavender-hued flowers create a pleasing accent to the somber leaves. One superb combination pairs Bowle's golden grass, *Milium effusum* 'Aureum', with Labrador violet. The bright chartreuse yellow grass blades are a fabulous foil for the dark leaves of the violet.

Sweet Violet, *Viola odorata*
Though naturalized and growing wild in the United States, this violet came from Europe as a florist's flower. In bloom, sweet violet is most fragrant when a small bouquet is picked and enjoyed indoors. The cool weather early in the spring makes the perfume less noticeable in the garden. Heart-shaped, regularly scalloped leaves are attractive. A stemmed violet, the new plantlets are easily divided from the parent plant after blooming time. A site in half-shade, in somewhat acid soil suggests placement near rhododendrons, mountain laurel, or pieris.

Stemless, Yellow-flowered, Round-leaved Violet, *Viola rotundifolia*
This violet is an excellent choice for cool, coniferous woods with acid soil. From New England to North Carolina, in the spring the ground-hugging leaves are perfectly in scale with the clear yellow flowers striped with brown on the lower petals. As the season con-

Whether you call them "weed" or "wildflower" depends on how neat and tidy your garden is kept—violets do spread themselves around!

tinues, the leaves continue to grow, and by the summer, still ground-hugging, they are the size of a teacup's saucer. Round-leaved violets serve as a fine ground cover in a suitable site.

Northern Blue Violet, *Viola septentrionalis*
As its name suggests, this violet is found in the northern portion of the United States, along the edge of thickets, in moist, open, coniferous woodlands, even on gravelly mountain ledges. A stemless violet, the pale to deep violet-colored flowers have a dense white beard on the three lower petals. The pointed, spade-shaped leaves are slightly hairy on the backs and edges, and also on the stems. This species is a good choice for acid soil in part shade near evergreens, but will not accept dry conditions.

Common Violet or Dooryard Violet, *Viola sororia*
The common violet is found across much of the United States. There seems there is no such thing as "typical" flower color, for the sister violet (as this species is also called) can be purple, purple-centered, red, white, or

even charmingly speckled as in the cultivar 'Freckles'. This last is a stable color break, for seedlings are also purple polka-dotted on a grayed ground color. Common violet is a good doer, growing in shade, semishade, or even sun. This makes it an excellent choice for those difficult transition areas from shade to sun. The leaves are approximately triangular, pointed at the tip and rounded at the base, each with their own stalk, for this is a stemless species.

Creamy Violet, *Viola striata*
This purple-striped white-flowered stemmed violet is found wild in the eastern half of the United States. In the spring it looks very dainty and refined, with dark green leaves and charming flowers, but then, like Topsy, it just grows, and grows some more, and by midsummer can reach 18 inches tall, flowering all the while. It makes a useful ground cover in shade, as the runners spread around, and leaves stay in good condition until quite late in the fall.

Flowers—Summer

Summer flowers are scarce in shady gardens. Foliage quite nicely furnishes the garden and keeps it attractive.

Goatsbeard, *Aruncus dioicus*
Goatsbeard, *Aruncus dioicus*, is a moisture-loving plant discussed in Problem Shade/Problem Trees, beginning on page 21.

Astilbe, *Astilbe* Species and Cultivars
Along with hosta and epimedium, astilbe forms the predominant triumvirate of perennials for the shady garden. Astilbes have attractive foliage, handsome flowers, require minimal maintenance, and their only exacting requirement is for adequate, continuous moisture. Hardy in zones 4 to 9, astilbes can grow in sun if water is abundant, but thrive in partial to moderate shade, with a fertile soil high in organic matter. When conditions are too dry, astilbes' leaves first crisp at the edges, then become dry little cornflakes. Should drought be broken by rain, new leaves will form in the same season, but such conditions really stress the plants. Astilbe flowers are excellent for cutting, and the attractive dry seed plumes may be left through the winter.

Readily available, the hybrid astilbes, *Astilbe* x *arendsii*, are as popular today as when they were developed by Georg Ahrends of Germany early this century. Hybridized from four Asian species, today we find cultivars in bloom from early June to

Astilbe chinensis 'Pumila'.

PERENNIALS

mid-August, with clear or creamy white, soft pink, shell pink, right pink, rose, or blood red flowers, on stems from 2 to 4 feet tall. About the only attribute astilbes might be said to lack is fragrance. Though all have green leaves at maturity, some astilbes have copper to bronze leaves as they emerge in the spring. This is especially frequent with deep pink- to red-flowered forms. Though new cultivars are introduced, many of the older ones (some close to a century old) have great staying power.

White-flowered cultivars include dense, erect, early-blooming, 2-foot-tall 'White Gloria' and 'Deutschland'; looser, more open,

Astilbe chinensis 'Pumila', detail.

somewhat nodding, early-flowering, 2½-foot-tall 'Bridal Veil'; similar, 3½-foot-tall 'Bergkrystall', which is slightly later blooming, in midseason; and stately, 3- to 4-foot-tall 'Professor van der Wielen' with arching, open, graceful plumes. Pink-flowered cultivars include early flowering, deep pink 'Gloria', which grows 2 foot tall; 'Reinland' which has 2-foot-tall, dense, compact, upright spikes of bright, clear pink flowers; late blooming, bright red 'Glut' (= 'Glow') which grows 2 to 2½ feet tall; 3-foot-tall 'Erica' with upright, open spikes of clear pink flowers; 3-foot-high 'Ostrich Plume' with large, arching, open sprays of coral pink flowers; and 3½-foot-tall 'Bressingham Beauty' with arching, open sprays of clear pink flowers at midseason. Red-flowered cultivars—most with copper, bronze, or mahogany leaves in the spring—include early blooming, dark crimson red 'Fanal', with dense, compact, 2-foot flower spikes; 'Garnet', which has carmine red flowers and grows 2 feet tall; late-blooming 'Feur' (='Fire'), which has feather, 3-foot spikes of coral red flowers; and 3-foot-tall 'Spinell' with open, graceful spikes of salmon red flowers.

Japonica hybrids begin the astilbe season, blooming from late spring to early summer. These cultivars include the popular 'Deutschland', with dense, erect spikes of white flowers; light pink, dense-flowered 'Europa'; and bright red 'Red Sentinel'. All are 2 feet tall, and early blooming. 'Koblenz' has deep salmon red flowers in a more open, 3-foot spike.

As well as these taller cultivars, there are some dainty miniature astilbes that are absolutely charming. Given woodsy soil and ample moisture, these *Astilbe simplicifolia* hybrids are as easy to grow as their larger relatives, merely slower-growing and maturing at 12 to 18 inches. All have sharply dissected, glossy foliage, often with bronze to mahogany hues right through the summer. Gather three or more next to a rock at the curve of a woodland path, or set them by some steps where their graceful plumes may arch over. 'Sprite' has glossy, bronzed foliage (even at maturity). Airy open sprays of shell pink flowers on 15-inch stems are followed by attractive, rusty red seed heads. Late-flowering, 12-inch-tall 'Bronze Elegance' has clear pink flowers and bronze-tinted foliage; 'Dunkellachs' has lacy, elegant mahogany leaves, and 14-inch plumes of dark, salmon pink flowers in midseason; tiny 'Willy Buchanan' grows 8 inches tall and has pink finish. Similar, *A. glaberrima* 'Saxatilis' flowers in midseason with dainty sprays of clear pink flowers on 6-inch plants.

Though the species *Astilbe chinensis* is rarely seen in gardens, its dwarf form, *A. chinensis* 'Pumila', is deservedly popular. Very late flowering, in September plants produce narrow, 8-inch panicles of crushed raspberry pink flowers. Rhizomatous, and tolerant of average moisture (though never drought), 'Pumila' is a useful ground cover. The dull-surfaced, mid-green, fernlike astilbe leaves combines nicely with the glossy, dark green, linear shape of liriope foliage, and liriopes also flower late. 'Intermezzo' has 20-inch spikes of salmon pink flowers in August and September, while 'Serenade' has 16-inch airy sprays of rose red flowers. Light pink-flowered, 2- to 2½-feet-tall, end-of-season 'Finale', once considered an arendsii hybrid, is now also classified as an *A. chinensis*.

False Goatsbeard, *Astilbe biternata*
This is a statuesque, 3- to 5-foot-tall, native North American perennial resembling an astilbe on steroids. Large panicles (branched, compound cluster of flowers) of small, creamy white flowers appear on the ends of 5- to 8-foot-tall stems, making their appearance in the late spring or early summer. The compound leaves appear alternately up the stem, each two or three times divided into sets of three leaflets that are cut and toothed along the edge. Set new plants or divide established ones in the spring, in a moist site with soil high in organic matter. Avoid placing false goatsbeard with plants that have look-alike leaves, such as aruncus, bugbane, doll's eyes, or ferns. Consider pairing this big beauty with a trio (or more) of a bold hosta such as 'Krossa Regal'.

Foxglove, *Digitalis* Species

Yellow Foxglove, *Digitalis grandiflora*
Yellow foxglove, *Digitalis grandiflora* (= *Digitalis ambigua*), is a pleasing perennial addition to the woodland garden. Evergreen rosettes of oval to lanceolate dark green leaves produce 18- to 30-inch stems of bell-like, soft, cream yellow flowers often with brown, netlike markings inside. Plants begin flowering in June, and, if kept from seed production by deadheading, will continue to flower through August. Charming in lightly shaded sites such as a woodland glade or forest edge, yellow foxglove prefers soils high in organic matter that remains moist, and is hardy in zones 4 to 7. Consider pairing it with a chartreuse hosta such as 'Lemon Lime', or one whose leaves have a creamy yellow edging such as *Hosta helenoides* 'Albopicta'.

Common foxglove, *Digitalis purpurea*, is discussed in Annuals, Biennials, and Tender Perennials, which begins on page 187.

Bugbane, *Cimicifuga* Species
The different species of summer-flowering bugbane, *Cimicifuga americana* and *C. racemosa*, are moisture-loving plants discussed in Problem Shade/Problem Trees, which begins on page 21.

Hosta
Whether we use the old name of funkia or plantain lily, or just accept hosta as both

PERENNIALS

common and Latin name, these marvelous perennials add bold foliage texture to the summer shade garden. They are available in a multiplicity of sizes from thumbnail to umbrella, and leaves that vary in color from plain green to glaucous blue or golden yellow, variegated with white or yellow as a central band or blotch, or as an attractive, contrasting edge. *Hosta* spp. and cultivars also have attractive flowers. Sturdy stems with bell-like lavender, purple, or white flowers appear in July through September, the exact time depending on the species and cultivar.

Hostas produce their leaves and flowers from a substantial crown growing just below the soil surface. Fleshy thonglike roots spread horizontally. While hostas prefer dappled shade and a regular supply of moisture, they accept conditions from full sun (but often some bleaching or burning occurs, especially with thin-leaved cultivars) to heavy shade. Extended dry periods can kill the plants. Hostas are easily propagated by division early in the spring before leaf growth begins. Dig the clump up, an arduous chore for established specimens of the larger cultivars, and hose off enough soil that you can see the

Not some rare cultivar with extremely narrow leaves, these hosta stems are all that's left when Bambi visits the salad bar in our gardens.

Hosta looks good when paired with different plants, in this case silver-splashed *Lamiastrum galeobodoleon* and *Geranium robertianum*.

purplish growing points or eyes on the crown. Small cultivars can often be divided using a pair of clippers but the big ones take more effort. With a serrated knife, saw the crown into three- to five-eye divisions. Replant promptly, taking the opportunity to rejuvenate the soil where the plants were originally growing with compost or leaf mold, and some 5-10-5 fertilizer. Water and mulch. It really is that easy.

You'd think every shade gardener would grow these sturdy plants, but there is one major problem that faces suburban and rural gardeners. Deer love hostas. Their affection is culinary, rather than aesthetic, and the varmints eat the leaf blade right off, leaving only the denuded petiole. All sorts of home remedies and repellents have been tried:

Big, bold leaved *Hosta sieboldii* looks even more massive by contrast with the dainty leaves of *Geranium robertianum*.

smelly cakes of soap hung among the plants, mesh bags of human hair, putrefied eggs in water laced with cayenne pepper and sprayed on the plants. I resorted to an electric fence. Repellents and fencing are discussed in more detail in Appendix 2, Deer, Oh Dear!

When hostas are combined with hostas, the results may be a great collection but, to my mind, not a garden. Pair them with plants having linear, straplike foliage such as liriope and sedges, and lacy-leafed plants such as ferns, astilbes, and sweet cicely. Just remember to keep things in scale—liriopes and sedges would vanish into insignificance teamed with 'Abiqua Elephant Ears', a very large *montana* x *sieboldiana* hybrid that needs a stately-leaved rodgersia as its partner.

Japanese Roof Iris, *Iris tectorum*

To my eye, Japanese roof iris is rather like a large-scale version of crested iris. Fans of fresh green leaves, 15 inches long by an inch or so wide, appear in the spring and stay through the first frosts. Branched flower stalks appear in early June, producing two or three flowers. Soft lavender, lavender spotted with blue-purple, or white, the somewhat flattish blossoms are 3 to 4 inches across. In time, the thickened greenish rhizomes hump themselves out of the ground and benefit from a nice topdressing of coarse compost in the spring and fall. Japanese roof iris grows best in somewhat acid fertile soil with adequate

moisture. Plant in the spring, and divide established clumps immediately after flowering. Large columbines make an excellent companion, both for synchronous flowering and attractive foliage combination throughout the growing season.

Sweet Cicely

Sweet cicely, *Myrrhis odorata*, is about the only herb I know that grows in the shade. The deeply cut, fernlike leaves, with just a touch of hoarfrost silver color, have a delicious licorice scent, while the ribbed, dark brown seeds have an anise flavor. Both leaves and seeds can be used for flavoring. Numerous tiny white flowers in a Queen Anne's lacelike umbel appear on 3- to 4-foot-tall stems early in the summer. Deadhead if you do not want self-sown plants to volunteer in the area. Seed should be fresh for good germination. As mature plants have fleshy, thonglike roots and transplant poorly, choose young plants and move them in the spring. I interplanted sweet cicely with *Hosta* 'Krossa Regal', quite enjoying the intermingling of

A woodland species with cool white flowers, Japanese roof iris, *Iris tectorum* 'Album', naturally prefers to grow in shade.

PERENNIALS

the hosta's vaselike form and grayish leaves with the herb's lacy leaves and delicate white flowers.

Flowers—Fall (September/October)

It is accepted as gospel truth that herbaceous woodland plants that grow in temperate climates flower in the spring. Native North American and European plants follow this pattern, having evolved in deciduous woodlands. It is to their advantage, for this period before the trees leaf out is when light is most available; however when we look at Asia, and especially Japan, the pattern changes. Though temperate, the forests of Japan are rich in broad-leaved evergreen trees and shrubs. And if there is not this seasonal shift in light availability, there is no strategic evolutionary advantage to spring bloom. Fall-flowering perennials for woodland gardens are often Japanese in origin. Perennials with attractive fruit can also add to the fall display.

Doll's Eyes and Baneberry,
Actaea pachypoda and *A. rubra*

Doll's Eyes, *A. pachypoda*
In the spring, doll's eyes, *Actaea pachypoda*, a native North American perennial, resembles an astilbe with similar leaves and a squatty white spike of flowers. Any similarity disappears in the fall when doll's eyes come into fruit—terminal, loosely spaced white berries, each with a black "eye," carried on pink pedicels. Often the cluster is heavy enough to swing the stem into a graceful curve. Lovely for woodland shade where they can have the organic-rich, moist but well-drained soil it prefers, doll's eyes make a lovely companion for any of the small- to medium-leaved white-

Fruits can be as showy as flowers, as demonstrated by doll's eyes or white baneberry, *Actaea pachypoda*, with its glistening white berries.

variegated hosta, or *Pachysandra* 'White Edge', and are also attractive arising from a carpet of Canada ginger. Avoid planting together with astilbe, bugbane, or goatsbeard, as the four plants all have look-alike leaves.

Red Baneberry, *Actaea rubra*
This perennial is equally easy to grow and very similar in leaf and flower. Its sealing-wax red berries on slender pedicels appear earlier, in July.

White Wood Aster, *Aster divaricatus*, Blue Wood Aster, *A. cordifolius*, and Large-leaved Aster, *A. macrophyllus*
The majority of daisy-flowered perennials are sun lovers, since, like grasses, they are at home in meadows and prairies. Just as there's a trio of grasses for shady sites, there's an aster trio that enhance the fall woodland.

White Wood Aster, *Aster divaricatus*
This perennial can be a bit of a thug, self-sowing with abandon. Dense root clumps and creeping rhizomes can easily be divided in the spring. Considering how this plant self-sows, especially on disturbed ground, you will need only to divide and multiply when you first begin to grow white wood asters. Moderate shade and average moisture are preferred, though plants are tolerant of dry soil that makes the species a useful ground cover for such sites. In August and September, continuing into early October, plants bear small white daisies with purplish centers, rather handsome against the dark, 2- to 3-foot-tall stems and heart-shaped, saw-toothed-edged leaves. A low rosette of leaves remains through the winter. This North American native grows wild from southern Canada through the eastern United States. One alone is sparse; plant in groups.

Blue Wood Aster, *A. cordifolius*
This aster accepts similar conditions, is also good for naturalizing, and has small, pale violet flowers in loose panicles on 4-foot-tall stems in August and September. Coarsely toothed large leaves have heart-shaped

The brilliant fruits of the red baneberry, *Actaea rubra*, make a vivid contrast against its leaves.

bases, and are carried on long petioles. Easy to transplant, established plants can be divided in the spring.

Large-Leaved Aster, *A. macrophyllus*
This aster has clusters of lavender flowers on 2½-foot-tall stems in mid- to late summer. This species colonizes with abandon.

Hardy Begonia, *Begonia grandis*
The name hardy begonia sounds like a contradiction as we think of the numerous tender kinds grown as houseplants. *Begonia grandis* (= *B. evansiana*) is a tuberous-rooted geophyte discussed in more detail in Geophytes, which begins on page 165.

Blue Cohosh, *Caulophyllum thalictroides*
Blue cohosh is a useful plant in two regards: In the spring purple-flushed shoots quickly develop thalictrumlike leaves, very functional for camouflaging dying daffodil foliage if you've interplanted the two. The small, yellowish greenish brown flowers are decidedly underimpressive and very easy to overlook when they appear in the spring. The real reason to grow this northeastern native is its fruits, large round blueberries with a whitish bloom. You'd never be tempted to eat one, for the thin skin covers a single, brown, hard seed.

Bugbane, *Cimicifuga rasmosa* and
C. simplex
Both late-blooming bugbanes, *Cimicifuga ramosa* and *C. simplex* are plants that prefer damp to moist soils. They are discussed in Problem Shade/Problem Trees, which begins on page 21.

Willow Gentian, *Gentiana asclepiadia*
Willow gentian is a plant of the Central

PERENNIALS

Inconspicuous in flower, blue cohosh, *Caulophyllum thalictroides*, has wonderful fruiting interest in the fall.

European mountains. It grows 16 to 24 inches tall, with clusters of gently arching dense leaves and stems. In late August and September each stem produces two or three flowers in a terminal cluster, with additional flowers in the upper leaf axils. The bell-like flowers are most often deep blue or light blue, though pink and white forms are also known. Willow gentian needs semishade, and a soil high in organic matter, moist but not soggy. Self-sown seedlings are easy to move, provided they are carefully dug in the spring with some soil around the roots; older plants dislike disturbance. Ferns make good companions, along with hardy begonias.

Hosta, *Hosta tardiflora*
Late-flowering hosta begins to bloom in my garden as trees first begin to drop their leaves. The tidy clumps of glossy green leaves produce a compact spike of lavender flowers, often jauntily decorated with a yellow birch leaves. I like to group a few plants of this hosta with other fall-interest plants: autumn cyclamen, *Cyclamen hederifolium*, a

geophyte with pink badminton shuttlecock flowers, and *Liriope muscari* with straplike dark green leaves and a spike of purple bead-shaped flowers, which also bloom in September.

Kirengesholma, *Kirengesholma palmata*
Kirengesholma palmata reminds one of an abutilon, that popular houseplant with big maplelike, green leaves. It has no common name other than its ponderous genus epithet, so perhaps we should give it one. How does "yellow fall bellflower" sound? Easily satisfied with part shade and a moist yet freely draining soil rich in organic matter, established plants have the stature of shrubs. In September each of the many 3- to 4-foot-tall stems produces clusters of nodding, bell-like, soft yellow flowers, a color much preferable to the harsh, taxicab yellow that marigolds display. Hardy from zones 5 to 9, plants will self-sow if cold weather holds off long enough. Blooming as late as it does, immature seed can be damaged by early frosts. One combination to consider pairs yellow fall bellflower with Japanese bugbane, *Cimicifuga japonica aserina*, whose slender white wands of flowers make a lovely embellishment.

Birch leaves are already falling as *Hosta tardiflora* blooms in the fall.

Kirengeshoma, *Kirengeshoma palmata*, comes into flower in early fall, a time of year when most perennials are focusing on approaching dormancy.

Lilyturf, *Liriope muscari*

Lilyturf may be used in a small grouping as an accent plant, or en masse as a ground cover. Requiring only an annual clipping over in the early spring, this workhorse perennial displays its tidy, straplike leaves year-round, and, as a bonus, produces attractive fall flowers. The dense spikes of purple or white flowers create an attractive renovation for the end-of-season garden, perhaps in combination with lavender, purple, violet, or white impatiens.

Nippon Lily, *Rohdea japonica*

Nippon lily might well be placed with evergreen plants or foliage plants, for its evergreen leaves are these plants' most attractive feature. The small, dense, ivory white flower cluster appears in early June, carried at ground level tucked away in the leaves, and is hardly showy. The resulting sealing-wax red berries, in a coblike cluster, add lovely color to the fall garden and remain through the winter. New growth appears in the summer. Tolerant of heavy shade and, once established, of dry sites, Nippon lily is hardier than once thought, growing quite nicely at the Arnold Arboretum in Boston, as well as in Washington, D.C., and Georgia. The typical form has smooth green leaves. There are also crested, "dragon-backed" forms and variegated ones. Exceptional forms command prices in the yen equivalent of hundreds of dollars in Japan, where there is a society devoted to the Nippon lily. Seed-raised plants are plain green, and division is slow. Ferns make the obvious partner, perhaps an evergreen species to provide year-round interest.

Blue-stemmed Goldenrod, *Solidago caesius*

If you think of goldenrods as sun-loving,

PERENNIALS

A close-up view reveals the simple beauty of kirengeshoma's yellow bell flowers.

Plants in combination. Japanese bugbane, *Cimicifuga acerina japonica*, makes a fine companion for kirengeshoma since both plants flower at the same time.

allergy-causing wildflowers, think again. They have showy flowers, indicating sticky pollen waiting for an insect to carry it from flower to flower, rather than being blown by the wind with resulting sneezing. And, one of my favorite native woodland wildflowers happens to be blue-stemmed goldenrod. This charmer has mostly unbranched, glaucous blue stems 12 to 30 inches tall, clad in light green, narrow, willowlike leaves toothed along the edge. The stems become wreathed with flowers in late September, with clusters of blooms produced in nearly every leaf axil. This is not a plant for deep shade, growing and flowering better in an edge of woodland or glade opening situation. Consider blue-stemmed goldenrod as a companion, and then successor, to willow gentian.

Toad Lily, *Tricyrtis* Species and Cultivars
With the unappealing name of toad lily it is a wonder that any tricyrtis made their way into our gardens. It makes me think of warty

brown flowers on a squatty plant. The Japanese name of *hototogisu*, for the speckled feathers on a cuckoo's breast, is far more appealing. Grow toad lilies in a lightly shaded site such as the forest edge or glade opening. Shallow rooted, they resent drying out so amend soil with compost or humus, mulch, and be sure to water whenever conditions are dry, especially in hot weather. In time they make large colonies, spreading with rhizomatous roots. It is tempting to consider dividing them but plants resent disturbance. I like them near a path, where the late season flowers can be enjoyed close up. Pair them with mid- to late-blooming white wood aster, *Aster divaricatus*, or the blue counterpart, large-leaved aster, *Aster macrophyllus*.

In the spring and summer the plants maintain a low profile. Erect or arch stems, a foot or more long depending on the species, are clothed with oval mid-green leaves. It is when they bloom in the fall that plants deserve center stage.

Tricyrtis hirta is the most familiar. Soft fuzzy leaves are the reason for its sometimes common name of hairy toad lily (even more unappealing!). Upright unbranched stems, from 1 to 3 feet tall, have clasping, broadly oblong, 5- to 6-inch-long leaves. In early to late fall several upright flowers cluster in the upper leaf axils, the place where each leaf clasps the stem. Basically white, flowers are finely speckled and spotted with purple. Var. *albescens* is an unspotted pure white selection.

Tricyrtis latifolia grows about 2 feet tall and has smoother, more heart-shaped leaves approximately 6 inches long. In the early fall branched pedicels (flower stalks) at the end of each stem and in the axils carry inch-long yellow flowers speckled inside with purple.

There is some confusion about *Tricyrtis macropoda*. Clauson and Ekstrom's *Perennials for American Gardens* says it is similar to *T. latifolia* with softer, creamy yellow flowers, Ohwi's *Flora of Japan* describes it as having purple-spotted white flowers; while the Heronswood catalog offers plants with purple-spotted, light lavender flowers. I'm more than happy to leave such entanglements to taxonomists. Whatever the true identity, it will be attractive and worth growing in your garden.

T. macranthopsis has arching rather than upright stems about 2½ feet long. When planted to drape over a low wall, it is easier to enjoy the brownish purple speckling inside radiant yellow bellflowers that dangle individually from the upper leaf axils. Leaves are smooth, and average 5 inches long. Part shade, rich soil high in organic matter, and adequate moisture are necessary for the best display. *Tricyrtis macrantha* is very similar, with somewhat smaller leaves. Flowering occurs from late summer to October.

Foliage

When choosing perennials for the shade you need to look for plants that offer more than pretty flowers. You must also consider plants for their foliage interest; otherwise, the garden will be boring after the concentrated period of spring bloom. Fortunately, some familiar shade-tolerant plants can do double duty. Spotted lungworts have attractive flowers in the spring, and silver-spotted leaves right through the worst of the winter. Flowers are almost an afterthought on hostas. Picture, if you will, *Hosta* 'Krossa Regal', a tall cultivar with grayish green leaves on long petioles, resulting in an overall vaselike form. I pair this hosta with ostrich fern, *Matteuccia pensylvannica*, which is similar in size and form to the hosta, with the lacy texture we expect of ferns. Elsewhere in my garden I combine 'Blue Cadet', which has smallish, glaucous blue leaves, with Japanese painted fern, *Athyrium nipponicum* 'Pictum', choosing this fern not only for its lacy texture but also its silvery color. There are other hostas that have been selected for their green, blue, or golden yellow leaves, often streaked, splashed, or margined with white or yellow. Foliage considerations can be carried even further, to the point of selecting plants with inconspicuous flowers and those that never flower at all. Be sure to read Foliage Effects for the Shady Garden, which begins on page 47,

PERENNIALS

to gain a better understanding of foliage and its uses in the shady garden. The following plants may have flowers, but their most important attribute is their leaves.

Ferns

In the wild, ferns don't grow in pine forests, or under hemlocks, so don't assume that the dark corner where you can't get anything else to grow is just the place for ferns. Generally they prefer conditions of dappled light, a moderately moist soil high in organic matter with good drainage. Those that grow best with really moist soil are: ostrich fern, *Matteuccia struthiopteris*; sensitive fern, *Onoclea sensibilis*; cinnamon fern, *Osmunda cinammomea*; interrupted fern, *O. claytonia*; royal fern, *O. regalis*; marsh fern, *Thelypteris palustris*; netted chain fern, *Woodwardia aureolata*; giant chain fern, *W. fimbriata*; and Virginia chain fern, *W. virginica*, all described in Problem Shade/Problem Trees, which begins on page 21, as is hay-scented fern, *Denndstaedia punctiloba*, grouped with plants for dry shade.

Maidenhair Fern, *Adiantum pedatum*
Dainty and elegant, maidenhair fern finds a welcome in every shady garden. A cluster of thin, black stems, 12 to 30 inches long, support a fan-out cluster of fingerlike branches. The shell-shaped pinnae are coppery-bronze when they first unroll in the spring, maturing to a delicate, fresh apple green. Hardy in zones 2 to 8, easy to grow, this clump-forming fern is a good mixer. I've planted maidenhair fern in an established ground cover of Japanese pachysandra, and the fern holds its own after some assistance and maintenance the first year. Another attractive combination pairs the fern with Canada ginger, *Asarum canadense*. The ubiquitous hosta is enhanced with this particular fern, as are Jack-in-the-pulpit, violets, and almost any other woodlander you care to choose. Moist to average soil, high in organic matter, in partial to heavy shade are suitable conditions. Maidenhair fern is hardy in zones 3 to 9.

Southern Maidenhair Fern, *Adiantum capillus-veneris*
More tender, southern maidenhair fern is only hardy to zone 6. Cascading, triangular, 12-inch-long, arching fronds cloak the ground, spreading from the creeping rhizome. Some discussion has been raised as to whether the plants hardy in zone 6 are truly this species, or a hybrid. Not being a pteridologist, I can't say, but I know that the plants have been in my garden for years, thriving with the usual woodland moist but well-drained, high in organic matter situation I provide. Growing on a slight slope, I also try to remember to mulch southern maidenhair's apparently evergreen fronds with pine boughs some time after Christmas, in case weather is severe and snow is lacking, a good practice for most marginally hardy perennials. If they do turn brown over the winter, I trim the damaged fronds back to the ground in the early spring before new growth begins. The typical southern maidenhair purchased from a greenhouse is definitely not hardy. Mine came, if memory serves correctly, from a North American Rock Garden Society local chapter's plant sale, source for many uncommon, good plants.

Japanese Painted Fern, *Athyrium niponicum*
Japanese painted fern 'Pictum' runs maidenhair fern a close race for "most popular fern." Readily available, easy to grow, gor-

A small concrete lantern in an oriental style shelters beneath the tall fronds of ostrich fern. In turn, the lantern is a backdrop for Japanese painted fern and European ginger.

geous, this deciduous, clump-forming fern has triangular, 8- to 16-inch fronds with burgundy red central leaf stems, and silver-gray and green pinnae. Plants in moderate shade have the best color, as too much sun bleaches them out. New fronds are produced all summer and into the early fall, as long as there is adequate moisture and fertility available to the plants. Plants grow well, and with a two- or three-fold increase in size each year. Established plants can be dug in the early spring, divided into four or five pieces, and replanted and make a good display that same year. There are several different color forms, with varying amounts of silver gray coloration, no doubt the result of plants produced from spores, as vegetative increase results in identical, cloned plants. I think Japanese painted fern is elegant with small to medium, glaucous blue-leaved hosta such as 'Halcyon', 'Hadspen Heron', or 'Blue Cadet'. White-flowered impatiens are subtle, burgundy-leaved coleus refined, black, strap-leaved *Ophiopogon planiscapus* 'Nigrescens' sophisticated partners for these charming ferns.

Autumn Fern, *Dryopteris erythrosora*

Autumn fern is another Japanese species that is popular for shady gardens. The new fronds are a handsome, glossy, bronze to coppery pink when they first appear in the spring.

PERENNIALS

They hold that color until they are fully mature in the early summer when the color turns to glossy dark green. Mature fronds are 18 to 24 inches long. Unlike many other evergreen ferns whose fronds weaken at the base and fall down in the winter, autumn fern remains proudly upright and green right through the winter. The common name comes from the color of the spore cases on the underside of the fronds, which are bright red. Autumn fern is clump forming, and hardy in zones 5 to 8. I use this fern with colchicum, for the fern fronds accent the geophytes' naked flowers, and are sturdy enough to survive the collapse of the colchicum's coarse foliage in June.

Goldie's Wood Fern, *Dryopteris goldiana*
Stately is the word that best describes Goldie's wood fern, *Dryopteris goldiana*. At 3 to 4 feet long, it is easily the biggest of our native species of wood ferns. In the spring the shaggy-haired fiddleheads, covered with brownish gold scales, uncoil and expand to form compact clumps of large, oval to triangular fronds tapering abruptly at the tip. Paler green along the edges, young fronds have an attractive, shimmery, two-tone effect. The deciduous fronds turn yellow in the fall. Over time the stocky rhizomes develop a somewhat elevated crown. Rooted firmly into place, older, established plants are difficult to move, so decide where you want it, singly as an accent or in a small group, and prepare the ground for long-term occupancy. A site in partial to full shade, high in organic matter, with adequate constant moisture is best. This fern is hardy in zones 3 to 8. Goldie's fern can cover for absent Virginia bluebells or dormant pink-flowered bleeding heart. It is stately with the giant Solomon's seal, *Polygonatum biflorum* (= *Polygonatum*

Wood ferns, the various different species of *Dryopteris*, have elegant fronds.

commutatum) whose 6-foot stems and colonizing habits allow it to hold their own with this ferny giant.

Marginal Wood Fern, *Dryopteris marginalis*
There is nothing borderline about marginal wood fern; the name merely refers to placement of the sori (spore cases) along the margin of the pinnae. Otherwise this evergreen fern is a useful addition to the shady garden. Attractive, erect to arching bluish green fronds, 18 to 30 inches long, make up the full clump that plants develop over time. Since the rhizome is slow to branch, plants tend to remain single-crowned. In the wild I find this fern growing on wooded slopes, generally next to one of the boulders that stud the Connecticut landscape. It looks particularly elegant against the granite backdrop, and I try to duplicate such settings in my garden.

Christmas Fern, *Polystichum achrostichoides*
This fern was one of the few plants that greeted me in the woods of our new house in New Jersey when first I saw it in the winter. The evergreen fronds were a sign that the soil was reasonably good, with rich moist nutrients. Christmas fern is good for slopes, as the

fronds' collapse with cold weather, coupled with their evergreen nature, helps protect the ground against erosion. In fact, a friend of mine used this fern as a ground cover, spacing plants about 15 to 18 inches apart on center, so the 1- to 2-foot leaves would blanket the area. Christmas fern is unusual among the sword ferns because its rhizomes do branch and make multicrowned plants. Older plants actually benefit if you dig them up, separate the crowns with a sharp knife, and replant, doing this in the early spring before the new croizers begin to uncoil. Christmas fern is hardy in zones 3 to 9, but grow poorly in the Pacific Northwest. That's fair enough—its northwestern counterpart grows poorly in the Northeast.

Western Sword Fern, *Polystichum munitum*
Elegant, evergreen, the western sword fern is found among the redwoods of California and the Oregon coast. The long, narrow, arching fronds grow from 3 to 5 feet tall in luxuriant clumps. Found in steep coastal canyons (Fern Valley outside Mendecino comes to mind), good drainage is a must since winter crown rot can be a problem. Once established, plants will tolerate drought but prefer moist, humus-rich soil with year-round moisture. Anything from partial shade to the Stygian gloom under giant redwoods is acceptable. One pleasing combination I saw in the wild displayed this fern's vertical fronds as an accent arising from a carpet of clover-leaved wood sorrel, *Oxalis acetosella*. Superb in northwestern gardens, this fern, though hardy in zones 6 to 9, will only languish, diminish, then die in the east.

Grasses and Grasslike Plants

Ornamental grasses are deservedly popular in gardens, valued for their elegant yet subtle linear texture and attractive flowers. Evolving as they did in the great prairies of the American Midwest, the steppes of Central Asia, and similarly sunny sites in Europe and elsewhere, familiar grasses such as miscanthus, *Miscanthus sinensis*, and pennisetum, *Pennisetum alopecuroides*, just won't grow in the shade. There are, however, a handful of players that merit a place on stage in shady gardens. These include true grasses, with leaf blades arising from swollen nodes on their hollow stems; sedges, easily distinguished by their triangular feel as you gently run your fingers up a cluster of stems; and rushes, whose growth is rounded, almost quilled. Sedges, *Carex* species, and woodrushes, *Luzula* species, are discussed in Problem Shade/Problem Trees, which begins on page 21. In addition to grasses, sedges, and rushes, do not overlook other plants with linear foliage such as lilyturf or mondo grass, *Liriope* species, or *Iris tectorum*. You'll want to use their spare pattern as a contrast to the bolder foliage of Siberian bugloss, *Brunnera macrophylla* and/or the lacy form of ferns, as discussed in Foliage Effects for the Shady Garden, which begins on page 47.

Northern Sea Oats, *Chasmanthium latifolium*
This is an excellent choice for light shade in rich, moist soil at woodland edge or a glade opening, the type of site where northern sea oats are found growing wild. Though rare, they are found in New Jersey and Pennsylvania, more frequently as you go west to Illinois and Kansas and south to Florida and Texas, so you see they are useful over much of the country. Plants grow about 3 feet tall, tidy and nicely upright, and trim, 8-inch-long, ¾-inch-wide leaves. These are an attractive soft green during the growing season, turning a rich warm brown in the fall. It is the seed heads that are northern seas oats' most attractive feature. Flattened as if pressed, each inch-long, oatlike spikelet dangles on a thin stem and trembles in the breeze. They are attractive when first formed and, while still green in early July, even more charming as they change to bronze, then tan.

PERENNIALS

If cut in the green or bronze stage, the seed heads are wonderful for fresh or dried arrangements. About the only necessary maintenance is a quick clipping down to the ground in late March before new growth begins. Of easy cultivation, northern sea oats do self-sow; however this is only a problem in a more formal garden.

Japanese Forest Grass or Hakone Grass, *Hakonechloa macra*

Japanese forest grass or hakone grass, *Hakonechloa macra* 'Aureola', is a superb grass for our gardens, thriving in partial to heavy shade. Arching, 8-inch-long, rich yellow leaves thinly striped with green form a foot-high mound. When nights turn cool in the fall— early to mid-October for me in New Jersey— the leaves become flushed with pinkish red. Slow growing, plants do best in sites high in

organic matter, moist yet well drained. If it were not for the high price that goes along with slow growth, I'd advise this as a ground cover. Even one makes a wonderful accent. Consider planting this grass as the Japanese do, in a deep forest green glazed pot. Because this shallow-rooted grass is subject to winter heaving, spring planting is advisable. You wouldn't want to take it out of the pot and plant in the garden in the fall. Plants in decorative containers need cold but frost-free conditions in the winter, perhaps in an attached, unheated garage.

Bowle's Golden Grass or Golden Wood Millet, *Milium effusum*

Bowle's golden grass, also known as golden wood millet, 'Aureum', is an upright, foot-tall, mounded, clump-forming grass with bright chartreuse yellow leaves in the

Japanese forest grass makes a soft, graceful mound, inviting a closer look as one wanders down this woodland path.

spring that turn medium green by midsummer as trees leaf out and light levels decrease. Best transplanted in the spring, the sunny new growth of this deciduous grass makes a charming accent in the shady garden. Except where summers are hot, this self-sowing grass soon makes a nice patch to complement the look-alike blue flowers of forget-me-not or Siberian bugloss, or the dark leaves of Labrador violet. Though charming with small-leaved blue hosta, Bowle's golden grass blends in and disappears if you pair it with yellow-leaved forms. If mine are an example, cats like to chew the tender leaves in the spring.

Other Perennials for Foliage Effects

Alumroot
Coralbells, *Heuchera sanguinia*, and their hybrids are familiar in gardens as flowering plants, producing airy panicles of small red or pink flowers. An occasional mention paid lip service, alluding to decorative foliage, especially when young with lighter or darker markings. At last, development and selection are being made based on the evergreen, shade-tolerant foliage, often gray-marbled or beautifully flushed with red. Leaf margins may be entire, lobed, even wavy.

Rock Geranium or Alumroot,
Heuchera americana
This alumroot can have leaves from 1½ to over 4 inches across. Typically, it is broad and somewhat ivylike, with rounded to triangular lobes, medium to dark green mottled with white. New leaves, produced all season if conditions are suitable, are often mottled with purple. Alumroot is a reliable plant needing only periodic division and replanting to keep it thrifty. In time, the woody rootstock thrusts the plant out of the ground, and should be separated and replanted with only the crown of foliage above the soil. Late summer or early

fall is a good time for this. Hardy from zones 4 to 9, alumroot grows 18 inches high and wide, needs moderate shade, and prefers average to constantly moist soil with good drainage, fertile and high in organic matter. Foliage looks best in the spring, fall, and winter, often appearing shabby in the heat of the summer, particularly in the warmer portions of its range. 'Dales Strain' has striking, silver blue marbled foliage and is drought-tolerant. This is a seed-raised strain; hence it is variable in the extent of marbling and depth of color. A cross between 'Dales Strain' and 'Palace Purple' resulted in 'Montrose Ruby', with deep, glossy, purple leaves marbled in silver. It is striking when planted with Japanese painted fern and silver-spotted lungwort. 'Garnet' has glossy, deep wine red leaves in the winter, and even brighter garnet red new leaves in the spring. Hardy in zones 5 to 9, plants prefer even moisture but accept dry conditions in shade. Fading in heavy shade, light shade, or sun results in the most intense leaf coloration. 'Pewter Veil' has purple-flushed, coppery pink new leaves hazed with silver and accentuated with silver veining, turning pewter silver as leaves mature. Hardy in zones 4 to 9, the evergreen leaves can reach 6 inches across.

If you are curious, what fun to try some of the most recent cultivars of alumroot in your garden. 'Eco-magnififolia' has a silver gray leaf with a dark gray edge, all streaked along the veins with red. Tolerant of heat and humidity, leaves are semievergreen. Especially dark-leaved cultivars include 'Chocolate Ruffles' with a somber dark upper surface, burgundy beneath, with some ruffling along the edges to reveal the brighter color; 'Chocolate Veil' with smooth, dark leaves up to 8 inches across, highlighted with purple; and 'Velvet Night', again with exceptionally dark leaves and purple accents.

Small-flowered Alumroot,
Heuchera micrantha
This would hardly be given a place in the

PERENNIALS

garden for its aptly named flowers are minute. Rather, it is the heart-shaped, multilobed leaves, from 2 to 4 inches long, beautifully gray-marbled, which are the plant's best feature. Native to the Pacific Coast, from British Columbia to Sierra Nevada, small-flowered alumroot dislikes especially hot summers and cold, snowless winters. Even temperatures, adequate, even moisture, and partial shade are preferred. Though hardy from zones 4 to 8, winter protection in zones 4 and 5 is necessary. Small-flowered alumroot is more often used as a parent in the development of garden-worthy cultivars and hybrids.

H. americana, H. micrantha

One such selection is 'Palace Purple', about which controversy still storms. Is it *H. americana*, *H. micrantha*, or a hybrid? Taxonomists care, but gardeners are unlikely to worry, having found a handsome foliage plant with large, lobed, deep purple leaves. Color is deepest in the cooler temperatures of the spring and fall, fading to olive drab in the summer. Seed-raised plants also vary in the depth and richness of coloration. To maintain the superior forms, those with the best color should be propagated asexually, by division or tissue culture. In a more formal design, think of 'Palace Purple' together with the black, straplike leaves of *Ophiopogon planiscapus* 'Arabicus', accented with clear red impatiens for an exciting combination of foliage and flowers. Or, 'Palace Purple' with the purple-flushed leaves of Labrador violet, and frothy mass of chartreuse flowers on lady's mantle.

Heuchera villosa

Yet another species, *Heuchera villosa*, does not have fancifully colored gray or purple leaves.

Rather, the leaves of hairy alumroot are large, a fresh clear green, cleft into triangular lobes, and pleasantly, softly stubbled. Hardy from zones 6 to 9, this large-leaved southern species (native to Arkansas, Tennessee, Kentucky, and the Appalachian Mountains) is more tolerant of summer heat than the others described here. It pairs beautifully with the compound leaf of astilbe, red baneberry, *Actaea rubra*, or doll's eyes, *A. pachypoda*, and is useful for disguising the absence of summer-dormant ephemerals.

Lungwort

Spotted Lungwort, *Pulmonaria saccharata*

An old-fashioned plant that had fallen into neglect, I'm glad to see the resurgent popularity of spotted lungwort, *Pulmonaria saccharata*. Silver-spotted leaves provide a decorative touch to the shaded garden, and variation in the intensity and quantity of spotting allows the discerning gardener to have his or her own "house selection." The softly hairy leaves are longer than wide, up to 8 inches long by 3½ inches wide, tapering toward the petiole that adds as much as 4 inches to the overall length. Spotting is always larger, sometimes overlapping blotches. Some plants have leaves nearly entirely silver with a thin green margin. Narrow, bell-like flowers appear that in spring are pink in bud, maturing to a clear sky blue. Mildew can be a problem in humid summer weather. Leaves become covered with a fuzzy gray coating, but are not harmed. If the sight distresses you, cut plants down to the ground and feed lightly with a liquid fertilizer. New growth is usually unaffected. Otherwise, plants are mostly trouble-free, needing only a shaded, sufficiently moist site with humus-rich soil in zones 3 to 8. Transplant self-sown plants after

Perennials can be quite at home in your shady garden.

Pulmonaria longifolia

Pulmonaria longifolia has the familiar dark green, silver-spotted leaves, but they are strikingly different in shape, being six times as long as they are wide, and very pointed. Crowded racemes of purplish blue flowers appear somewhat later than the other lungworts. Hardy from zones 4 to 8, this long-leaved lungwort is more tolerant of summer heat and humidity than the other species. 'Bertram Anderson' is a cultivar with vivid blue flowers and narrow, silver-spotted leaves, as 'Roy Davidson' has.

New cultivars of lungwort with elegant leaves are gaining approval for their commendable enhancement of shady gardens: 'British Sterling' has luxuriously silver leaves with a very minimum of dark green contrast; 'Excaliber' is mildew-resistant, and has silver leaves that are narrowly margined in dark green, with some speckling where the two colors adjoin, 'Milky Way' has large, heavily silver-spotted leaves and wine red flowers, 'Spilled Milk' has silver leaves with a small amount of irregular dark green mottling. Rose red buds fade to pink as the flowers open, 'Little Star' has long, thin, dark green, lanceolate leaves suggestive of *P. longifolia* parentage, strewn with tiny white spots and silver blotches, and large, cobalt blue flowers when in bloom.

If the simple shape of lungwort is paired with the simple shape of a hosta, even one with a white-streaked or margined leaf, there is little contrast of shape; instead, a more intricate, complex leaf should be chosen to set the two apart. There are two possibilities: For example, either allow the silver-spotted or -mottled leaf of the lungwort to become the dominant factor, and choose evergreen Christmas fern, or select silver-gray Japanese painted fern. The disparity of shape remains the same, enhanced with the elegance of silver fern and mercury-spotted lungwort.

the foliage matures when they move most readily without wilting. If the lungworts must be moved sooner, cut some of the leaves in half (crosswise, not lengthwise) to reduce transpiration losses and wilting. There are several fine cultivars among which to choose: 'Sissinghurst White' has white flowers, but the leaf markings are mediocre; 'Margery Fish' is vigorous with particularly nicely silver-spotted, long, elliptical leaves; 'Janet Fisk' has bright, light, white-marbled leaves, 'Mrs. Moon' is an old, adored cultivar with large, well-spotted, silver-dappled leaves. It may be a hybrid with common lungwort.

Spotted lungwort can be confused with common lungwort, *Pulmonaria officinalis*. The leaves of common lungwort are heart-shaped and do not taper toward the petiole. They have smaller, quite regular spots, and the flowers are red to rose violet or blue. 'Cambridge' (= 'Cambridge Blue') has silver-spotted heart-shaped leaves and masses of pale blue flowers.

PERENNIALS

Foam Flower

While foam flower, *Tiarella cordifolia*, is discussed in Ground Covers and Vines, which begins on page 111, there are some recent foliage selections that are effective when used as specimen or accent plants. Use these cultivars in zones 3 to 8, placing them at the edge of a path, together with small hosta, smaller ferns, violets, primroses, epimedium and bleeding heart for foliage contrast. Foam flowers' blossoms, while lovely, are here considered as a bonus. *Tiarella cordifolia* 'Montrose' has tidy clumps of maplelike leaves marbled in purple. In mid- to late spring small spires of soft pink flowers add to the display. I particularly like 'Montrose' with the spotted leaves of *Pulmonaria saccharata*, and with bleeding hearts. 'Oakleaf' has dark green, distinctly lobed, serrated leaves, and good fall color. The creamy, pinkish white flowers in May to June provide a long period of bloom. 'Eco Rambling Tapestry' is also a vigorous, spreading foam flower, with a deep burgundy purple blotch in the center of each bright green, slightly puckered leaf. 'Tiger Stripe' has glossy leaves heavily splashed with purplish red.

Tiarella wherryi

Tiarella wherryi is a clump-forming plant without any stolons, making it even more suitable as an accent plant. 'Dunvegan' has deeply cut, palmately dissected, velvety, medium green leaves that form a tidy clump. Suitable for shaded to partially shaded sites, production of the pinkish white flowers is better with more light. 'Eco Red Heart' is a selection with medium green heart-shaped leaves that have a remarkable burgundy blotch in the center. Abundant light pink to white flowers appear from May to June. 'Eco Splotched Velvet' also has green leaves with red centers and a soft velvety texture.

An interesting cross with *Tiarella trifoliata* (whose leaves are three-lobed) has resulted in 'Filigree Lace', with finely serrated, multi-lobed leaves that have dark lines penciled down the center along the main veins, and airy white flowers.

Elegant as an accent plant, *Tiarella wherryi* is a clump-forming, non-spreading foam flower.

GEOPHYTES

Everybody's favorite, snowdrops make a white cascade in early spring.

GEOPHYTES

Winter aconite, close up.

Winter ends, and only the last remnants of snow persist in shady hollows. The first small geophytes pierce the frozen ground, assurance of the spring season that will follow. *Geophyte* is a convenient noun, an umbrella under which shelter true bulbs, corms, and tubers. Stored within their lumpy underground structures are food reserves that give these early flowers a head start before more moderate conditions arrive. This early growth indeed encourages impatient gardeners. Many spring-blooming geophytes are like well-behaved house guests—they arrive, flower, complete their cycle of growth, and then depart in time for other herbaceous perennials to take center stage. The geophytes can readily be combined with shrubs, adding interest to the earliest-blooming kinds, and providing color and interest

beneath bare branches. Geophytes shelter nicely beneath a carpeting ground cover. In partnership with perennials, geophytes add their own special charm. All it takes is a little advance planning, and the selection of appropriate varieties of geophytes, perennials, ground covers, and shrubs.

For most attractive results, the small, familiar, spring-blooming species of geophytes are best planted with a lavish hand—never fewer than 10, 25 is a good number, but hundreds are admirable. Generally, their small size is matched by a modest price. Even so, if you covet masses of geophytes but budget constraints limit your horticultural greed, take heart. Many are "good doers" and, when planted in a suitable site, multiply quite rapidly either by seed or off-set, or both.

Early Spring

Persian Violets, *Cyclamen coum*

The Persian violet, *Cyclamen coum*, is an early visitor, or a lingering one, depending on your point of view. It makes its presence known along about September, when rounded to heart-shaped leaves, elegantly marked with silver, appear. At the same time the tuber-corms set their flower buds. Winter arrives, with snow and freezing temperatures. No matter, the cyclamen leaves are close to the ground, perhaps mulched with fallen leaves. Plump flowers resembling somewhat flattened badminton shuttlecocks of vivid cerise pink open in late February in my New Jersey garden, earlier in the Southeast. Plants go dormant along about June, to repeat the cycle again in a few weeks time.

Hardly among the most common geophytes, Persian violet is well worth the search.

Persian violets like moist but well-drained sites, drier in summer, with humus-rich soil. They even tolerate the dark dry shade beneath beech trees. In suitable locations, plants set seed freely once they are established. Each seedling plant develops a little pearl of a tuber-corm, with a tiny, solitary leaf tethered by a threadlike stem. They can be carefully dug up and replanted in a nursery area, with less competition and more attention to watering. You'll get a greater number of flowering-sized plants this way than if you leave the seedlings to make it on their own. Seed is the only means of increase, as this geophyte makes no offsets. A bright, first spring color scheme would be to combine Persian violets with winter aconites and spring snowflakes, all nestled together with Christmas rose, *Helleborus niger*.

Snowdrops, *Galanthus*

Certainly one of the most familiar early geophytes is the common snowdrop, *Galanthus nivalis*. My father said that for him its name was *schneeglockchen*, tiny bells in the snow, the name he learned as a child in Germany. Called *perce neige*, snow piercer, in France, and fair maids of February in England, snowdrops obviously are regarded with affection in many places. Among the best of the little bulbs for naturalizing in woodland, or in shaded borders, snowdrops' dainty white flowers have a delicate scent of honey, best appreciated close up. Found wild in open woodland throughout central Europe to the Balkans and Russia, one of the first plants into bloom, snowdrops perform reliably, unharmed by frost or snow. The leaves and flower bud emerge together in a sturdy bundle, piercing through frozen soil. A solitary flower dangles on a wire-fine pedicel, three clean white petals surrounding a central tube tipped with green. Insignificant by ones and twos, masses of snowdrops in an established

As though nestled up for protection, a mass of snowdrops cuddles to an oak tree.

GEOPHYTES

For all its dainty size, snowdrops have a bravura character. After all, they freeze, yet flower all the same, unharmed.

planting are an unforgettable sight. One such stands out in memory—literally hundreds of flowers emerging from the carpeting, glossy, dark green foliage of running myrtle, *Vinca minor.*

Snowdrops are readily available at local nurseries in the fall. They should be promptly purchased and equally promptly planted when they arrive at the nursery, around Labor Day. Small geophytes shrivel and dry up more quickly than larger ones. The brown-jacketed snowdrop bulbs have a basal plate at the bottom from which the roots emerge. Plant in humus-rich, average to moist but well-drained soil, at a depth twice that of the bulb's height. Snowdrops in an established planting can be readily moved soon after flowering while their leaves are still in good condition. Dig and replant with the same care you would provide any other actively growing herbaceous perennial.

I like snowdrops in multitudes, perhaps at the base of a mature, mossy-trunked oak in my woods, or, in smaller groups, with the chaste white flowers of Christmas rose, *Helleborus niger.* One of the most vigorous cultivars I grow is the green-tipped snowdrop, *G. nivalis* 'Viridapicis', which differs from the species in having green markings at the tip of the three outer petals. A clump I dug that had been in for a number of years contained over a hundred bulbs, packed three layers deep. Mind, they'd been flowering well enough as they were; I just thought I'd move some elsewhere. Soon enough I was stuffing them in all around the garden, feeling rather like a squirrel barraged with too many acorns. But ah, the next spring there were snowdrops in all sorts of magical places where I'd forgotten having planted them.

The giant snowdrop, *G. elwessi*, is also superb, a couple of weeks earlier in bloom, larger flowers with a green blotch at both base and tip of the inner tube—sometimes the markings run together—and gray-green leaves. Not as easy to find in the marketplace, the giant snowdrop is well worth the search. It, too, multiplies by offsets and seed, and adds its early flowers to the garden's declaration of spring.

Spring Snowflake, *Leucojum vernum*
Similar at the first hasty glance, a closer look reveals the differences between snowdrops and spring snowflake, *Leucojum vernum.* The flowers of spring snowflake look like starched petticoats, plump green-tipped bells of flowers, one, perhaps two, to a stem. Their leaves are also a brighter, more grass green color than the grayish green of snowdrop foliage. Spring snowflake likes a moist site, one that never becomes dry, even in the summer when they are dormant. Bulbs multiply underground by offsets, in time making large clumps that can be lifted and separated for

immediate replanting as the flowers fade in the spring.

Winter Aconite, *Eranthis hiemalis*

Winter aconite is one of my favorite flowers of first spring. Bright yellow buttercups of flowers open in late February, one to a stem with a tidy saw-toothed green ruff of foliage as an accent. Alas, the dried tubers available in the fall are usually so dried out that they often fail to grow; only about 5 out of 25 make their appearance the following spring. But all is not in vain, for those five will produce generous amounts of tan, BB-sized seeds, all of which seem to germinate the next year, and reach flowering size the year after that. Plants in growth—"in the green" as the English call it—can be transplanted

Cats dislike snow more than winter aconite, which will bloom before spring truly arrives.

around the garden with ease. Because winter aconites flower so early, there really is not much in growth to combine them with, except for other geophytes. Try a planting of winter aconite with spring snowflake, perhaps with several green-flowered bear's foot hellebore, *Helleborus foetidus*, behind which are the polished red-barked stems of red-twig dogwood, *Cornus alba*.

Spring

By late March or early April the second surge of spring begins to crest, and all sorts of small geophytes enhance the shady garden. By now, the first of the herbaceous perennials begin their blooming period, and the imaginative gardener has more options and possibilities for plant combinations with geophytes.

Glory-of-the-snow, *Chionodoxa luciliae*

Glory-of-the-snow has its common name for its habit of blooming in the wake of retreating snow in the mountains of Turkey. In gardens it would be unusual indeed to see its blue flowers against a coverlet of snow. No matter, the upward-facing blue flowers with a white eye are welcome against a mulch of last year's brown leaves. Bulbs are readily available in the fall, and accept the move into a new location with ease. Once settled in, these glory-of-the-snow will self-sow and create a gently flowing tide across the forest floor (even if the "forest" consists of a single dogwood tree).

The March Walk at Winterthur, in Maryland, is the result of 50 years of self-propagation: glory-of-the-snow following winter aconites and snowdrops, followed in turn a couple of weeks later by scillas, replaced in turn by wood hyacinths, then summer's rest.

Blue and chartreuse is a favorite color combination of mine, so I combine bear's foot hellebore with glory-of-the-snow. The geophyte is a fine companion for Lenten rose,

GEOPHYTES

The viburnum's berries remain from last fall as glory-of-the-snow bursts into bloom in welcome of spring.

Helleborus x *orientalis*, whose flowers may be apple green, white, pale pink, or plum red. I particularly like the deep, darker colored hellebores with 'Pink Giant', a large, clear pink-flowered cultivar of glory-of-the-snow.

Siberian Squill, *Scilla sibirica*

Many gardeners know Siberian squill, perhaps noticing the blue flower shadows over the thin grass of a somewhat shaded lawn. Really thick turf is a problem, and the bulbs

A crisp Delft color scheme of white and blue is created with bloodroot and Siberian squill.

will weaken and decline. Perhaps in an older garden you've seen bulbs nestle amid shrubs, adding their display to the first azalea blossoms. Three to five nodding flowers fill the spike, and bulbs often send up more than one flower stem. Siberian squills are excellent for the vermin-ridden garden, for nothing eats them—not chipmunks, not rabbits, not deer. Like snowdrops, they seem immune to depredation. The dark purplish blue-jacketed bulbs are readily purchased in the fall, and easily planted in any rich, reasonably well-drained, fertile soil. Combine Siberian squill with bloodroot, *Sanguinaria canadensis*, for a charming, crisp, blue and white display. The bloodroot's leaves remain through the summer, filling the space left vacant by the dormant bulbs.

Siberian squill has a "cousin," an earlier flowering, much paler species with a nearly unpronounceable name, *Scilla mischtschenkoana*. This free-flowering little scilla has flowers as pale as skim milk, with a

In detail, glory-of-the-snow has flowers of an electrifying, luminous blue.

turquoise line down the center of each petal. The effect of the early spring sunlight streaming through the translucent petals is charming.

Guinea Hen Flower, *Fritillaria meleagris*
This geophyte is a quiet charmer. The sturdy pendant bells on narrow-leaved slender stems are checkered in a fine mosaic of purple and white. Some plants have flowers so suffused with purple that the markings blur, others are lightened to white with faint, green, ghostly markings. The small, few-scaled bulbs lack a tunic or covering. When purchased in the fall the base of the bulb has a beard of dried-out roots. The small size,

lack of tunic, and permanent roots suggest planting sooner, rather than later. Guinea hen flowers like damp sites, so that low spot that never dries out in the woods is a good location. They happily accept average moisture also; just avoid planting them in sites that dry out in summer. Plant at least 25, using them in groups of 5 to 10, even in the smallest garden. Try a clump of guinea hen flowers with Lenten roses in pink or plum, or use one of the green-flowered hellebores. I have a small, fuchsia-colored violet that a client gave me several years ago. It doesn't seem to seed, just makes an ever-enlarging elegant clump with the more somber hue of guinea hen flowers.

GEOPHYTES

You'll agree that *Scilla mischtschenkoana* has a hard-to-pronounce name, but this early flowering relative of the familiar Siberian squill is just as valuable in shady gardens.

Dog-tooth Violets, *Erythronium* Species and Cultivars

Perhaps in northeastern forests you've seen our native dog-tooth violet as large patches of green and brown mottled leaves, with here and there a solitary yellow flower resembling a miniature lily. This is not the best species for the garden, as flowering is sparse for the number of plants that are growing. Cultivars of the European dog-tooth violet, *E. dens-canis*, are far more satisfactory.

There are some charmingly named forms of dog-tooth violets: 'Frans Hals' has mottled leaves and large, pale purple flowers; 'Lilac Wonder' has soft lavender to darker, purple flowers; 'Purple King' has heavily mottled leaves and large, deep plum purple flowers, mottled brown and white in their center; 'Rose Queen' has mottled leaves and deep pink flowers, 'Snowflake' has pure white flowers and mottled leaves; 'Charmer' has white petals with a brown blotch at the base. These cultivars are quite hardy, to zone 3. The Japanese dog-tooth violet, *E. dens-canis* var. *japonicum* is an excellent, vigorous plant, with violet-purple flowers.

Two attractive yellow-flowered hybrids are 'Jeannine', with large, clear sulfur yellow flowers, marked at the center with a pale brown ring that fades with age; and 'Kondo', with lightly mottled leaves and light yellow flowers, again with a brown marking in the center.

Another species of dog-tooth violet with several beautiful cultivars for the garden is *E. revolutum*, from northern California up into Oregon. 'Citronella' has mottled leaves and cool, lemon yellow flowers; 'Pagoda' has leaves with bronze markings and sulfur yellow flowers with a plum-colored blotch at

The charming flowers of dog-tooth violet are handsome *en masse*, and also effective in smaller groupings.

A mass planting of dog-tooth violet, *Erythronium* 'Pagoda', creates a lovely effect in this Dutch garden.

the base of each petal; 'White Beauty' has heavily mottled, white-veined leaves and large white flowers with a yellow center. *E. tuolumnense*, a species from central California, has plain green leaves and small, bright yellow flowers veined with green. It is among the earliest to flower. Both of these West Coast species are hardy to zone 5.

This little geophyte is occasionally offered at nurseries in the fall. The pointed, fleshy corms readily dry out, and are also easily bruised, requiring gentle handling and prompt planting. Their corms resent disturbance, and generally flower poorly the spring after they have been moved, even if it is within the same garden. Dog-tooth violets need woodland conditions with moist but well-drained, fertile soil, dappled light with ample moisture in the spring, and shade in the summer when they are dormant. They bloom in April.

Epimedium, ferns, and hosta are suitable companions, their leaves expanding to fill the space left bare when the dog-tooth violets go dormant in June.

Daffodils, *Narcissus* Species and Cultivars

Whether you call them daffodils, narcissus, or jonquills, *Narcissus* species and cultivars are excellent bulbs for the shady garden. It doesn't matter if you plan an informal, natu-ralistic design, or a more formal, precise,

orderly display, daffodils can work in either design style. Plant groups of ten in an orderly display marching through an evergreen ground cover, even those as vigorous as pachysandra or English ivy. Plant an irregular drift among birches for a casual, country garden effect. Daffodils bloom early enough to flower and come back even under mature oaks. A simple, reduced-maintenance design would have dogwoods as understory trees, evergreen rhododendrons for shrubs, and scattered groups of daffodils adding color as the dogwoods begin to bloom. Herbaceous perennials to complete the picture might include Siberian bugloss, epimedium, astilbe, and hosta.

A good value for the money, many if not all daffodil cultivars not only come back year after year, they multiply while they are at it. About the only thing they don't like, in common with almost all geophytes, is excessive moisture while they are dormant. Again, like snowdrops, critters don't eat daffodils. If deer eat your tulips, the adjoining daffodils will be untouched.

A soft, pleasing combination pairs *Erythronium* 'White Beauty' with the plum-colored flowers of *Helleborus* x *orientalis* 'Early Purple Group.'

GEOPHYTES

Daffodils are marvellous bulbs. Attractive, hardy, reliable—and pests leave them alone!

There are so many cultivars, in ten different divisions, plus another just for the wild species, that singling out this daffodil or that one seems unreasonable. There are trumpet daffodils, the kind we buy as cut flowers as a sign winter is almost over. They perform better in cold winter regions, the Northeast, the northern tier of states, the Midwest, than they do in the Deep South. They have a single flower to the stem and a trumpet equal to or longer than the perianth segments. These days 'King Alfred', thought of as the standard yellow, is more often a King Alfred type, with 'Dutch Master' or 'Golden Harvest' supplied instead. No matter, these are the yellow daffodil of Wordsworth. But not all trumpet daffodils are yellow. 'Beersheba' has excellent, pure white flowers; 'Mount Hood' starts off with white petals and a trumpet the color of old, yellowed ivory, fading to white at maturity; 'Spellbinder' has petals of that hard-boiled egg yolk color, a greenish, sulphur yellow, and a white trumpet, showy and effective in the more formal landscape.

Short-cupped daffodils have one flower to a stem, with the trumpet reduced to a cup only one-third the length of the perianth segments. They repeat well in the landscape, reliably coming back year after year. 'Barrett Browning' is early flowering, white with an orange-red cup; 'White Lady' with white petals and a yellow cup has been around in gardens for over a century.

I find the cyclamineus hybrids, which reveal their parentage by the swept-back angle of their perianth in relation to the trumpet, are highly satisfactory both in their appearance and perennial character. 'February Gold' may not bloom that early—late March or early April is more like it—but this sturdy 12- to 14-inch-tall yellow daffodil has been a reliable member of my garden for close to 20 years; 'Jenny' is a bit smaller, opens creamy, ivory white then fades to pure white at maturity; 'Dove Wings' is similar. I like either of these coming through pink lungwort, *Pulmonaria rubra*, with a soft blue grape hyacinth, *Muscari armeniacum* 'Cantab', or as a cool companion to bear's foot hellebore.

Not all daffodils are yellow. *Narcissus poeticus* has crisp white petals.

Poeticus narcissus, with white petals and a short ruffle of a cup banded red at the edge, then yellow, last green, also seems to accept neglect. 'Actaea', 'Cantabile', and 'Felindre' add fragrance to their good looks and are charming in combination with biennial white-flowered honesty, *Lunaria annua*, in May.

Southern gardeners do better with jonquilla and tazetta hybrids, which are better adapted to hot summers and mild winters. There are several jonquilla cultivars named for birds: bright orange-cupped, yellow-petalled 'Bunting'; lemon yellow-cupped white-petaled 'Canary'; 'Curlew' with ivory white cup and petals, white-cupped yellow petalled 'Dickcissel', and rich metallic yellow 'Quail', all with several small, fragrant flowers to a stem, flowering mid- to late in the daffodil season. Tazettas, used for forcing in the north, have numerous strongly scented flowers to each stem: 'Cragford' has a charming small orange cup and luminous white petals; 'Geranium' is similar.

The checkerboard markings of the guinea hen flower create a distinctive pattern on the boxy, bell-like flowers.

Muscari, Grape Hyacinths, *Muscari*
Species

Grape hyacinths are vigorous, bold, and a bit thuggish. Their leaves come up in the fall and flop around all winter getting a bit chewed up by the cold weather. With the arrival of spring, the bulbs send up flower spikes that somewhat resemble miniature hyacinths. Grape hyacinth has more bead-like, rounded flowers, somewhat constricted at the mouth. They're usually a rich smoky blue, though white forms are also available. If you find the blue grape hyacinths invasively spreading, as they grow by both seed above ground and bulb offsets below ground, go for the white as it is more restrained in habit.

Grape hyacinths make good markers for other bulbs. Their fall leaves will remind you where those daffodils were planted last year. They make a pleasing partner for all

Grape hyacinths are safe with real rabbits, not just a statue.

GEOPHYTES

A pot of grape hyacinths makes an attractive addition to the garden.

sorts of woodland perennials, from the short-lived Canada columbine, *Aquilegia canadensis,* to the more permanent garden residents such as bear's foot hellebore, *Helleborus foetidus.* Another advantage for those who garden in deer country, as do I, is that grape hyacinths are not eaten by those overgrown rats with cloven hooves. Plant grape hyacinths in bright shade, allowing them room to run.

Coda

Gardeners tend to categorize their plants—this is an herb, that's a perennial. Similarly, we class as "bulbs" those geophytes that arrive from Holland, and native geophytes are categorized as "wildflowers." Lumpy underground roots are lumpy underground roots, and geographic origin has

The smoky blue flowers of grape hyacinth make a pleasing combination when paired with Canada columbine.

nothing to do with it. Certain of our herbaceous woodland native plants have fibrous roots, and may be appropriately classed as perennials. Others have tuberous, cormous, or bulbous roots, and are properly assigned to geophyte.

Jack-in-the-pulpit, *Arisaema triphyllum*

When in flower, Jack-in-the-pulpit is an unmistakable plant. The green or brown hood, properly named a spathe, rises protectively over the erect spadix it encloses. Three leaflets form a "T" arrangement. If you have a plant with a single set of leaflets, it is a male. But when the self-same plant gains maturity and the underground tuber stores more food, it will send up two sets of leaflets and flowers as a female. Females (should we call them Jill-in-the-pulpit?) produce vibrant red berries in the fall. Though subdued in foliage and flower, our native *Arisaema* is useful in the garden as it grows in shaded, moist soils, preferably high in organic matter. Untouched by mice, rabbits, deer, or other vermin, consider a combination of Jacks and Jills with fern, astilbe, gingers both evergreen and deciduous, as well as naturally occuring flowering woodland partners such as bloodroots and violets.

As well as species native to North America (a second species, the green dragon or *Arisaema draconitum*, is native to the southeastern states) there are 20 or 30 species from China, Japan, and the Himalayas that are becoming increasingly popular, and more readily available. Perhaps the best is snow-rice cake plant, *Arisaema sikokianum*, with a jauntily erect chocolate brown spathe surrounding a snow white, club-like spadix. Easy to grow, snow-rice cake plant is still on the pricey side for mass groupings. It is, however, quite easily raised from seed, if you can obtain any.

Dicentra, *Dicentra* Species

Dutchman's breeches, *Dicentra cucullaria*, received its common name for the fanciful

Maybe you think all bulbs come from Holland. A quick look at the Jack-in-the-pulpit shows this woodland native has a sturdy tuber nestled underground.

resemblance of its small, two-horned, yellow-mouthed, white flowers to pants hung on the washline to dry. Among the first of our woodland natives to flower, ferny gray-green leaves emerge in April from a true bulb that resembles clustered grains of rice. In the wild I find plants growing on open stony slopes, and I mimic their habitat by planting them on a slope in my garden. Over time, the bulbs have increased, spilling downhill in company with primroses and early trilliums. After flowering plants go dormant in late May or early June, this is another of those ephemerals that come early, then rest until the next spring comes around.

Squirrel Corn, *Dicentra canadensis*

This is a close relative, with similar leaves, white locket-shaped flowers, and a bulb

GEOPHYTES

Perhaps we should say "Jill-in-the-pulpit" for this Jack-in-the-pulpit has a rich array of striking red berries in fall, showing it is a female plant.

Jack-in-the-pulpit has three leaflets, as does trillium. Here they are arrayed in a "T" arrangement rather than equally spaced as in trillium.

that looks like the clustered kernels of mustard-yellow field corn. I like squirrel corn in partnership with the glossy, dark green, rounded leaves of European ginger, *Asarum europeum*.

Bloodroot, *Sanguinaria canadensis*

Fortunately, bloodroot has attractive leaves. The flowers are quite pretty, eight-petaled white daisies with a squarish outline but they last for less than a week, and four or five days of bloom hardly secures them space in the garden. If you choose bloodroot for its handsome orbicular, more- or fewer-lobed, grayed green leaves, then the brief period of bloom becomes a welcome bonus. The horizontal tubers grow just below the soil surface, forking and spreading to create expanding clumps. Plants also readily increase by seed. I like bloodroot as foliage contrast to a carpet of running myrtle, *Vinca minor*, or in combination with ferny and linear leaves—astilbe, ferns, and epimedium

178

The dainty white flowers and ferny leaves of Dutchman's breeches have a clear relationship to other species of dicentra.

Though the name, and the bulb, might lead you to think it came from Holland, this little woodland gem is native to North America.

for the former, liriope for the latter. There is an exquisite double-flowered form like a miniature peony, *S. canadensis* 'Multiplex'. Sterile, it can only be increased by division. This is also necessary for the health of the colony, as congested tubers may begin to rot. Division is best done as the leaves begin to yellow in the early fall. Separate plants at the fork, making sure there are one or two healthy shoots for next year's growth to

each division, and replant promptly. When cut, the tubers ooze an orange-red sap—so do broken stems for that matter.

Trillium, *Trillium* Species

Trillium cuneatum
Earliest of the trillium I've grown, *Trillium cuneatum* appears in March, flowering late that month or early in April. One year, a colder than usual frost turned their stems

Choice (and expensive!) double bloodroot is sterile, and consequently its flowers last longer than those of the single form.

A small colony of bloodroots looks quite charming. Remember though, the flowers last for only a few days.

179

GEOPHYTES

and leaves to rigid icy lumps, limp when they thawed the following morning. I was certain I'd lost that season's growth, but every single one came back and flowered, revealing an unexpected resilience. These are sessile trillium, with a single, three-petalled, dark, oxblood red flower perched directly on the whorl of mottled dark and light green leaves, also three in number. Flowers never open very wide, resembling a candle flame.

Plants are vigorous, in time sending up two, three, even four flower stems from each tuber. Fresh seed germinates well, and a careful search each spring reveals any number of tiny, single, spade-shaped mottled leaves from the seed I pushed into the ground around the parent plants two years earlier. These are triumphantly dug, lined out in a nursery bed for additional growth, then replanted in the garden when of blooming size. The mixed community in that part of my garden often overwhelms first-year trillium seedlings. These other plants include another geophyte, Grecian windflower, *Anemone blanda* 'White Splendour' with

Trillium cuneatum, with *Anemone blanda* 'White Splendour'.

white, daisylike flowers; ajuga with its ground-covering mats of foliage and spikes of rich blue flowers in May; and *Phlox divaricata*, with soft blue flowers. By the time Japanese maples are leafing out in early May, the flowers of *T. cuneatum* are fading to a softer, green-tinged maroon, attractive beneath the red-leaved Japanese maples. Trillium are usually offered as wild-collected plants, a practice that should be determinedly discouraged for the destructive pressure it places on wild populations. Deer eat any species of trillium, flower and foliage, to which they have access. This not merely spoils the display; loss of foliage seriously weakens the plants.

Trillium luteum
Very similar in overall appearance, though a month later in growth and flower, *Trillium luteum* has pale chartreuse to soft primrose yellow flowers that have a citrus scent. I like them emerging from a ground cover of soft blue- or lavender-flowered creeping phlox, *P. stolonifera*. Small, golden-leaved hosta such as 'Kabitan' or 'Wogan Gold' make charming companions.

Great White Trillium, *Trillium grandiflorum*
Great white trillium differs from the preceding species in that it is a pedunculate trillium, having a short peduncle or stem between the more widely opening flowers and plain green leaves. Dr. Richard Lighty of the Mt. Cuba Center for the Study of Piedmont Flora has selected a vigorous clone and named it 'Quicksilver'. It is believed that this can be multiplied briskly enough to supply eager gardeners with propagated (as opposed to wild-collected) plants. The snow-white flowers appear in early May, charming in combination with early azaleas, and

Most gardeners are thrilled with a small clump of great white trillium. Where they grow naturally, *Trillium grandiflorum* will make large colonies.

All parts in threes—leaflets, sepals, and petals alike—provide the Latin name for trillium.

GEOPHYTES

Sheltered woodland conditions are what is wanted by *Trillium grandiflorum*.

A roadside pairing of trillium and bloodroot suggests a similar combination would be equally effective in the garden.

herbaceous perennials such as Siberian bugloss, *Dicentra* 'Bountiful' or 'Luxuriant', and annual forget-me-nots.

Though the typical form is a rich ox-blood red, *Trillium erectum* 'Album' has appealing white flowers.

Birthroot or Wet Dog Trillium, *Trillium erectum*

This is the common trillium in New England. Typically, the pedunculate flowers are deep red and widely open to reveal the yellow stamens, but I've come across plants with white, ivory, or yellowish flowers, even two-tone bicolors with a pink reverse and white surface. In nature this species grows together with bloodroot, *Sanguinaria canadensis*, several different ferns, and various violets, the usual gamut of woodland dwellers. I like white and blue as a color combination, so I selected out the white forms of *T. erectum* in my garden to pair with phlox, Siberian bugloss, ajuga, and white violets. The deep red forms look good with the same companions (lavender rather than white violets though, as I wanted to avoid a red, white, lavender-blue association.)

Wood Hyacinth, *Hyacinthoides non-scripta*

Wood hyacinth, *Hyacinthoides non-scripta* (= *Endymion non-scriptus*, *Scilla non-scripta*), is a non-native geophyte that flowers in the second surge of spring, in May, decorating the woodland with its loose racemes of bell-like, soft blue flowers. Alas, it is a bit of a thug, quietly spreading, expanding, increasing its territory. In Holland one spring I saw a beech woods carpeted with wood hyacinth as far as the eye could see. Obviously, in more limited space some control is necessary. That is simple enough; as the flowers begin to wither, just trim back the stem. Then the only multiplication is by offsets, creating enlarging clumps of bulbs rather than seedlings spreading far and wide. The fleshy, naked bulbs will pull themselves rather deep into the ground, making it difficult to dig and move them after several years. Wood hyacinths are especially attractive when planted among hosta with creamy chartreuse markings to their leaves. The contrast of flowers and foliage is elegant, and then the hosta leaves cover the space when the bulbs are dormant. There are rose pink- and white-flowered forms but I don't care for them; the pink is a somewhat cool shade, difficult to pair with any pink azaleas, and the white forms I've had are weaker-growing.

Summer

Cyclamen, *Cyclamen purpurascens*
Cyclamen are most familiar to gardeners as the tender potted plants used as houseplants. The best-known hardy species are the Persian violet of early spring, and the ivy-leaved cyclamen that blooms in late summer and early fall. Hardy to zone 6, *Cyclamen purpurascens* flowers in the summer. Dark green, nearly evergreen, rounded leaves are sometimes marked with silver green, the marbling varies from prominent to faint and inconspicuous. If snow cover protects the old leaves in the winter, they may still be present when new ones unfold in the spring. Fragrant rose pink, carmine, or purple flowers, often veined in a deep pink, with a dark carmine mark at the base of the petals, appear from late June to September. In the wild, *C. purpurascens* is found in beech forests or mixed beech and

conifer woodlands. In gardens it likes a cool, shady site with ample humus, neutral to somewhat alkaline pH, and good drainage but not drought. This species does well in my zone 6 garden, planted almost 6 inches deep near the toe of a slope on the high side of a fallen oak limb used for edging. Once a year or so, I push a piece of white blackboard chalk into the soil near the tubers in the spring, to counteract my rather acid conditions.

Caladium, *Caladium*
Caladium, though a tuber and as such appropriate in this chapter, are discussed in the following chapter, which is concerned with annuals, since they are most frequently used for temporary, seasonal, summer color.

Fall

Lords and Ladies, *Arum italicum*
This interesting tuber has an unusual growth cycle. Leaves emerge in the fall, remaining green and fresh through zone 6 and milder winters. If conditions in the colder portion of its range are too severe, leaves will die off, and a second set will emerge in the spring, with flowers similar to those of Jack-in-the-pulpit appearing in the late spring. Leaves then go dormant for the summer, leaving the corncob-like seed clusters standing alone. Soon after the green seeds ripen and turn red, it is time for the cycle to begin all over again.

Beginning in the fall and extending into winter's snow, *Arum italicum* has attractive leaves that enliven the shady garden.

GEOPHYTES

The most attractive arum is the cultivar 'Pictum', whose dark green, arrow-shaped leaves are laced with a silvery tracing along the veins. It is charming in combination with Japanese painted fern for the brief period they overlap in the spring. In winter, look for evergreen partners, such as Christmas fern or liriope, or Christmas rose, *Helleborus niger*.

Begonia, *Begonia grandis* ssp. *evansiana*

A hardy begonia may seem unlikely, but *Begonia grandis* ssp. *evansiana* does quite nicely in my zone 6 garden, probably its northern limit of hardiness. While dormant it has survived single-digit temperatures in my garden, even an occasional drop below 0°F. Large, tapering, triangular leaves, verdigris copper green to green above, beefsteak red beneath, are sparsely spaced up the 2- to 3-foot-tall stem. Growth begins late in the spring, in mid-May, engendering concern

Astonishingly enough, there's a begonia hardy enough to take on winter, that flowers in September, in the shade.

that the previous winter was too cold for survival.

Note: There are no such fears in the Southeast; concern there is rather that plants will take over the entire garden.

Pink flowers, about 1 inch across, begin to appear in September, earlier in the South. Small tubers form in the leaf axils, falling to the ground and making new plants. Most years, Connecticut is just a little too cold for this, with the first hard frost usually turning the stems to mush before these aerial bulbils mature. The bay side of Long Island is mild enough and I remember one garden with a bed, first with masses of primroses in the spring, then equally filled with hardy begonias in early fall. Given their stature, combine hardy begonias with tall ferns. Given its late season of bloom, find other seasonal associations for hardy begonia, such as lilyturf and *Hosta tardiflora*, which flower at the same time.

Colchicum, *Colchicum speciosum*

Gardeners into instant gratification will appreciate *colchicum*. These corms are planted early in the fall like so many other geophytes. Rather than wait until the spring, however, they come up and flower within a matter of weeks. It is hard to explain why they are not grown in more gardens, unless it is their price. Expect to pay the same for a colchicum as you would for half a dozen tulips or daffodils. The one colchicum, flowering in the fall, will send up three to six lavender flowers shaped like a crocus but much, much larger. Leaves won't appear until the spring, big broad strappy things with a slightly pleated texture. Leaves remain until sometime in June, when they turn yellow and collapse in an unlovely manner all over their neighbors. Find big sturdy perennials to pair with colchicums, or use them in front of shrubs.

Colchicum speciosum is an attractively flowering, pest-proof addition to the fall garden.

Plant colchicum in bright shade in a site that won't dry too much in summer. Plant the corms three times as deep as the corm is tall, with the pointier end up and foot-like projection down. Three corms is a minimum to start with, five is nicer, and ten better yet. Anything more is luxurious!

Ivy-leaved Cyclamen, *Cyclamen hederifolium*

Ivy-leaved cyclamen is an excellent geophyte for flowers and foliage late in the gardening season. It begins to flower in August, sending up dancing butterflies of pink flowers unaccompanied by leaves. Appearing

GEOPHYTES

Not spring but fall brings forth the flowers of colchicum, seen here with the fruits of *Arum italicum*.

Foliage persists through the winter, finally becoming dormant in late May or early June.

The tuber-corms of ivy-leaved cyclamen root from the upper surface, so make sure they are correctly oriented, with the smooth, slightly rounded underside downward. The scant couple of inches of soil above the cyclamen should be fertile and high in organic matter. Good drainage is important. Using reasoning I cannot follow, dormant tubers are available at nurseries in the spring, with months of dormancy ahead of them. No matter what vendors say, I am convinced that these are often wild-collected plants, indicated by misshapen or damaged tuber-corms. Cyclamen is most successful if purchased and planted in growth, as potted plants in the early fall. The problem is finding a source. It is very easy to raise plants from seed, and they reach flowering size in 18 months.

Because they have an unusual growth cycle, I like to combine ivy-leaved cyclamen with a ground cover. This protects the dormant tuber-corms from accidental disturbance, and gives me something better to look at than bare ground or weeds. One excellent choice is *Ajuga repandens* 'Tricolor'. Another, which takes a bit more effort, is the tender, silver- and purple-leaved inch plant, *Tradescantia zebrina*, which is very popular as a houseplant. In mid-spring I root cuttings that are planted out in late spring, over *Cyclamen hederifolium*. When the cyclamen's pink shuttlecock flowers come dancing forth in August, there is foliage to complement them, conceal bare ground, and keep mud from splashing onto the flowers. With the advent of cold weather, the tender inch plant dies away, leaving the silver-marked cyclamen foliage pride of place through the winter.

first in September, shaped somewhat like those of English ivy, each plant with unique silver markings on forest green leaves.

ANNUALS, BIENNIALS, AND TENDER PERENNIALS

Cordyline and rex begonia are usually thought of as houseplants. Planted together with hardy perennial Japanese painted fern, when it comes to containers I think anything goes.

ANNUALS, BIENNIALS, AND TENDER PERENNIALS

Familiar annuals such as coleus and impatiens can be combined for effective results.

We all like to have a colorful summer garden. Since perennials usually flower for only a couple of weeks, annuals with their long season of bloom provide a continuity of color. In addition to true annuals—those plants that germinate from seed, mature, flower, produce seed of their own, and then die, all within the space of a single year—tender perennials that cannot survive the winter are also used for seasonal color. Some, such as coleus, are so coupled with "annual" in the mind of gardeners that they are best discussed here. In addition, a number of tropical perennials used as houseplants can add seasonal color to the shady garden. This also seems a good place to discuss biennials, plants that germinate from seed one year, flower and die the next.

Annuals

There is no point in complaining that only a few old, traditional, commonplace annuals thrive in the shade. Novelty alone does not guarantee an attractive garden—far from it. It is what you do with what you've got that makes a good garden. And the familiar trio of impatiens, begonias, and coleus can really enhance the perennials and ground covers that furnish your shady garden.

Impatiens

Impatiens are invaluable for their extended flowering period, from the late spring with mild, settled, night temperatures, until frost. Plants appreciate a soil high in organic matter, moist but well drained. That means you should add some compost or leaf mold to the soil and dig it in well. Water when the weather is dry, but avoid soggy situations that can lead to root rot. Sometimes I buy my plants a little early in the season, perhaps the first week of May here in Connecticut. I take the young plants out of their four- or six-plant cell-pack unit and pot them up individually in 2¼-inch pots. I keep the young plants under grow lights in my plant room. By giving them a little more root room, and fertilizing at half-strength with a liquid fertilizer twice a week, I get husky plants ready to take off and flower when they go out into the garden on the Memorial Day weekend, a safe planting date in my area. Just make sure you buy impatiens or patience plant or busy lizzies, or whatever local name *Impatiens walleriana* has where you live, and *not* New Guinea impatiens, which are sun lovers, unhappy in the shade. Generally, impatiens are only hardy in zone 10, but will occasionally reseed. A note of caution: Deer dine on impatiens.

There are all sorts of possibilities for enhancing the shady garden with impatiens. Impatiens in the Accent series compactly

The somber leaves of heuchera are enlivened by impatiens' vivid flowers.

Standard summertime fare, a corset of red impatiens encircles a tree. With a little more effort, you can achieve better, more interesting results.

grow about 12 inches tall, with large carmine, coral, salmon, scarlet, red, rose, pink, violet, lilac, or white flowers. Elfin series are lower growing, and Super-elfin are even smaller, from 6 or 8 to 10 inches. The Blitz series has extra-large, 2-inch-diameter flowers. Some impatiens, Starbright series, have a white streak down the center of each petal, creating a starlike pattern against the violet, orange, red, or rose flower. Double Confection series are double flowered, though some seedlings will be semidouble. The soft pink, violet, or white flowers resemble miniature roses. The doubles are usually sold as individually potted plants in larger sizes, rather than in smaller, multiple-cell-pack size.

For a more emphatic color combination, use violet and lavender impatiens with a small, golden-leaved hosta such as 'Wogan Gold' or 'Kabitan'. Plant the impatiens in an undulating ribbon, here thicker, there thinner, weaving in and out among the hosta. Allow the two flower colors to mingle rather than keeping them in separate bands or clumps. Try lavender and violet impatiens in a shaded window box, together with golden coleus and a trailing, green- and gold-leafed Swedish ivy, *Plectranthus coleoides*, which has reddish stems. If you want to get really fancy, use the double-flowered form of impatiens. Since double impatiens are not always as

Containers create a display by their very function: These plants are important enough to have been provided a special setting.

plantings. Instead, use the bright red flowers of the impatiens as a vivid accent for bronze-, copper-, and purple-leaved plants, such as ajugas. Together with the somber, olive-purple, summer hue of *Heuchera americana* 'Palace Purple' and the narrow, black, linear leaves of *Ophiopogon planiscapus* 'Nigrescens', the clear bright color of the impatiens supplies a necessary emphasis to lift the perennials from drab to delightful.

White is wonderful in shady gardens, lightening and brightening in the low light levels. There may be a narrow, shaded strip along your driveway, a foot-wide band of earth between the asphalt and a fence. Fill it with white impatiens, and watch how the flowers light up when you drive home at night. A very simple combination joins white impatiens with dark forest green Christmas fern, with the annual filling in for dormant geophytes. Just picture some white-flowered impatiens with silver gray Japanese painted fern, *Athyrium nipponicum* 'Pictum', or with frosty blue hosta, or all three together.

Coleus

At garden centers and nurseries throughout the country you find unnamed coleus, of mixed foliage color and shape. These members of the mint family can have yellow, orange, red, copper, mahogany, or lime green leaves, sometimes with two or three contrasting colors splashed on the same leaf. No wonder an older common name is painted nettle. Coleus in a rainbow range of colors are widely availability at nurseries in cell packs of mixed or individual types: 'Rainbow' with large, heart-shaped, multi-hued leaves irregularly striped with yellow, red, coppery red, and green; the Dragon series with oak-shaped, scarlet to purple and black leaves, edged in yellow green;

widely available as the singles, you might want to take cuttings in mid-August, or dig the plants in early September, to carry through the winter indoors. If the contrast of yellow and violet is stronger than you care for, choose a blue hosta such as 'Halcyon' or 'Blue Cadet', and the violet and lavender impatiens flowers will accentuate the foliage in a more subtle manner. In either instance, the combination of flowers and foliage will be showy all summer long. Another simple combination pairs the same violet- and lavender-flowered impatiens with the inch plant, *Tradescantia zebrina*, that familiar houseplant with silver- and purple-striped leaves, now given a summer vacation in the garden.

I like the clear red impatiens too, but not with silver dusty miller which is how the local businesses freshen up their foundation

'Carefree' is also an oakleaf type in a mix of colors, and the slower-growing Saber type (excellent for containers) that has long, deeply frilled, narrow leaves with a dark green edge.

When you pay a visit to botanical gardens and great public gardens such as Longwood Gardens in Kennett Square, Pennsylvania, in the summer you'll find them using specific clones. Look at the labels accompanying the attractive displays, and you'll find names such as 'Scarlet Poncho' with red leaves and the cascading branches typical of this series; 'Saber Golden' with chartreuse leaves; golden 'Pineapple Wizard'; pale green-edged, light red 'Wizard Sunset'; or somber, deep purple 'Othello'. There are even nurseries that specialize in coleus. At the Great Autumn Show of the Royal Horticultural Society, held in September at Vincent Square in London, I saw specialists' booths, nurseries selling antique and modern cultivars of coleus. Few of us need to go to such lengths to obtain particular forms but you may find

one at a garden center that really appeals to you. And, even on a home scale, more than one coleus plant will be needed. Take cuttings in the late summer, and keep the rooted plants indoors over the winter. These will provide stock plants in the spring for the next summer's garden.

Coleus need ample, even moisture. They are among the first plants to flag if the soil becomes dry, first displaying drooping leaves, then limp, flabby stems, then death. While some cultivars ('Wizard' series, in particular) can grow in full sun, coleus are really most satisfactory in shady sites. Like impatiens, coleus is a very tender perennial, only hardy in zone 10. Some plants have a trailing habit; others can reach 3 feet tall, especially where they live as perennials in subtropical gardens.

Golden coleus are rather monotonous with golden hosta, but really shine when paired with glaucous blue hosta. Their bright leaves are also fine with dark forest green foliage, glossy, round-leaved European ginger, the narrow finger lobes of bear's foot hellebore,

Hardy perennials like these can be combined with annuals, biennials, and tender perennials for an attractive grouping.

191

or even tucked into vacancies in a ground cover of running myrtle. In light shade 'Rainbow' looks absolutely wonderful paired with red and purple *Salvia spendens*, whose deeply colored spikes of flowers accent the red and purple splotches on the creamy coleus leaf. Red coleus with Japanese painted fern, *Athyrium nipponicum* 'Pictum' accent the burgundy color of the central axis on each of the fern's fronds. This pairing provides a very different mien than that contributed by white impatiens. Who said coleus and impatiens were boring?

Begonias

Wax begonia, fibrous-rooted begonia, bedding begonia—all these common names reflect the popularity of the semperflorenscultorum hybrid begonias. A half-dozen different species were involved in developing these vigorous, tender perennial plants with erect, clumping stems 6 to 15 inches tall, fibrous roots, and green, copper bronze, or blackish red leaves. In cooler climates the single or double white, pink, or red flowers appear in the summer, year-round in mild winter regions. Plants have both male and female flowers, the males readily distinguished by the golden pollen on the stamens. Wax begonias flower best in light shade, and prefer a humus-rich, moist but freely draining soil.

While flower color is certainly an important consideration in selecting cultivars, do not overlook leaf color. Copper bronze-leaved forms are sumptuous under the feathery, plum purple foliage of cut-leafed Japanese maple, *Acer palmatum* 'Dissectum Atropurpureum', or with copper-colored foliage of *Ajuga* 'Burgundy Glow', adding that extra-special effect missing from green-leaved forms in such situations. The Cocktail, Danica, and Devil series have dark bronze

Foliage shape and color work as effectively in containers as in the design of gardens.

leaves. Green-leaved, white-flowered wax begonias are elegant with glaucous blue hosta, ferns, and the white-edged leaves of *Cornus alba* 'Elegantissima'. Olympia series have green leaves. Organdy and Royale series have both bronze- and green-leaved varieties. Calla Lily begonias have variegated, white-marbled leaves that resemble calla lilies as they unfurl. Ample light is necessary for the best development. Water moderately, and then only when the soil is dry. These are best used as container, rather than bedding plants.

Rex Begonia, *Begonia rex*

These begonias are tender perennials more often grown as container plants indoors or in a conservatory or greenhouse. I've had good results planting them directly in the garden after the weather is mild and settled. Then, in the late summer I dig the plants and repot for their winter indoors. It is easy to distinguish rex from wax begonias, as the former have fleshy, creeping, rhizomatous roots that sprawl along the surface or burrow just underground. Also, rex begonias have 6- to 12-inch-long, obliquely triangular leaves of a rich metallic green marked with a broad silver blotch above, and beefsteak red on the underside. There are literally hundreds of named cultivars between the closely allied Asian species and *B. rex* itself. Leaf color is dark green, wine red, or bronze, with silver, gray, or purple zones and patterns. The strongest markings develop in good light, so use rex begonias in light shade. They are even more tender than wax begonias, and prefer night temperatures of at least 60°F. Water carefully, and try not to wet the leaves, which are susceptible to mildew. Rex begonias are elegant with silver and glaucous blue foliage, and even more somber purple and bronze leaves. You might also consider displaying a rex begonia in an attractive pot set on a supporting plinth, even a discreetly disguised cement block hidden by nearby hostas. One summer I used rex begonias in a half-height, double-rolled-rim terra-cotta pot. Together with Japanese painted fern and a hot pink ti plant, *Cordyline terminalis,* the container marked the path into the woodland garden.

Hardy begonia, *Begonia grandis* (= *B. evansiana*), is discussed in Perennials, which begins on page 125.

Scarlet Sage, *Salvia splendens*

Scarlet sage is most familiar in a bonfire red incarnation, with stiffly upright spikes of vivid red flowers. Plants provide long-lasting color, since the calyces are also deeply colored. Though scarlet sage is most frequently grown in sunny sites (together with lemon yellow marigolds for a riot of color), plants do quite well in light to moderate shade. Some of the most intensely red cultivars, ranging in height from 18 to 24 inches,

include 'Bonfire', 'Carabiniere', 'Rocket', 'St. John's Fire', and 'Tally-ho'. 'Laser Purple' and 'Mood Indigo' are splendidly Victorian, with deep purple, fade-resistant flowers. I've also purchased (but haven't found the name of) a lovely muted burgundy red, and a soft, shrimpy coral pink. There is a white but the color appears dingy to my eye, neither a clean white nor a soft ivory. What the hybridists are developing are runty, 8-inch-tall dwarfs. The erect spires of radiant flowers are the best thing about scarlet sage. Scatter them in group of three to five amid lower-growing perennials, where they can add a nice accent to summer foliage.

Biennials

Biennials take a little more planning to get into action in the garden. For one thing, if started from seed you cannot expect flowers until the following year. For another, you need to start them from seed two years running to get continuity of performance. Once that is accomplished, the biennials will self-sow in suitable locations. Individual plants die at the end of two years, but their offspring create a perpetuating perennial colony. Specific plants vanish, but you will have the biennials in that general area, perhaps even spreading out.

Foxglove, *Digitalis purpurea*

The tall wands of flowers produced by foxgloves lend stature and elegance to the garden. From a basal rosette of large, sturdy, oval-dark green leaves arises a tall unbranched flower spike, up to 6 feet tall. The bell-like flowers are purple to pink, usually heavily freckled inside with pale-edged darker purplish spots. They are charming as a backdrop to smaller shrubs, or counterpoint to larger ones.

I particularly like 'Alba', the pure white-flowered form, but you must be stern to establish a true-breeding strain, for white

193

foxglove flowers are a recessive color to pink or purple ones. In other words, if a white flower received pollen from anything but another white foxglove, many of the resulting seedlings will be pink or purple. As soon as the flower buds begin to swell and show color, rip out by the roots any plants that show other than white. Within a couple of years you'll have only 'Alba', like white candles glowing in the shade. Together with white-barked birches, the effect is stunning.

Honesty, *Lunnaria annua*

You may be familiar with honesty, *Lunnaria annua*, as dried material for winter arrangements. Flowers are followed by thin, flat, round fruits that have a central membrane. This attractive silvery membrane provides the other common names of money plant or silver dollar plant.

Sow seed directly where you want plants to grow, two years in a row. After that, the plants will renew the colony for you. Cold-hardy, self-sown seedlings appear in the fall, and, if the weather is mild, some may flower the following spring. In their second year, plants grow 3 feet tall, with clusters of white or purple flowers in late April and early May. I prefer the white-flowered form, combining

The silvery seed pods of honesty, *Lunnaria annua*, are an effective foil for this white variegated hosta.

them with later blooming daffodils such as 'Actaea'. 'Alba Variegata' has white flowers and the leaves are also white-variegated and have irregular white margins. It comes true from seed. 'Haslemere' has lots of lilac purple flowers and off-white, variegated leaves.

Woodland Forget-me-not, *Myosotis sylvatica*

Popular in many gardens, woodland forget-me-not is usually grown as a biennial. Though some plants may live a year or more, they should not be considered especially perennial. Since forget-me-not self-sow freely, it establishes permanent colonies. Upright, 6- to 8-inch-high stems with lanceolate, 2- to 3-inch-long hairy leaves make a nice background to the dense clusters of ⅜-inch-wide, yellow-eyed, sky blue flowers. Plants bloom prolifically in the late spring. Then, as seed matures, they blacken and die off. If your garden layout permits, walk over the stems to release seed for next year's plants, otherwise, collect stems just before they blacken and hang them upside down in a brown paper bag to collect seed as it ripens. Then broadcast the seed where it is to grow. I so prefer the true blue of forget-me-nots that I don't bother with the white- or pink-flowered forms that are available. I especially like woodland forget-me-nots' blue flowers with the brownish green leaves and yellow flowers of *Corydalis cheilanthifolia*.

Tender Perennials

So many of our summer annuals (in the horticultural sense) are really zone 10 perennials—coleus, impatiens, scarlet sage—that it is an author's guessing game as to where to place them in the text. My choice was to follow garden center placement—if they put a plant with annuals, then so shall I. Group them in the company of houseplants, and I'll call them tender perennials.

Caladium

Caladium seems more appropriate identified with annuals, even though technically it is a tuber, thus suitable for inclusion with geophytes. After all, caladiums are only hardy in those parts of the country with mild winters. Grown for summer color in colder regions, they are year-round garden residents only in Florida and similar subtropical precincts. Like coleus, caladiums provide foliage interest to the shady garden. Luxuriant arrow-shaped leaves in white, pink, red, perhaps veined and/or edged in green, provide color in beds, borders, and containers. Their bold shape contrasts nicely with linear grasslike foliage of sedges, and the lacy texture of ferns or astilbes.

Summer shade need not be boring, not with seasonal plants such as impatiens and caladiums to highlight the scene.

Obligingly, caladiums will happily grow in containers as well as the ground.

Caladiums prefer a hot, humid climate. Those dog days of August with torpid heat and sticky air are caladiums' prime weather. There is no point in planting them until conditions are really settled and warm.

Dormant tubers need a leisurely start. Mid-February is about right for an early June planting date. When your tubers arrive, look them over careful and decide which way is up. There will be a small bud shoot or two, indicating the growing points. Start them like this, and you'll get fewer, but larger leaves. Scoop the shoot out with your thumbnail, and plants will produce more, but smaller leaves. Set the tubers in pots or flats of a 50:50 peat moss:vermiculite mix, barely covering the tubers. Keep the medium quite moist but not soggy. Keep them warm, about 70°F, until tubers show signs of growth. (Often the top of a grow-light fixture or a refrigerator will provide the necessary bottom heat.) After leaves begin growing, 65°F is acceptable, but avoid chilling. Pot up when leaf growth is well established, and set out in June. Nurseries will usually have potted caladiums ready to plant out but their selection of cultivars is rather limited.

A cool, refreshing combination for a shady window box or patio container might combine green-edged, white-leaved *Caladium* 'June Bride' with white-flowered impatiens and Victorian brake fern, *Pteris cretica* 'Albolineata', tender fern with a broad white stripe on the frond segments, usually grown as a houseplant, or, as mentioned earlier, lighten a shady corner with white-leaved *Caladium* 'Candidum', again with white-flowered impatiens, and *Hosta plantaginea*, with elegant, glossy, fresh green leaves and deliciously fragrant white flowers in August. Plan on using about 10 or 12 impatiens to three caladiums and one hosta for appropriate balance.

Both 'June Bride' and 'Candidum' are classed as fancy-leaf caladiums, having large, rather broad, arrow-shaped leaves and a thin, translucent texture. Strap-leaf caladiums

ANNUALS, BIENNIALS, AND TENDER PERENNIALS

A cool, refreshing combination for a shady nook in summer: *Hosta plantaginea* with *Caladium* 'Candidum' and white impatiens.

The scarlet leaf of *Caladium* 'Frieda Hemple' accentuates the somber leaf of *Heuchera* 'Palace Purple'.

have narrower leaves, usually more noticeable, acute basal lobes, and often a ruffled edge to their leaves. I find they also have thicker, more substantial leaves. One of my favorites is *Caladium* 'Pothos', with a lance-like white leaf and green blotches. An attractive combination is 'Pothos' with white-edged *Pachysandra terminalis* 'Silver Edge', and dark green, evergreen, Christmas fern *Polystichum achrostichoides*.

Remember that the deeper the shade, the better white and light colors will stand out. Dark colors such as deep reds tend to merge with the shadows. For that reason I would suggest keeping dark red-leafed caladiums toward the lighter fringes of the garden. One standby favorite is *Caladium* 'Frieda Hemple' with bright red leaves marked with scarlet ribs and edged with a wide, dark green margin. Combine this with *Heuchera* 'Palace Purple' and its somber purple-green leaves, then accent the combination with bright scarlet impatiens.

There are other options for seasonal display in shady gardens that you might not have considered. Many houseplants perform better planted in the ground than they do in a pot, even when the pot is set out for the summer.

Inch Plant, *Tradescantia zebrina*
(= *Zebrina pendula*)
This is a creeping trailing plant with silver-striped leaves, usually purple beneath, popular for hanging baskets. I find it invaluable as a summer ground cover for shady places. Since it roots at the nodes along the stem, I just pinch off shoots from a mother plant and stick them in the ground. They root very easily, and then just happily scramble over the ground, rooting as they go. Plants die as soon as the first hard frost arrives. It is wise to take some cuttings in late August or early September and root them, keeping them indoors over the winter.

APPENDIX 1—Attracting Birds to the Shady Garden

Food

When someone wants to attract birds to the garden, they usually take the easy route and put out a feeder or two. There is a more natural approach, combining the human wish for an attractive garden, and the birds' needs for food, shelter, and a place to nest and raise their young. The two seemingly different objectives are easily reconcilable. Think about the birds' requirements along with aesthetics, and you can readily create a bird-friendly garden.

Ecologists and naturalists talk about "the carrying capacity of the land." That's a way of saying that the better (or more substandard) the conditions, the greater (or fewer) numbers and/or diversity of animals the site will support. A front yard with lawn, a single Japanese maple in a bed of mulch, and some azaleas boxed into the foundation planting has little to attract birds. Swap the maple for a dogwood, and robins will flock to the tree in the fall to eat the berries before migrating south. Choose a shadbush and you'll have summer visitors. Replace the azaleas with shrubs that fruit, and you're well on your way to creating a piece of prime real estate, in terms of its appeal for birds.

The beautiful berries on viburnum serve as winter bird food.

Birds have a high metabolic rate and need steady supplies of food. Those that live in woodlands have different requirements than those that live in grasslands or along the shore. Needs also differ between seed eaters or insect eaters and birds of prey. In the garden, just as in nature, this steady supply of food is provided not by a single source, but rather by a diversity of plants. Many birds that we tempt with seed-filled feeders in the winter can also be attracted year-round by planting suitable trees and shrubs that provide natural food sources.

Shelter

Birds need a place to spend the night. Wild turkeys roost in trees, and they'd better be sturdy for a flock of these substantial birds. Especially in inclement weather—winter cold, heavy rain—birds need shelter, and, again, will be readily attracted to a garden that provides this in a natural way, with conifers or other dense-growing trees and shrubs. Birdhouses are good; so are shrubs and trees. You can attract birds through their need for secure sites where they can lay eggs and raise their nestlings. Hummingbirds may nectar on sun-loving plants, but they nest in thickety shrubs of lightly shaded wet woodlands. Increasing the carrying capacity of the land with appropriate plants means offering birds more food, suitable places to hide and rest, protection from bad weather, and a place to raise their families.

Not all forest-dwelling birds inhabit the same neighborhood. Some choose the more open woodland edges, others prefer to dwell in small groves or thickets similar to a shady suburban backyard, still others require large tracts of old-growth forest beyond most home neighborhoods. How you manage what you have can make a difference. Ecotones, those

Attracting Birds to the Shady Garden

boundary areas where two different habitats come together, are rich habitats, highly suitable for attracting birds, where a woodland edge meets a lawn area, for example. If the lawn is more of a low meadow than a manicured turf, so much the better, as seed from annual "weedy" grasses and other low-growing plants provide an additional food source. Similarly, a tapestry hedge containing a mix of deciduous and evergreen shrubs will attract a wider range of birds than a clipped, single-species hedge of privet. Look at your garden and think in layers. Is there an abrupt transition from lawn to foundation planting to specimen tree? This familiar garden layout is less appealing to birds than a design that offers more options. A woodland community with canopy trees, understory trees, shrubs, perennials, and ground covers creates better habitat options. A natural mulch of last year's leaves is attractive to rufous-sided towhees, brown thrashers, and other birds that like to scratch in the litter hunting for earthworms and insects to eat.

Choose at least some trees and shrubs for your garden that provide food for the birds. This means selecting fruiting plants rather than merely pretty ones—azaleas may have attractive flowers but offer no seeds, nuts, or berries as do viburnums, dogwoods, and hollies. Plants with single flowers are often your best choice, since double-flowered perennials, shrubs, and trees are usually sterile and rarely set any seed. Another bonus of birds in the garden is that even seed-eating birds feed their young on insects, and a healthy bird population in the garden means dependable natural pest control, benefitting your entire garden.

Evergreens provide winter shelter: Conifers such as hemlocks, *Tsuga canadensis*; all species of spruces, *Picea* spp.; and eastern white pines, *Pinus strobus*, are especially useful. When you consider that birds' normal body temperature is about 105°F, it becomes clear how important such winter shelter is at night and during storms if birds are to survive. Conifers provide birds with the best shelter from wind and snow in the winter, and some protection from rain, and they supply food as well. A tremendous number of birds, such as black-capped chickadees, tufted titmice, red-breasted nuthatches, brown creepers, pine warblers, cardinals, evening and pine grosbeaks, pine siskins, red and white-winged crossbills, rufous-sided towhees, and northern juncos, consider the seeds to be a preferred food. Yew, *Taxus cuspidata*, is an evergreen shrub that provides dense cover not only for shelter from weather, but also for early-nesting birds before deciduous trees and shrubs leaf out, such as song sparrows, chipping sparrows, robins, and mockingbirds. Site new plantings of tall growing conifers on the north side of your property so trees will not add shade to the garden.

Nutritional Needs

The food needs of birds vary during the year. Different fruits are eaten at different times: soft fruits such as bramble berries, blueberries, elderberries, chokeberries, and shadbush berries in the summer; high-lipid fruits such as the bright red berries of flowering dogwood are taken early by migrating birds that need the energy for long flights. Flocks of robins will strip a dogwood of fruit in a day. Other, high-carbohydrate fruits persist into the winter, when they provide food in an otherwise bare larder. Virginia creeper, *Parthenocissus quinquefolia*, and American cranberrybush, *Viburnum trilobum*, fall into this category. Some fruits must freeze and thaw several times before they are palatable to birds. And you should not overlook the value of canopy trees such as oaks. Their acorns, together with nuts such as walnuts and hickories, are called "mast," and are an important food source for wild turkeys, ruffed grouse woodpeckers, blue jays, titmice, brown thrashers, robins, and others.

Since birches produce small brown seeds rather than anything showy, you may never have thought of them as especially fruitful trees. Wood ducks, turkeys, ruffed grouse, ring-necked pheasants, blue jays, tufted titmice, pine siskins, American goldfinches, and northern juncos are some diverse birds that disagree: all of them eat birch seeds from sweet birch, *Betula lenta*; paper birch, *B. papyrifera*; and gray birch, *B. populifolia*.

Serviceberry is almost as popular as flowering dogwood with birds as it is to gardeners. The latter appreciate both downy serviceberry, *Amelanchier arborea*, and shadblow serviceberry, *A. canadensis*, as small trees with attractive white spring flowers, sweet purple berries in summer, and attractive fall color. You will find the fruits difficult to gather. The birds relish the tasty fruits, which are not merely eaten but are a preferred food for ruffed grouse, eastern kingbirds, gray catbirds, mockingbirds, brown thrashers, robins, wood and hermit thrushes, veerys, cedar waxwings, scarlet tanagers, rufous-sided towhees, cardinals, and rose-breasted grosbeaks.

American holly, *Ilex opaca*, is one of the few broad-leaved evergreen trees that grows in northeastern gardens. Preferring partial to deeply shaded sites with open, moist soil, this highly ornamental native has scarlet red persistent fruits on female plants, which are a preferred food for mockingbirds, eastern bluebirds, and cedar waxwings, and are eaten by robins, cardinals, hermit thrushes, brown thrashers, gray catbirds, turkeys, bobwhites, common flickers and red-bellied woodpeckers. American holly is a preferred nest site for a few birds such as cardinals, catbirds, and mockingbirds.

Seed-eating birds are readily attracted by appropriate plantings. Yews have attractive red berries on the female plants, popular with robins, white-throated sparrows, song sparrows, chipping sparrows, ruffed grouse, and mockingbirds. As an understory tree, nothing is better than flowering dogwood, except perhaps serviceberry. The shrub dogwoods are also ideal. Alternate-leaf dogwood, *Cornus alterniflora*, grows as a shrub in shady sites with moist soil. Fruits mature in late July to September, clusters of blue-black berries on red stems. They are eaten by woodpeckers, mockingbirds, gray catbirds, robins, wood and hermit thrushes, eastern bluebirds, cedar waxwings, and many other birds. Another shrub for moist shady places is spicebush, *Lindera benzoin*. Dioecious, individual plants are either male or female, and the female bushes have bright red berries in the late summer to fall, which are eaten by thrushes, robins, gray catbirds, ruffed grouse, ring-necked pheasants, cardinals, and others.

Shade-tolerant inkberry, *Ilex glabra*, is an evergreen holly that grows on sandy, peaty soils. Female plants have very persistent, not especially showy, glossy blackberries eaten by robins, eastern bluebirds, rufous-sided towhees, mockingbirds, cedar waxwings, and others.

As a group, viburnums, like dogwoods, are a very popular food source for a number of bird species. Dockmackie or mapleleaf viburnum, *Viburnum acerifolium*; hobblebush, *V. alnifolium*; and witherod, *V. cassinoides*, are all native species with purple to blue-black fruits that persist into midwinter. They provide valuable winter food for ruffed grouses, brown thrashers, pine grosbeaks, and other birds. American cranberrybush, *V. trilobum*, has very showy, colorful, orange to bright red fruits that remain on the plants all winter, providing food for early returning migrants as well as over-wintering birds such as turkeys, ruffed grouses, ring-necked pheasants, eastern bluebirds, cedar waxwings, cardinals, and others.

Some shrubs, though quite attractive to birds, should not be planted because they escape from the garden and crowd native plants out of their natural habitat. Especially to be avoided are Japanese barberry, *Berberis thunbergii*, Russian olive, *Eleagnus angustifolia*, and multiflora rose, *Rosa multiflora*. Nor could I bring myself to deliberately plant poison ivy, *Toxicodendron radicans*, even though its white fruits are extremely popular with any number of birds!

Attracting Birds to the Shady Garden

Birds need more than food and shelter. Since they lack teeth with which to chew, birds need another way to break up their food. This is accomplished in a small muscular pouch or gizzard that contains sand and small gravel. Especially in the winter when the ground is frozen, birds may have a hard time obtaining such grit, and it is helpful to supply some, clean and free of salt. Pet stores that sell cage bird supplies are a good source, or, in more rural areas, feed and grain stores that sell various sizes of chicken grit. In the spring, when birds are laying eggs, you might want to provide crushed limestone or crushed oyster shell, if it is available, as both materials are good sources of extra calcium for strong eggshells.

Bathing

Birds need to bathe, and even seem to enjoy it. Water is fine for bathing as well as drinking in summer, provided it is changed frequently to keep supplies fresh. Birds are bathers, not swimmers, so supply water in a shallow container no more than 3 inches deep, with a rough, textured surface for secure footing. This can be as simple as a large clay plant saucer with a rock for birds to perch on located near the rim. Site the birdbath in the open, on the sunny side of the woodland edge. Wet birds cannot fly as well as when their feathers are dry, so any screening brush or overhanging trees that camouflage predators makes the birds easier prey. A nearby tree where birds can perch beforehand to check out the site is also suitable for preening and drying feathers after bathing. And if you suspend a leaking container such as a tin can with a small hole, or a plastic jug above the birdbath, the sound of dripping water should quickly attract birds as the drops splash down.

Birds also take dust baths both in the summer and in the winter. The fine silty particles remove excess oils, clean their feathers, and help rid the birds of lice and other insect pests. If you are preparing a special area for dry bathing, consider adding one part flowers of sulphur (very finely powdered sulphur) to 10 or 12 parts dust to act as a parasiticide. Mix the two together thoroughly. The dry, dusty dirt under a roof overhang works well as a "bathhouse" year-round, but birds need a clear view of what might be lurking nearby.

Nesting

Dead trees may seem an eyesore to the gardener, but are prime real estate to woodpeckers, owls, chickadees, titmice, and other birds. Obviously, if a snag poses a danger (say it might fall over onto your home, or is near a path), then it must be removed. If the dead tree is out of the way, at least 15 feet tall and 6 inches or more in diameter, then leave it. Some birds will even use a snag only 6 feet tall. If possible, allow dead trees to stand for cavity-nesting species. Woodpeckers are primary cavity-nesting birds, creating the original nest site in the snag. Secondary cavity-nesting birds that occupy abandoned cavities include eastern bluebirds, tufted titmice, house wrens at the forest edges, nuthatches and black-capped chickadees deeper in the forest. Dead trees provide more than nesting sites for cavity dwellers. They also serve as a grocery store; insect grubs under the bark and in soft dead wood provide food for woodpeckers, wintercreepers, and other birds. Hawks use the bare branches of a tall snag as lookout towers, since they make a suitable perch from which to survey the area.

Brush piles offer good cover for ground-feeding birds such as sparrows, towhees, juncos, winter wrens, and thrushes. The piles are not particularly attractive so they should go in an out-of-view part of the property, 10 feet or less from a glade opening or woodland edge. Mourning cloak butterflies overwinter as adults, and brush piles provide a good place for them to hibernate. They emerge and fly about with the first warm days of spring. Mourning cloaks have very dark brown-black wings edged with yellow. Brush piles also provide shelter for painted lady, red admiral, and buckeye butterflies, but only in southeastern gardens where the adult butterflies can survive through winter conditions. Chipmunks will also take advantage of the cover brush piles provide. A deluxe brush pile is created by stacking several layers of 4- to 8-inch-diameter tree branches in alternating directions to create an open grid. The thickest branches go on the bottom. Then pile a tepeelike heap of thin, 1- to 2-inch-diameter, twiggy branches on the platform to a height of about 6 feet. Brush piles are functional for about five or six years, gradually rotting away.

Shade Garden Trees, Shrubs, and Vines for Feeding Birds Naturally

Common Name	Latin Name	Type of Plant
Shadbush	Amelanchier arborea	small tree
Serviceberry	Amelanchier canadensis	small tree
Running shadbush	Amelanchier stolonifera	shrub
Chokeberry	Aronia arbutifolia	large shrub
Sweet birch	Betula lenta	small tree
Paper birch	Betula papyrifera	small tree
Gray birch	Betula populifolia	small tree
Alternate leafed dogwood	Cornus alternifolia	large shrub
Silky dogwood	Cornus amomum	shrub
Flowering dogwood	Cornus florida	small tree
Japanese dogwood	Cornus kousa	small tree
Redtwig dogwood	Cornus stolonifera	shrub
Wintergreen	Gaultheria procumbens	ground cover
Inkberry	Ilex glabra	evergreen shrub
American holly	Ilex opaca	broad-leaved evergreen tree
Spicebush	Lindera benzoin	shrub
Virginia creeper	Parthenocissus quinquefolia	vine
Boston ivy	Parthenocissus tricuspidata	vine
Spruces	Picea spp.	large coniferous trees
White pine	Pinus strobus	large coniferous tree
Pin cherry	Prunus pensylvanica	small tree
Black cherry	Prunus serotina	small tree
Chokecherry	Prunus virginiana	small tree
Oaks	Quercus spp.	large trees
Snowberry	Symphoricarpus albus	shrub
Yew	Taxus cuspidata	coniferous shrub
Hemlock	Tsuga canadensis	coniferous tree
Lowbush blueberry	Vaccinium angustifolium	shrub
Highbush blueberry	Vaccinium corymbosum	shrub
Mapleleaf viburnum	Viburnum acerifolium	shrub
Hobblebush	Viburnum alnifolium	shrub
Witherod	Viburnum cassinoides	shrub
Arrowwood	Viburnum dentatum	shrub
Nannyberry	Viburnum lentago	shrub
American cranberry bush	Viburnum trilobum	shrub
Wild grape	Vitis riparia	vine

APPENDIX 2—Deer, Oh Dear!

Your Garden—A Deer's Delight

I say it's a garden, they think it's a restaurant, and a wide range of nonnative perennials, including but not limited to day lilies, hostas, tulips, and lilies, serve as a tasty meal for Bambi and his brethren. Natives are not safe; deer eat trilliums. They dine on such shrubs as azaleas, rhododendrons, yews, and mountain laurels. Small trees and shrubs may be thrashed to pieces as bucks rub off the velvet on their newly grown antlers as, not only does the velvet itch at this point, the bucks are scent-marking their territory.

Deer are no longer wary creatures that are visible at dawn and dusk and that shy away from human habitation. Deer have become an increasingly major problem in suburban gardens, botanical gardens, parks, arboreta, and forests, especially in the Northeast. Typically, suburban houses are set in landscapes that provide gladelike openings in a mostly wooded setting. This creates an ideal habitat for herbivorous deer, which are browsing, rather than grazing animals. Given the absence of predators and good habitat, a herd of deer can almost double its number every year. Without wolves or mountain lions, and few if any hunters, the deer population explodes. Does have a single fawn with their first pregnancy; subsequent pregnancies generally result in twins if adequate food is available, and triplets are common. Connecticut's deer population swelled from 19,700 in 1975 to 55,000 in 1993.

Gardens, with plants carefully grown to perfection—weeded, watered, fertilized—are a hungry deer's delight. A former Connecticut state game biologist, Jay McAninch, told me that deer are known to selectively feed on fertilized plantings and can pick out the most nutritious food. If you fertilize two rows in the middle of a 2-acre crop field, he said, the deer will eat those two rows first. However most

Lovely to look at, but not in my backyard!

gardeners have at least a few favorite plants, also popular with the deer, that they are reluctant to discard. I find deer's passion for trilliums something I just cannot accept.

Gardening with plants that are resistant to deer browsing is a low-impact approach that is most suitable where you are willing to compromise. There is a wide range of trees and shrubs, perennials and flowers, that are apparently unpalatable (or at least a food of last resort) on the deer lunch line. They do not eat any geophyte in the Amaryllis family, such as daffodils and snowdrops. Ferns are seemingly unappetizing to them, as are ornamental grasses. Deer ordinarily do not eat pungent, scented foliage; most herbs are deer-proof. Pieris is a shrub that has long been recognized as "safe," even by the Japanese who used it centuries ago in the deer park at Nara and on temple grounds.

Deer eat all manner of spiny and prickly plants such as junipers and roses. The point of origin, native or exotic, seems to have little if any influence on whether they eat a plant or not. Deer are especially fond of such exotic, nonnative woody and vining plants as yews, rhododendrons, and ivies, all of which happen to be highly toxic to domestic livestock.

Many plants are not exactly deer-proof; rather, they are resistant to browsing by deer, or have a seasonal palatability. If such plants can be protected when they are at risk, they are safe the rest of the year. Obviously, the time when food is scarce in the winter will be when woody trees and shrubs need extra protection. The young shoots that grow in the spring are preferred to last year's woodier branches. Pregnant does need extra nutrition in the late winter and the early spring, and through the spring while nursing.

The absence of hunting and predators has resulted in burgeoning deer populations in such places as Fairfield County, Connecticut, much of New Jersey, and even cities such as Philadelphia and Baltimore. Knowing why this is happening does not help the hapless gardener who needs to know how to cope. The three basic solutions are growing those plants that deer usually do not eat, repellant sprays to protect plants favored both by gardener and deer, and fencing to keep deer off the site.

Shade-tolerant Plants Resistant to Deer Browsing

Trees	Ground Covers
Acer palmatum, Japanese maple (seemingly immune to browsing, sometimes damaged by bucks rubbing the velvet off their antlers in late summer)	*Ajuga reptans*, bugleweed
	Asarum canadensis, Canada ginger
	Epimedium, barrenwort
Carpinus, hornbeam	Ferns in general
Cornus florida, flowering dogwood	*Galium odoratum*, woodruff
Cornus kousa, Japanese or kousa dogwood	*Lamium*, dead nettle
Ilex opaca, American holly	*Pachysandra procumbens*, Allegheny spurge
	Pachysandra terminalis, pachysandra
Shrubs	*Vinca minor*, running myrtle
Aucuba, aucuba	**Perennials**
Cephalotaxus harringtonia, Japanese plum-yew	*Actaea pachypoda*, doll's eyes
Clethra alnifolia, summersweet	*Actaea rubra*, red baneberry
Cornus alba, red-twig dogwood	*Aquilegia canadensis*, Canada columbine
Hydrangea (*H. quercifolia*, oak-leaf hydrangea, severely browsed)	*Aruncus dioicus*, goatsbeard
Ilex cornuta, Chinese holly	*Astilbe* species and cultivars
Ilex crenata, Japanese holly (occasionally nibbled, but not severely damaged)	*Brunnera macrophylla*, Siberian bugloss
	Caulophyllum thalictroides, blue cohosh
Ilex glabra, inkberry (nibbled, but not severely damaged)	*Cimicifuga racemosa*, snakeroot
Kalmia latifolia, mountain laurel (browsed to a certain extent, even though toxic)	*Cimicifuga simplex*, snakeroot
	Geranium macrorrhizum, geranium
Kerria japonica, kerria	*Helleborus* species
Leucothoe fontanesiana, drooping leucothoe	*Heuchera* species and cultivars, alumroot
Lindera benzoin, spicebush	*Kirengeshoma palmata*
Mahonia, Oregon holly-grape	*Mertensia virginiana*, Virginia bluebell
Pieris japonica, Japanese pieris or andromeda	*Myrrhis odorata*, sweet cicely
Pieris floribunda, mountain pieris	*Pulmonaria rubra*, red-flowered lungwort
Skimmia japonica	*Pulmonaria saccharata*, spotted lungwort
Viburnum	*Rodgersia* species and cultivars
Vines	*Tiarella cordifolia*, foamflower
Parthenocissus quinquefolia, Virginia creeper	*Viola*, violets
Parthenocissus tricuspidata, Boston ivy	
Schizophragma hydrangeoides	

Deer, Oh Dear!

Shade-tolerant Plants Resistant to Deer Browsing (continued)	
Geophytes	*Hyacinthus orientalis*, hyacinth
Arisaema triphyllum, Jack-in-the-pulpit	*Leucojum vernum*, spring snowflake
Begonia grandis, hardy begonia	*Lycoris radiata*, red spider lily
Caladium, caladium	*Lycoris squamigera*, magic lily or rain lily
Chionodoxa lucilliae, glory-of-the-snow	*Narcissus*, daffodil
Colchicum speciosum, naked ladies	*Sanguinaria canadensis*, bloodroot
Cyclamen coum, Persian violet	**Annuals and Biennials**
Cyclamen hederifolium, autumn cyclamen	*Begonia* x *semperflorens-cultorum*, fibrous-rooted begonia
Eranthis hiemalis, winter aconite	*Digitalis purpurea*, foxglove
Fritillaria meleagris, guinea hen flower	*Lunaria annua*, honesty or money plant
Galanthus nivalis, snowdrop	*Myosotis sylvatica*, forget-me-not
Hyacinthoides hispanicus, wood hyacinth	

Deer Repellents

Repellent sprays have varying effectiveness. Factors to consider include:

- How high is the deer population?
- How hungry are the animals?
- What are the tastes of the local herd (which varies from group to group, since each doe teachs its fawns what is palatable)?
- What other browse is available?
- How efficiently are you renewing the repellent over time as plants put on new growth or after rainfall reduces effectiveness?

For most effective results, begin application of repellents *before* deer damage is apparent. Deer are creatures of habit, so it is easier to keep them away if they have not already learned you are growing savory treats. Alternate your use of repellents rather than rely on only one. My friend John Horn, a talented, experienced gardener and designer living in Wilton, Connecticut, uses a rotating schedule of commercial repellents. For example, in May, when hostas are growing quickly and are at their most succulent, he uses Hinder on a weekly basis. Mixing the repellent at the recommended dilution, John adds a teaspoon of liquid dish detergent per gallon of prepared spray. The detergent acts as a spreader/sticker and both enhances and prolongs the repellent action without harmful effects. In June, John switches to Milorganite, a fertilizer made from processed sewerage sludge, applied every 10 days. Using an inexpensive hand-held broadcast spreader, he dusts the fertilizer right onto the hosta leaves. Just after a rainfall is best, he told me, so the granules stick rather than bounce off. If the weather is dry, apply the Milorganite right after you water. Then, in July, John switches to Bobbex, developed originally as a fertilizer, and that has been found to be a highly effective repellent for use on non-food plants. Available as a liquid concentrate, John dilutes the Bobbex just before application. Longer lasting, Bobbex needs to be applied only every three to five weeks.

For dormant season protection of woody plants, apply repellents in mid- to late fall and early winter. Remember, heavy snow will allow deer to stand higher than ground level, and I've seen them balance on their hind legs like a ballet dancer to reach higher, more succulent branches. Also, snow loading can bend branches down to hungry mouths. Apply spray from the ground level to above the browse line. In the tri-state area of New York, New Jersey, and Connecticut, for example, timing would be late November or early December. You want to apply the spray when the air temperature is above 40°F, and the spray will stay there until it dries. If temperatures are near or below freezing, leaves can be damaged as the water freezes. Reapply in January, replacing repellent that has washed off in rain and snow. No matter what you use, remember that under harsh winter conditions when food is scarce, starving deer will browse despite any repellent you might apply.

Odor Repellents

Many gardeners use repellents that work on scent. Human hair was highly recommended at one time, a couple of handfuls stuffed in a mesh bag or panty hose, and hung on bushes.

Note: A couple of caveats: Barber shops are a better source than beauty parlors, as hair that has been washed first is less effective. Renew the hair several times during the growing season as rain reduces effectiveness.

Another favorite for a while was highly perfumed soap. Just walk down the supermarket aisle and give the different brands a "sniff" test.

Some suggestions: Leave the paper wrapper on so the soap won't dissolve in rain. If you cut the bars in half, do so right through the wrapper and hang them cut-end down. Keep the soap above the reach of skunks, who'll eat it. Another method that I find more effective is to shave the soap into flakes. Put a cup or so into quart-sized Ziploc vegetable storage baggies, which have microperforations that allow the scent to escape while protecting the soap shavings from rain. Hang the bags of soap or hair about 30 inches off the ground, about deer nose height.

Supposedly, manure and urine from lions, tigers, cougars, or other large cats (unlikely to be available unless you have a zookeeper in the family!) are reported to scare deer off a site. Bobcat and coyote urine is commercially available. I have no idea how it is collected, nor have I spoken to anyone who has tried carnivore manure or urine as repellents. I have dumped the more solid contents of my house cat's litter pan (the old-style, nonclumping litter) down vole holes with good results.

Commercial and Homemade Odor Repellents	
Putrescent Egg Solids	
Commercial	MGK Big Game Repellent, Deer-away. Odor and taste repellent, recommended as a spray for conifer seedlings, and as a powder for ornamental shrubs.
Homemade	Six eggs, shell and all, 5 ounces of Tabasco sauce, 1 gallon of water. Use a blender to crush the eggs in a pint of water. Combine remaining ingredients. Let sit for a week. Strain through a coffee filter to avoid clogging the sprayer, and apply as a spray. Useful during the growing season. *or* Two eggs, shell and all, 1 to 2 cups coarsely chopped green onion tops, 2 garlic cloves, 1 tablespoon chili powder or red pepper, 2 cups water. Chop in the blender at high speed until well pureed. Let sit for a few days. Pour into gallon plastic bucket. Add a cake of yellow laundry soap (Fels Naptha). Fill with tepid water. Let sit for an hour or so. Stir, strain, and spray.
Higher Fatty Acids	
Commercial	Hinder. Contains ammonium soaps of higher fatty acids and is recommended for a wide range of ornamentals, fruit trees, and vegetable crops.
Homemade	Smelly soap, whole or shaved, hung at the approximate height of a deer nose.
Sewerage Sludge	
Commercial	Milorganite. Scatter on ground or hang in bags. Useful in the winter and also during growing season.
Dried Blood	
Commercial	Organic nitrogen fertilizer. Scatter on the ground. Replace after rain or irrigation.
Bone Tar Oil	
Commercial	Magic Circle (highly effective for me, no longer available in this formulation in the United States; sold in England under the brand name Reynardine).

Deer, Oh Dear!

Commercial and Homemade Taste Repellents	
Thiram	
Commercial	Gustafson 42-S, Science Rabbit and Deer Repellent, Chew-not, Chaperone, Bonide Rabbit-Deer Repellent, Magic Circle (current formulation). Thiram is a lawn fungicide.
Homemade	One-half cup Thiram to 1 gallon water. Make a slurry of Thiram with some warm water first, then add remaining water. Add Vaporguard at 5 tablespoons per gallon as a sticker. Apply late November/early December and again in a January warm spell. Keep agitating the sprayer tank during application, and be certain to rinse the sprayer nozzle thoroughly afterwards. Thiram leaves a whitish coating on leaves and branches. Useful for winter protection of trees and shrubs.
Capsaicin (pepper spray)	
Commercial	Miller Hot Sauce.
Homemade	3 tablespoons crushed hot pepper per cup of water. Let sit overnight, strain. Add water to make up 1 gallon. Add a spreader/sticker at the recommended rate. Useful during growing season.

Fencing

Mechanical barriers work, but I find spot treatment for individual plants generally spoils the appearance of the garden. Cages of chicken wire protecting primroses are practical, but hardly add to the garden's ambience. Fencing can be extremely effective but it is often a last resort solution due to cost.

Electric Fences

The most effective and most inconspicuous fencing makes use of several strands of high-tensile steel wire and a high-voltage, low-impedance electric charger. Inadvertent contact is unpleasant to humans and pets, but far from lethal unless you have a cardiac pacemaker implanted. Regular stock fence chargers, such as those used with cows and horses, are less effective. Deer have hollow hair, which provides some insulation against the shock. In Connecticut I used this style of electric fence for years. In combination with decorative wooden fences, the house itself, and my 18-foot-long tool shed, I was able to protect approximately three-quarters of my one-acre suburban property. The house and wooden fence allowed access to the garage without any gates. Before installation of the electric fences, two different deer herds used to stroll through my property, one in the morning, another in the afternoon, and even take postprandial naps in my garden. Since the acreage was small and game biologists count the pressure as low, I was able to use a pair of fences, spaced 24 to 30 inches apart. The outer fence was 3 feet high with two wires; the inner fence is 40 inches high with three wires. Deer have widely spaced eyes that provide good peripheral vision as they watch for predators; as a result they have poor depth perception. The two-dimensional aspect with wires at different levels, coupled with the electric shock and the fact that deer are not broad jumpers, kept deer out of my garden for well over a decade.

Except for the corners, the wires were inconspicuous, especially in my informal, naturalistic garden. The cost of materials was also significantly lower than that of woven wire or wooden fences. Though construction may take several days, be sure that your fence is completed and electrified the same day. If the fence is up but the electricity is not turned on for several days, deer may go through it. In such situations, even after the fence is charged, some deer will continue to go through it. Deer are very much creatures of habit. Try to have your electric fence installed early in the spring before deer are attracted to the garden by succulent new growth. Use reinforcement. Cut strips of tinfoil approximately 2 inches by 6 inches, smear peanut butter on half the length. Turn your fence off, and crimp the uncoated tinfoil around the uppermost strand of outer fence wire. Place the baits every 10 or 15 feet. Turn the fence back on. When they lick the wire, the deer will get a shocking reminder to stay away. Think of it as an above-ground version of the invisible fencing for dogs. Birds are unaffected, as, with both feet on the wire they are not grounded and receive no shock. (I have not had a fence installed in the New Jersey garden for reasons of topography—the site slopes, steeply in places, and there is an intermittent drainage creek that further complicates the situation, and resulting high cost.)

Where aesthetic considerations preclude the use of paired wire fences, as in a more formal garden, you might try a combination of electric fence on the perimeter, with an inner hedge. From within the garden you would see the fence, while the deer would be on the outside, electrified wire edge. Be careful to leave enough clear space between hedge and fence that the hedge can be clipped, for branches must not touch the wire if the fence is to operate in the most efficient manner. Casual contact will be a shocking reminder to be more careful, but I would (from personal experience) rate it as unpleasant, nothing worse. The critical, essential exception would be individuals with cardiac pacemakers, who must avoid any contact.

One electric fencing style, developed by the Institute of Ecosystem Studies in Millbrook, New York, will control high deer population pressure and is most suitable for moderate to large properties. Taking up approximately 6 feet of horizontal space, with corners that look like cat's cradles, this fencing system utilizes too much space to be practical on small properties. It makes use of a high-tensile, seven-wire, electrified fence that slants outward toward the perimeter. The wires are spaced 12 inches apart and the high side is 4 feet off the ground.

Paired Fences

Paired fences can be effective at a lower height than a single unit. Deer are high jumpers, and white-tail deer in Connecticut have been seen to stroll up to a 6- or 7-foot-tall woven wire fence and bound right over it. Minimum height should be at least 8 feet, and 9 feet or higher is better. In my experience, a wooden fence that blocks their view is effective; apparently deer are understandably reluctant to blindly jump where they cannot see how they'll land. My fence in Connecticut had solid sections 5½ feet high topped with a 12-inch-high decorative lattice. Be sure that the fence is also close to the ground; deer, especially fawns and yearlings, have been known to do a "commando-style crawl" through amazingly narrow gaps between the ground and the fence. Deer can go through a barbed wire fence with strands 12 inches apart and rarely touch the wire. Yearlings can pass through the 8-inch by 12-inch mesh of a standard cattle fence.

APPENDIX 3—Nursery Sources

Sparse yet elegant, a winter pairing of Japanese maple and bamboo.

Mail-order nurseries offer a way to obtain plants you cannot find at local garden centers. They may be specialists, offering a single kind of perennial. Perhaps they supply unusual trees and shrubs. In any event, they open the door to a greater selection of plants than exists in your neighborhood.

A couple of caveats: Mail-order nurseries cannot send plants, especially trees and shrubs, as large as those you'll find locally. No one's happy when shipping costs more than the merchandise! However, those I've gotten are large enough to make a show in my garden right away. If plants are small, it should say so in the catalog.

And speaking of catalogs, some of my best plants have come from nurseries whose catalogs do not have pictures. That's fine with me; I'm interested in the plant, not its portrait. But if you're ordering something you've never seen before, check it out in one of the books listed in the bibliography (see page 215). And, since catalogs cost the nursery to print and mail, there's often a charge of a dollar or two (or five), which is sometimes, but not always, refundable against your first order.

Trees, Shrubs, and Bamboo

Broken Arrow Nursery
13 Broken Arrow Road
Hamden, Connecticut 06518
Tel: 203-288-1026
Fax: 203-287-1035
Hybridizer and specialist in kalmias; also offers species and hybrid rhododendrons, and other woodland trees and shrubs such as enkianthus, fothergillas, pieris, and more. Catalog: $2.00

Brown's Kalmia Nursery
8527 Semiahmoo Drive
Blaine, Washington 98230
Tel: 360-371-2489, 360-371-5551
Fx: 360-371-3516
Kalmia specialist offering hybrids from small, liner size to flowering size. Catalog: $1.00; will ship to Canada

Burt Associates Bamboo
P.O. Box 719
3 Landmark Road
Westford, Massachusetts 01886
Tel: 508-692-3240
E-mail: bamboo@tiac.net
Web: www.tiac.net/users/bamboo
Bamboo specialist offering hardy and tender species. Catalog: $2.00, deductible from first order; will ship to Canada

Camellia Forest Nursery
125 Carolina Forest Road
Chapel Hill, North Carolina 27516
Tel: 919-967-5529
Fax: 919-967-5529
E-mail: camforest@aol.com
Web: home.aol.com/camforest
Camellias and a wide range of unusual Asian trees and shrubs. Catalog: $4.00; first-class stamps or international reply coupons; will ship to Canada

Carroll Gardens
444 East Main Street
Westminster, Maryland 21157
Tel: 410-848-5422, 1-800-638-6334
Fax: 410-857-4112

Huge selection of trees, shrubs, vines, perennials. Very informative catalog: $3.00; will ship to Canada

Fairweather Gardens
P.O. Box 330
Greenwich, New Jersey 08323
Fax: 609-451-0303
Diverse selection of trees and shrubs, including camellias, hollies, Japanese maples, viburnums. Very informative catalog: $3.00; will not ship west of the Rockies

Forestfarm
990 Tetherow Road
Williams, Oregon 97544-9599
Tel: 541-846-7269
Fax: 541-846-6963
E-mail: forestfarm@a1pro.net
An extraordinary range of trees and shrubs, mostly smaller sizes for growing in your home nursery, with some 1- and 5-gallon size. Very informative catalog: $4.00; will ship to Canada but not Hawaii

Gossler Farms Nursery
1200 Weaver Road
Springfield, Oregon 97478-9691
Tel: 541-746-3922
Fax: 541-744-7924
Especially wide selection of magnolias, other woody plants. Catalog thoroughly describes plants, provides cultural suggestions: $2.00; will ship to Canada

Greer Gardens
1280 Goodpasture Island Road
Eugene, Oregon 97401-1794
Tel: 541-686-8266
Fax: 541-686-0910
E-mail: greergard@aol.com
Large selection of rhododendrons and azaleas, Japanese maples, ericaceous shrubs and more. Enthusiastic, informative catalog: $3.00, $5.00 overseas; will ship to Canada and abroad

Heronswood Nursery Ltd.
7530 NE 288th Street
Kingston, Washington 98346-9502
Tel: 360-297-4172
Fax: 360-297-8321
Wide range of uncommon ornamental woody plants and a variety of unusual perennials. Very descriptive catalog: $4.00 ($5.00 overseas); will ship to Canada and overseas

Lamtree Farm
2323 Copeland Road
Warrensville, North Carolina 28693
Tel: 910-385-6144
Small nursery with excellent selection of native rhododendrons and azaleas, franklinias, halesias, leucothoes, stewartias, styrax, others. Catalog: $2.00; cannot ship to California, Oregon, or Washington

Linton & Linton Bamboo
310 Woodbine Road
Savannah, Georgia 31410
Tel: 912-897-5755
Fax: 912-921-5890
E-mail: coastal@uga.cc.uga.edu
Web: www.atlgarden.com
Bamboo specialist offering field-grown as well as container stock. Catalog: free; will ship to Canada and overseas

Mountain Maples
P. O. Box 1329
Laytonville, California 95454-1329
Tel: 707-984-6522
Fax: 707-984-7433
Selection of over 200 Japanese maple cultivars (many listed only by their Japanese names), some species maples. Catalog has nice descriptions: $2.00

Musser Forests, Inc.
P.O. Box 340
Route 119 North
Indiana, Pennsylvania 15701-0340
Tel: 412-465-5685, 1-800-643-8319
Fax: 412-465-9893
Wide range of trees and shrubs, some perennials and ground covers in small, transplant sizes. Catalog: free; will ship to Canada and overseas

Steve Ray's Bamboo Gardens
250 Cedar Cliff Road
Springville, Alabama 35146
Tel: 205-594-3438
Hardy bamboo specialist. Catalog: $3.00; minimum order $20.00; will not ship to California or Hawaii

Roslyn Nursery
211 Burrs Lane
Dix Hills, New York 11746
Tel: 516-643-9347
Fax: 516-484-1555
E-mail: roslyn@concentric.net
Web: www.cris.com/~Roslyn/

Nursery Sources

Specialty list of hybrid and species rhododendrons and azaleas, hollies, pieris, kalmias, Japanese maples, and other deciduous and evergreen shrubs, some perennials. Catalog: $3.00, $5.00 overseas; will ship to Canada and overseas

Woodlanders, Inc.
1128 Colleton Avenue
Aiken, South Carolina 29801
Tel: 803-648-7522
Fax: 803-648-7522
Specialist in southeastern native trees, shrubs, vines, ground covers, ferns, perennials, and rare, hard-to-find exotics. Catalog: $2.00, $3.00 overseas; minimum order $15.00; will ship to Canada and overseas Specializes in rare and hard-to-find native plants.

See also:
Kurt Bluemel, Inc. (under Perennials),
Rhododendron Species Foundation (under Perennials)

Ground Covers

With the amount of plants needed to cover ground, it seems likely that you'd do best to find something locally. If that doesn't work, buy enough to start propagating the quantity necessary.

Garden Vision
63 Williamsville Road
Hubbardston, Massachusetts 01452-1315
Tel: 508-928-4808
Epimediums only; over 40 different species, varieties, and cultivars with new kinds added all the time. Catalog: long SASE; will ship to Canada but not Hawaii

Ivies of the World
P.O. Box 408
Weirsdale, Florida 32195-0408
Tel: 352-821-2201
Fax: 352-821-2201
E-mail: rookh@aol.com
Ivies galore; over 250 cultivars sold mostly as rooted cuttings. Catalog: $2.00; will ship to Canada

Oregon Trail Groundcovers
P.O. Box 601
Canby, Oregon 97013
Tel: 503-263-4688
Fax: 503-266-9832
All they sell is *Vinca minor* (vinca, periwinkle or running myrtle); ten different cultivars with red-violet, blue, or white flowers, double-flowered, or variegated leaves. Minimum order of 50 plants. Catalog: $3.00, deductible from first order; will ship to Canada

Peekskill Nurseries
P.O. Box 428
Old Yorktown Road
Shrub Oak, New York 10588
Tel: 914-245-5595
Ground cover specialist, offering pachysandra, vinca, euonymus, Baltic ivy, in quantities from 10 to thousands. Catalog: $1.00

Prentiss Court Ground Covers
P.O. Box 8662
Greenville, South Carolina 29604
Tel: 864-277-4037
Fax: 864-299-5015
E-mail: EMcND@aol.com
Family business offering ajuga, euonymus, ivies, liriope, vinca, and others. Plants offered bare-root in 50-plant minimum or in pots. Catalog: $1.00; cannot ship to Alaska or Hawaii

See also:
Bluestone Perennials (under Perennials), Musser Forests Inc. (under Trees and Shrubs), Savory's Gardens, Inc. (under Perennials), Woodlanders, Inc. (under Trees and Shrubs)

Perennials

Kurt Bluemel, Inc.
2470 Greene Lane
Baldwin, Maryland 21013-9523
Tel: 410-557-7229
Fax: 410-557-9785
E-mail: kbi@bluemel.com
Web: www.bluemel.com.kbi

Specialist with very extensive list of ornamental grasses and grasslike plants, as well as bamboos, ferns, and herbaceous perennials. Catalog: $3.00; will ship to Canada and overseas

Bluestone Perennials
7211 Middle Ridge Road
Madison, Ohio 44057
Tel: 1-800-852-5243
Fax: 216-428-7198
E-mail: bluestone@harborcom.net
Web: www.bluestoneperennials.com
Wide selection of hardy herbaceous perennials; small plants at modest prices, also ground covers. Catalog: free

Busse Gardens
5873 Oliver Avenue S.W.
Cokato, Minnesota 55321-4229
Tel: 320-286-2654, 1-800-544-3192
Fax: 320-286-6601
Wide selection of hardy herbaceous perennials including astilbes, ferns, heucheras, lots of hostas, and others. Catalog: $2.00, refundable with first order

Bridgewood Gardens
P.O. Box 800
Crownsville, Maryland
Tel: 410-849-3916
Fax: 410-849-3427
Hosta specialist. Catalog: free; cannot ship to Alaska, Arizona, California, Hawaii, Oregon, and Washington

Fancy Fronds
P.O. Box 1090
Gold Bar, Washington 98251-1090
Tel: 360-793-1472
A plethora of hardy ferns, fancy and plain, from England, Asia, New Zealand; thoroughly described in a catalog from a knowledgeable, enthusiastic grower. Ferns raised from spores or by vegetative division and raised to 4-inch pot size for shipping. Catalog: $2.00, refundable with first order

Foliage Gardens
2003-128th Avenue S.E.
Bellevue, Washington 98005
Tel: 206-747-2998
E-mail: FoliageG@juno.com
A wide selection of both hardy and greenhouse ferns and their cultivars. Catalog: $2.00; will ship to Canada

Highfield Garden
4704 N.E. Cedar Creek Road
Woodland, Washington 98674
Tel: 360-225-6525
Very wide selection of hardy geraniums (including shade-tolerant species), other perennials, and ornamental grasses. Catalog: $1.00

Limerock Ornamental Grasses
70 Sawmill Road
Port Matilda, Pennsylvania 16870
Tel: 814-692-2272
Fax: 814-692-9848
Broad selection of ornamental grasses, sedges, and rushes (including shade-tolerant species), some perennials. Catalog: $3.00; will not ship to California

Lower Marlboro Nursery
P.O. Box 1013
7011 Flint Hill Road (Owings)
Dunkirk, Maryland 20754
Tel: 301-812-0808
Fax: 301-812-0808
Specializing in native plants of northeastern United States, many shade-tolerant. Catalog: $2.00; will not ship to Alaska, Arizona, California, Hawaii, Oregon, or Washington

Naylor Creek Nursery
2610 West Valley Road
Chimacum, Washington 94701
Tel: 360-732-4983
Fax: 360-732-7171
Nice selection of hostas, astilbes, pulmonarias and epimediums. Catalog: free; will ship to Canada and abroad

Niche Gardens
1111 Dawson Road
Chapel Hill, North Carolina 27516
Tel: 919-967-0078
Fax: 919-967-4206
E-mail: nichegdn@ipass.net
Web: www.nichegdn.com
Perennials, ornamental grasses, southeastern native plants, trees and shrubs, some suitable for shady gardens. Catalog: $3.00; $15.00 minimum order

Plant Delights Nursery
9241 Sauls Road
Raleigh, North Carolina 27603
Tel: 919-772-4794
Fax: 919-662-0370

Nursery Sources

E-mail: tony@plantdel.com
Web: www.plantdel.com
A plantaholic's delight, incredible selection of perennials, especially hostas, heucheras, pulmonarias. Catalog: 10 first-class stamps or a box of chocolate; will ship to Canada and overseas

The Primrose Path
R.D. 2, Box 110
Scottsdale, Pennsylvania 15683
Fax: 412-887-3077
Nice selection of woodland plants, especially good in (what else) primroses, as well as heucheras and tiarellas. Catalog: $2.00, refundable on first order

Rainforest Gardens
13139-224th Street
Maple Ridge, BC, Canada V2X 7E7
Tel: 604-467-4218
Fax: 604-467-3181
E-mail: info@rainforest-gardens.com
Web: www.dsoe.com/rainforest
Herbaceous perennial specialist with good selection of hardy geraniums (including shade-tolerant species), hostas, astilbes, ferns, hellebores, primroses, and others. Catalog: $4.00, refundable on first order; ships only within Canada

Red's Rhodies
15920 S.W. Oberst Lane
Sherwood, Oregon 97140-8436
Tel: 503-625-6331
Fax: 503-625-6331
Offers arisaemas and some terrestrial orchids such as bletillas and calanthes. Catalog: $2.00; will ship to Canada and overseas

The Rhododendron Species Foundation
P.O. Box 3798
2525 S. 336th Street
Federal Way, Washington 98063-3798
Tel: 206-838-4646
Fax: 206-838-4686
This nonprofit organization offers unusual rhododendrons and choice, rare, companion plants as a fund-raising effort. Members have priority; anyone can order. Catalog: $3.50; will ship to Canada and overseas

Robyn's Nest Nursery
7802 N.E. 63rd Street
Vancouver, Washington 98662
Tel: 360-256-7399
Choice selections of astilbes, epimediums, hostas, and others. Catalog: $2.00, $5.00 overseas; will ship to Canada and overseas

Savory's Gardens Inc.
5300 Whiting Avenue
Edina, Minnesota 55439-1249
Tel: 612-941-8755
Fax: 612-941-3750
List of approximately 200 hostas, as well as other perennials and ground covers. Catalog: $2.00, $4.00 overseas; will ship to Canada and overseas

Shady Oaks Nursery
112 10th Avenue S.E.
Waseca, Minnesota 56093-3122
Tel: 507-835-5033, 1-800-504-8006
Fax: 507-835-8772
E-mail: shadyoaks@shadyoaks.com
Web: www.shadyoaks.com
Our kind of nursery—they specialize in plants for the shade! Herbaceous perennials, ferns, ground covers, hostas, wildflowers. Catalog: free

Underwood Shade Nursery
P.O. Box 1386
North Attleboro, Massachusetts 02763-0386
Tel: 508-222-2164
Fax: 508-222-5152
E-mail: shadeplant@ici.net
Small nursery specializing in shade-tolerant plants—our kind of place! Aroids, species violets, wildflowers, and others. Catalog: $2.00, refundable with first order; will not ship to Arizona, Nevada, or Wyoming

Andre Viette Farm & Nursery
P.O. Box 1109
State Route 608
Fishersville, Virginia 22939
Tel: 540-943-2315, 1-800-575-5538
Fax: 540-943-0782
E-mail: viette@viette.com
Web: www.viette.com

Very broad selection of herbaceous perennials for sun and shade, the latter including astilbes, epimediums, liriopes, and others. Catalog: $5.00; cannot ship to California

See also:
Woodlanders, Inc. (under Trees and Shrubs)

Geophytes (Bulbs, Corms, and Tubers)

It is becoming more difficult to find local nurseries that sell bulbs, corms, and tubers loose in bins. And I really dislike purchasing geophytes in nasty net bags at discount stores where they're often kept in overheated (to the geophyte) conditions, I cannot see their quality, and quantity is determined by the packager rather than my garden needs. Additionally, the selection is generally limited to commonplace varieties. Mail order is often a viable solution.

Caladium World
P.O. Box 629
121 Caladium Row
Sebring, Florida 33871-0629
Tel: 941-385-7661
Fax: 941-385-5836
You probably never imagined there were this many kinds of caladiums. Minimum 25 tubers per variety. Catalog: free

The Daffodil Mart
85 Broad Street
Torrington, Connecticut 06790-6668
Tel: 1-800-255-2852
Fax: 1-800-420-2852
Now owned by White Flower Farm, this nursery continues to list an especially wide range of geophytes in a non-illustrated catalog. Not just daffodils, but a very extensive catalog of bulbs of all descriptions. Catalog: free; will ship to Canada

Dutch Gardens
P.O. Box 200
Adelphia, New Jersey 07710-0200
Tel: 1-800-818-3861
Fax: 908-780-7720
E-mail: cs@dutchgardens.nl
Web: www.dutchgardens.nl
Good color catalog of spring-flowering geophytes; second catalog for summer-blooming kinds. Catalog: free; will not ship to Alaska, Hawaii, Puerto Rico

Gardenimport, Inc.
P.O. Box 760
Thornhill, Ontario, Canada L3T 4A5
Tel: 905-731-1950
Fax: 905-881-3499
E-mail: flower@gardenimport.com
Web: www.gardenimport.com
Separate spring and fall, color-illustrated catalogs offering a good selection of familiar geophytes with a smattering of less common genera. Catalog: $5.00, refundable with first order; will ship to the United States

McClure & Zimmerman
P.O. Box 368
108 West Winnebago
Friesland, Wisconsin 53935
Tel: 920-326-4220
Fax: 1-800-692-5864
Extensive selection of familiar spring-flowering geophytes and less common species; for example, solid selection of colchicums. No photographs, some line drawings, very good descriptions. Catalog: free

Grant Mitsch Novelty Daffodils
P.O. Box 218
Hubbard, Oregon 97032
Tel: 503-651-2742 (evenings)
Fax: 503-651-2792
E-mail: havens@canby.com
Rare and uncommon hybrid daffodils. Good descriptions, many color illustrations. Catalog: $3.00, refundable with first order, $5.00 Canada and overseas; will ship to Canada and overseas

Oakwood Daffodils
2330 West Bertrand Road
Niles, Michigan 49120
Tel: 616-684-3327
E-mail: scr@stb.infi.net
Midwestern-bred, -grown, and -acclimated daffodils. Catalog: $1.00, refundable with first order, $2.00 Canada and overseas; will ship to Canada and overseas

Old House Gardens
536 Third Street
Ann Arbor, Michigan 48103-4957
Tel: 313-995-1486
Fax: 313-995-1486
E-mail: ohg@arrownet.com
Specializing in geophytes from the nineteenth and early twentieth century. Catalog: $2.00

Nursery Sources

Rainbow Acres
P.O. Box 1543
Sebring, Florida 33871-1543
Tel: 941-382-4449
Fancy-leaf caladiums by name or in mix of red-leafed, pink-leafed, white-variegated types. Catalog: free

John Scheepers, Inc.
23 Tulip Drive
Bantam, Connecticut 06750
Tel: 860-567-0838
Fax: 860-567-5323
Nice range of spring-flowering geophytes, lilies, and amaryllis described in color-illustrated catalog. Owned by Van Engelen, but sells in smaller quantities. Catalog: free

Van Bourgondien Bros.
P.O. Box 1000
245 Farmingdale Road, Route 109
Babylon, New York 11702-0598
Tel: 516-669-3500, 1-800-622-9997
Fax: 516-669-1228
E-mail: blooms@dutchbulbs.com
Web: dutchbulbs.com
Separate color-illustrated catalogs of spring- and summer-flowering geophytes and a few perennials. Catalog: free; cannot ship to Alaska, Hawaii, Puerto Rico, or Guam

Van Dyck's Flower Farms, Inc.
P.O. Box 430
Brightwaters, New York 11718-0430
Tel: 1-800-248-2852
Fax: 516-669-3518
Spring-flowering geophytes; lots of "minor" species as well as daffodils, tulips, hyacinths and some hybrid lilies. Catalog: free; ships only to contiguous 48 states

Van Engelen, Inc.
23 Tulip Drive
Bantam, Connecticut 06750
Tel: 1-860-567-8734
Fax: 860-567-5323
Wide selection of spring-flowering geophytes in lots of 50 and 100 per variety. Catalog: free

Annuals

I cannot justify buying impatiens by mail when they can be purchased at discount stores and supermarkets. It can be worthwhile to start unusual annuals from seed. Nor should you overlook the houseplant aisle. However, there are a couple of mail-order sources to investigate.

Color Farm Growers
2710 Thornhill Road
Auburndale, Florida 33823
Tel: 941-967-9895
Coleus specialists offering old-fashioned heirloom varieties as well as new hybrids: black, dark purple, red, orange, yellow, fancy-edged and variegated. Custom-grown plants shipped as rooted cuttings. Catalog: $1.00; will ship to Canada

Glasshouse Works
P.O. Box 97, Church Street
Stewart, Ohio 45778-0097
Tel: 614-662-2142, 1-800-837-2142
Fax: 614-662-2120
E-mail: plants@glasshouseworks.com
Web: www.glasshouseworks.com
Lists many tropical genera suitable for use as shade-tolerant summer bedding or accent plants; specializing in variegated plants. Catalog: $2.00, $5.00 overseas; will ship to Canada and overseas

Logee's Greenhouses
141 North Street
Danielson, Connecticut 06239
Tel: 860-774-8038
Fax: 860-774-9932
E-mail: logees@neca.com
Web: www.logeesplants.com
Incredible selection of greenhouse and conservatory plants with an astonishing diversity of fibrous-rooted and fancy-leaved rex begonias. Catalog: free; will ship to Canada and overseas

BIBLIOGRAPHY

Plants

Trees and Shrubs: General

Dirr, Michael A. *Dirr's Hardy Trees and Shrubs.* Portland, Oregon: Timber Press, 1997.

Flint, Harrison L. *Landscape Plants for Eastern North America, Exclusive of Florida and the Immediate Gulf Coast.* New York, New York: John Wiley & Sons, 1983.

Poor, Janet Meakin, and Nancy Peterson Brewster. *Plants That Merit Attention, Volume I: Trees.* Portland, Oregon: Timber Press, 1984.

Poor, Janet Meakin and Nancy Peterson Brewster. *Plants That Merit Attention, Volume II: Shrubs.* Portland, Oregon: Timber Press, 1996.

Perennials: General

Armitage, Allan M. *Herbaceous Perennial Plants.* Watkinsville, Georgia: Varsity Press, 1989.

Clausen, Ruth Rogers, and Nicolas H. Ekstrom. *Perennials for American Gardens.* New York, New York: Random House, 1989.

Hansen, Richard and Friedrich Stahl. *Perennials and Their Garden Habitats.* Portland, Oregon: Timber Press, 1993.

Perennials: Specific

Bath, Trevor, and Joy Jones. *The Gardener's Guide to Growing Hardy Geraniums.* Portland, Oregon: Timber Press, 1994.

Grenfell, Diana. *The Gardener's Guide to Growing Hostas.* Portland, Oregon: Timber Press, 1996.

Klaber, Doretta. *Primroses and Spring.* New York, New York: M. Barrows & Company, Inc.

Distributed by William Morrow & Company, Inc., 1976

Mathew, Brian. *Hellebores.* London, England: Alpine Garden Society, 1989.

Mickel, John. *Ferns for American Gardens.* New York, New York: Macmillan Publishing Company, 1994.

Rice, Graham, and Elizabeth Strangman. *The Gardener's Guide to Growing Hellebores.* Portland, Oregon: Timber Press, 1993.

Geophytes: General

Glattstein, Judy. *The American Gardener's World of Bulbs.* New York, New York: Little, Brown and Company, 1994.

Mathew, Brian. *The Year-Round Bulb Garden.* London, England: Souvenir Press, 1986.

Technique

Cramer, Harriet L. *The Shadier Garden.* New York, New York: Crescent Books, 1997.

Druse, Ken. *The Natural Shade Garden.* New York, New York: Clarkson Potter, 1992.

Fish, Margery. *Gardening in the Shade.* London, England: W. H. and L. Collingridge Limited, 1964.

Glattstein, Judy. *Garden Design with Foliage.* Pownal, Vermont: Storey Communications, Inc., A Garden Way Publishing Book, 1991.

Schenk, George. *The Complete Shade Gardener.* Boston, Massachusetts: Houghton Mifflin Company, 1984.

Taylor, Jane. *Gardening in Shade.* London, England: J.M. Dent & Sons Ltd, 1991.

METRIC CONVERSION TABLE

Weights and Measures

Converting from English to Metric System			Converting from Metric to English System		
1 in.	=	25.4 mm	1 mm	=	0.039 in.
1 in.	=	2.54 cm	1 cm	=	0.39 in.
1 ft.	=	0.3 m	1 m	=	3.28 ft.
1 yd.	=	0.91 m	1 m	=	1.09 yd.
1 mi.	=	1.61 m	1 km	=	0.62 mi.
1 liquid oz.	=	29.6 ml	1 l	=	1.06 qt.
1 liquid qt.	=	0.95 l	1 l	=	0.26 gal.
1 gal.	=	3.79 l	1 g	=	0.04 oz.
1 oz. (weight)	=	28.3 g	1 kg	=	2.2 lb.
1 lb.	=	0.45 kg			

Temperature

Multiply Celsius by 1.8, then add 32 to obtain Fahrenheit. Subtract 32 from Fahrenheit reading, then multiply by 0.55 to obtain Celsius.

Converting from Fahrenheit to Celsius

Example: 98.6°F

Step 1: Subtract 32 from 98.6.

The result is 66.6.

Step 2: Multiply 66.6 by 0.55.

The result is 36.63 or

approximately 37°C.

Converting from Celsius to Fahrenheit

Example: 0°C

Step 1: Multiply 0 by 1.8.

The result is 0.

Step 2: Add 32 to 0.

The result is 32 or 32°F.

INDEX

Jack-in-the-pulpit, in fruit.

Grape hyacinths with Canada columbine.